ALPS

Turin

Po R.

Trebia R.

Arminium

Arretium

Tiber R.

Corsica

Rome

Cannae

Capua

Tarentum

Sardinia

nean Sea

Messina

Sicily

Carthage

Syracuse

N

- - - → HANNIBAL'S INVASION ROUTE

50 0 100 200 300 400 MILES

Praise for *Hannibal*

"Leckie seeks not to bury Hannibal in analysis but to portray him. He gives readers a taste of an outsized man whose obsession to conquer Rome made him as bloodthirsty as he was bold. This is a ripping good read whose lesson in ancient history is yet another reward."

—*Publishers Weekly*

"What remains in the mind is not a mere record of battles, or even the brief telling of Hannibal's famous crossing of the Alps, elephants in tow. Instead, it is the vagaries of the great general's mind that are most vividly described, raising the novel above historiography. Hannibal is a man who has sworn to destroy Rome, but who falls some way short."

—*The Sunday Times*

"One of the most cracking reads of the year...rips along at great pace and conveys not only the history of the period but the in-built brutality of those who fought for and against the Roman Empire."

—*The Daily Express*

"Leckie's first-person narrative portrays Hannibal as a noble savage, whose tenacity swiftly turns to brutality. In his meticulous recreation of an ancient way of life, he passes the first test facing any historical novelist; and his semi-poetic style can carry a rawness appropriate to the rust and dust of the military setting, the immediacy of battle. This debut largely succeeds in maintaining suspense within the constraints of the historical evidence."

—*Times Literary Supplement*

"*Hannibal* is carefully constructed; pieces of his background and character are fitted together like a jigsaw. This is an energetic novel, at best when the canvas is widest, describing places or battles, describing the matter-of-fact cruelties and detailing the politics which dominated [Hannibal's] life."

—*The Herald*

HANNIBAL

ROSS LECKIE

REGNERY PUBLISHING, INC.
Washington, D.C.

Library of Congress Cataloging-in-Publication Data

Leckie, Ross, 1957–
    Hannibal / Ross Leckie.
      p.   cm.
    ISBN 0-89526-443-9
    1. Hannibal, 247-182 B.C.—Fiction. 2. Punic Wars, 2nd, 218-201
B.C.—Fiction. 3. Carthage (Extinct city)—Fiction. 4. Rome—
History—Republic, 265-30 B.C.—Fiction. I. Title.
PR6062.E337H36   1996
823'.914—dc20   96-35048
                                           CIP

Published in the United States by
Regnery Publishing, Inc.
An Eagle Publishing Company
422 First Street, SE
Washington, DC 20003

Distributed to the trade by
National Book Network
4720-A Boston Way
Lanham, MD 20706

First published in Great Britain in 1995
by Canongate Books Ltd.

Printed on acid-free paper.
Manufactured in the United States of America.

10 9 8 7 6 5 4 3 2

Books are available in quantity for promotional or premium use. Write to Director of Special Sales, Regnery Publishing, Inc., 422 First Street, SE, Suite 300, Washington, DC 20003, for information on discounts and terms or call (202) 546-5005.

FOR
SOPHIA

οἱ μὲν ἰππήων τρότον, οἱ δὲ πέσδων,
οἱ δὲ νάων φαῖσ' ἐπὶ γᾶν μέλαιναν
ἔμμεναι κάλλιστον, ἔγω δὲ κῆν' ὄτ-
τω τις ἔραται

— Sappho

CONTENTS

Nullus amor populis nec foedera sunto . . .
Litora litoribus contraria, fluctibus undas
Imprecor, arma armis: pugnent ipsique nepotesque.

Neither love nor treaty shall there be between the nations . . .
Let your shores oppose their shores, your waves their waves,
your arms their arms. This is my prayer: let them fight, they and
their sons' sons, forever.

> Dido, Queen of Carthage's curse upon the Romans.
> Virgil, *Aeneid* IV, 624 ff.

Bellum maxime omnium memorabile quae unquam gesta sunt . . .
Hannibale duce Carthaginienses cum populo Romano gessere.

The war fought by the Carthaginians under Hannibal against
the Romans was the most memorable of all wars ever waged.

> Livy, *Ab Urbe Condita*, XXI.1

PROLOGUE

I am old now, and the time of my people is past. No more will the lineage of Barca fight the Romans whom we hate. The Paradise of Mithra holds all those that I have loved, souls whom the River of Ordeal could not scald. Soon I shall join them.

The ravens and the vultures gather over Carthage. I see its doom. Our ships have long been sunk or captured. Their oars of the oaks of Bashan and the Ashurites are broken, sound no more. My army is dispersed. I am far away.

I sit now naked from the heat in a borrowed room in a foreign land alone. They sent for me. I would not go. Soon they will come. They have thought it too hard, too hazardous a task to wait for the death of an old man.

My body stiffens. My wounds throb. I am as an old and wizened oak tree in a field, against which cattle have rubbed too long. Yet shall I tell my story, and be done. I see my body and its many, many scars. All are in front. The Romans shall not have me.

I

CARTHAGE

Children's memories are deep and strange. Grown men must struggle through the past to reach and to know them. It is best done while one lives, but if postponed will surely come with or after death. I have often seen it so, for I have known too many deaths. My friend Maharbal took three weeks to die after a sword thrust caught him in the stomach. We were deep in Campania, high in the hills when a Roman patrol surprised us. Only I was with him at the end. No-one else could bear the stench of his putresence. In his death-fever he returned to our childhood in Spain, calling out to me as we raced our ponies hard along the strand of Gadez. Through that last night he turned over such many things. Then, at dawn, he gave up his spirit, but in peace.

Tanit-pene-Baal, the god of dreams and death, would have it thus. We must first cross the River of Ordeal, then the River of Forgetfulness, Ashroket in our Punic tongue, and remember all our lives before our spirits can be free. If we do not, we linger for eternities with the undead by Ashroket's banks. There stands a great and giant elm tree, its branches spreading like arms, full of years. The undead make their home there, clinging everywhere beneath its leaves, as many as the leaves of the forest which fall with autumn's chill, and stretch out their hands in longing for the farther bank.

Let me now prepare to cross. I, who have always been fighting, now give the god his due. Time for me, time for the thousands who died for me and need me now to account for their memories so they too may pass in peace. There is so much blood.

Blood. And hate. I must have been three, turning four. I was playing with marbles in the courtyard of our home in Carthage, my brother Mago with me. A breeze stirred the palm trees all around. Suddenly the wail of the corynx, the Carthaginian war-trumpet, filled the air. My mother, heavy with child, ran to us. "Come quickly, boys. Your father is home. He has sent for you. Come."

We followed her to my father's hall, rising from its massive foundations to a terraced storey. Onto its walls of bronze were set diamonds, beryls, the three kinds of ruby, four kinds of sapphire, twelve of emeralds, topazes from Mount Zabacra, opals from Bactria, glossopetri fallen from the moon. Never before had I passed through its scarlet doors quartered with a black cross, beyond its grilles of beaten gold which kept out scorpions.

It was silent inside, despite the press of people. As well as Carthaginians, there were Ligurians there, Balearics, Negroes, Numidians, Lusitanians, Cantabrians, Cappadaocians, Lydians, Celtiberians, Dorians, men from every corner of the earth, for this has always been the way with us. They parted to let us pass. Standing on a dais at the far end of the hall was Hamilcar, my father, tired and dirty from journeying, his sweat making lines through the grey dust on his forehead.

Before my father stood a man, strange of dress and skin. "I ask you, Marcus Atilius Regulus, what mercy you should have of us. Answer me!" In the stillness, the man's reply was clear: "I answer you, Hamilcar Barca, as will many greater than you could ever be: *Summa sedes non capit duos.* Do with me as you must."

Of course I did not have enough Latin then to understand. Only later did my tutor, Silenus of Caleacte, explain: "*Supreme power cannot be shared,*" words which form the more so now, I fear, the policy of Rome. I smile as I remember how I returned the words of Regulus in kind, the cry of fear, "*Hannibalis ad portas, Hannibal is at the gates,*" filling the thoughts of Romans for the many years in which I made them dance.

What I did understand was the roar of anger that rose to meet the man's reply. My father stood still. He held up his hands for quiet. "Carthaginians, allies, friends, you have heard what this man has said. You know him, Regulus, the Roman consul we defeated and captured when he invaded our own Africa ten years ago. We should perhaps have crucified him. Yet we sent him to Rome to treat for peace on condition he would return. For what have we ever sought of the Romans, we who knew the bounds of the world before they were even a people, than that they should leave us in peace? When have we ever sought out war, unless when these vipers, these conquerors and colonisers of greed tamper with our trade and seize our lands? Three times has Carthage made solemn treaties of peace with Rome. Three times have the Romans broken their word. As we must, we resist them."

A murmur of agreement, of anger, rose and died away, as hiss of pebbles on the shore when wave recedes.

"This Regulus we sent to Rome. And what did he urge on their Senate? Why, not peace but more war. Then war he shall have. As Sufet of Carthage I speak for the Council of Elders and I say: let that which is customary be done."

It was as all had expected. Two men came forward and seized Regulus by the arms. A third gave to my father a short sharp knife and turned Regulus towards us. In one swift movement my father seized the Roman's long nose with the thumb and finger of his left hand. With the knife in his right he cut it off. Regulus screamed and sank to the floor. The pool that gathered in the dust beside him was my first sight of Roman blood. I felt nothing. Mago beside me began to sniffle. My mother grabbed him by the hair and made him watch.

Next my father knelt. The Roman was pinned down on his back. I knew as my father began to reach out. I was to cut out tongues myself in years to come. The Roman's screams were drowned in his own blood. My father rose, said: "Send him

3

again to Rome. Then will he treat for neither peace nor war," and left.

My mother sent us to our room. Mago cried. I lay on my bed. I did not understand. I understood somehow that I did not need to. The door opened. My father was there, washed, in clean clothes. I sat up, quickly. "Hannibal, Mago," he said, "you are young. But what you learn today you cannot learn too soon. Come in, Hamilax."

Hamilax was my father's High Steward. How long he had served our house, I do not know. But he was old, his face deep-lined. "My sons," said my father, "there are many things that words cannot capture. What you have seen today is one. Here is another. Hamilax, take off your tunic."

Standing before us, Hamilax took off his shirt. From the waist up his skin was angry, red and rippled, like the surface of the sea when the wind ruffles it in a dying sun. He turned. His back was the same, but for the welts that crossed it. We looked. "Thank you, Hamilax. You may go," commanded my father. I saw the Steward wince as he knelt to pick up his tunic. His skin, I saw, was stuck to his ribs.

"The Romans did this to him." My father sat down on my bed. "He served my father Hasdrubal before me and was captured fighting the Romans at the great sea battle of Mylae. My father offered an exchange: ten of them for Hamilax. They agreed. When the ship bearing him came to Carthage, I was with my father waiting at the docks. But we could not see Hamilax standing on the deck. He was carried ashore on a litter.

"Understand this: yes, the Romans had released him, but first they had flayed him with red-hot sand. It was to be weeks before we knew if he would live or die. This, I learned, is Roman faith. What you saw done to Regulus was right. The gods demand it. Do not forget." Then he was gone. There was only the creak of the great wheel which carried water through the palace, turning, turning.

As I grew, I felt alone not least because my father was so seldom with us. He was away, fighting the Romans in Sicily. He would come when he could, perhaps three times each year, sometimes for a night and a day, sometimes for more. Even then, he had no time. Strange men would arrive, borne to our palace on rich litters. They and my father would talk and argue late into the night. I heard snatches of discussion about trade, about money, for I slept in a room above that in which they met. One I came to know as Gisco was always loud. "Let the Romans have Sicily, yes, and Sardinia too. All we need from them is freedom to trade as did our fathers' fathers' fathers. Let us look south, to Africa."

"And will the Romans stop," my father scoffed, "with Sicily? What about Spain and our mines there?"

"They can have all that, if they leave us Africa . . ."

I slipped into a fitful sleep.

It was during one of these visits — was I four, five? — that my father woke me. It was still dark, but from the garden I heard the calling of the storks that marked each dawn and, through the window, carried on a gentle breeze, the sound of Eschmoun's horses, safe in their sacred glade, whinnying towards the sun. "Hannibal, get up." Shivering, I rose, slipped on my tunic, sandals. "Come with me."

Through the sleeping house I followed my father down. We passed through the great front doors of porphyry, on down the staircase of ebony, the prow of a defeated galley in the corner of each step. On the main path of black sand mixed with powdered coral we went along the avenue. The double rows of cypresses swayed softly in the breeze. In the garden, past the orchards of fig trees and pomegranates, white-tufted cotton shrubs, roses and vines, we walked, on beyond the fish ponds and the great pits where the elephants, smelling us, stirred.

The wall, the great wall of Carthage where I was forbidden to go, rose up from the darkness. It was, I knew already from

Silenus, a marvel of the earth. Of dressed stone, forty feet high and thirty feet thick, the wall ran for twenty-two miles round Carthage. Double-storeyed, it held within its bulk the stables for 300 elephants with stores for their caparisons, their tethers and their food. Above were more stables for 4,000 horse, their harness, gear. There were barracks too for 20,000 soldiers and 4,000 cavalry. A city within a city above which soared up towers, each of strong battlements, shrouded in bronze shields. My servants said it was the work of our god Baal, but I knew that man had made it.

Reaching forward in the darkness, my father felt the great smooth stones. He paused and heaved. One swung open, startling me. He stepped forward, into the wall. I followed. He turned and pulled shut the stone behind us. "This is a way, Hannibal, known only to me and to Hamilax. You will tell none of it." In the dark, I followed him, as I was to follow through much greater darknesses to come.

Pushing up another stone, my father climbed onto the rampart, I behind. No sentries called. We were on a stretch of wall defended by the sea, impregnable. "I have brought you here, Hannibal, to look and to learn. Be silent now, and see."

In the east, pink light swelled. White foam girdled the peninsula and the sea was still. Dogs barked. Birds called. As the light grew, the water-courses of Megara in the city below unwrapped their white coils, serpents against the greenery of the gardens that they served. Houses grew, taking shape and massing from the darkness amid the lengthening, empty streets. On the roofs, water tanks caught the brimming sun and shone like stars. The lighthouse on the promontory of Hermaeum grew pale. Baal Hammon was pouring over Carthage the golden rain of his veins.

Now I could make out below the wall the rampart of turf and, beyond that, a great ditch, deep and wide and dark. In the shadow of the rampart was Malqua, the sailors' and dyers' quarter, a place of dirt and ugly hovels. About it lived the

Un-named, people of no Punic blood but of unknown race and origin, eaters of porcupines and shellfish, hyenas, snakes. Their huts of seaweed and slime clung to the cliff like nests. They had lived so, without rulers or religion, execrated, naked, sickly and wild, as long as the memory of man.

Turning, I looked over the city within the wall on which I stood. Cube-shaped houses rose in tiers towards the Acropolis. Public squares stood levelled here and there. The greenery of temple precincts broke up the uniformity of grey. First the golden tiles of Khamon's roof caught the rising sun, then the coral of Melkarth's. My eye was drawn on, up to the Acropolis hill, in the centre of Byrsa. The strengthening light caught its copper cupolas, its capitals of bronze, the white Parian marble of its architraves, its obelisks of azure stripes, its buttresses from Babylon. Here, drawn together from the corners of the earth, was the soul of Carthage.

As day broke, the city stirred to life. Great wagons and laden dromedaries approached the gates. Passing in, they moved lurching on the flagged streets to the market. At the cross-roads, the moneychangers rolled up the awnings of their booths. From the potters' quarter, Mappalia, the kilns began to smoke. From Tanit's sacred glade came the sound of the chants and tambourines of her holy harlots.

My father spoke. "You are a Barca, Hannibal, and my son. You see this great city unfold before you. You feel its call, yes?" I nodded. "It calls you because its life is your life. Your forefathers came to this place from Tyre in Phoenicia and found poor and huddled huts. See what we have made. Always has our family been pre-eminent among the Carthaginians.

"But do not be deceived. Carthage has no friends. We rule through fear and greed, not love. What you see is an island, alone against the world. We must trade to live and the Romans would pen us in" – and his voice grew rough and angry – "like cattle. Of the Elders, I see this and fight. When I am gone, this fight will be yours." He held my shoulders. I can still see his burning eyes. "Do you understand?"

I held his gaze. "Yes, Father," was all I said. It was done.

"Good. Then your training will begin. Go back to your room. Hamilax will come for you."

Within the hour, Hamilax and I were gone, I knew not where. We slipped out of Carthage through an obscure wicket gate, then walked east through terraces of olives and vines. A man met us. We mounted mules, went on.

Peaceful were the months that followed. Hamilax took me to a distant beach, three days' ride from Hadrumetum, to a shore of turtles and high palms. Above the beach were cliffs of sandstone, caves. In one of these we made our home and the learning began.

Hamilax began to teach me, as he had been told, such things as I had need to know. I learnt of our gods, of Melkarth first, honoured by the Phoenicians, our ancestors, and how he waged a great war against Masiasbal to avenge the serpent queen. For forty ages they fought, then forty more, locked in bitter combat. From the depths of Tartessus they fought, to the high mountains of Ersiphonia until they came to the utmost bounds of the world. There the she-monster Masiasbal turned at bay, against the flaming walls of the world and, under a blood-red moon in the sight of women dragon-tailed, Melkarth slew her.

All this I learned and more. It was for Silenus to teach me Greek, but Hamilax was versed in the old Canaanite tongue of my people and this too he began to teach me, that which is written in the books of Sakkun-yathon.

> *Aesneth karith nago*
> *Walkhah um ubefo*
> *Karith an shem . . .*
>
> *Being but a man I walk alone*
> *Seeking in the darkness*
> *Under the eye of god . . .*

By day, I began to learn the ways of animals and how to trap them, the art both of the javelin and the sword. I went barefoot, like a shepherd. Of all my childhood, these were golden days.

Hamilax was a man of grudging words. One evening we were sitting on the beach, watching a huge and flaming sun set in the sky. I asked him what was the sun, and why it was leaving. "Ask your own heart, Hannibal," he said. "Many things become clear to those who learn to ask their own hearts in silence."

We returned to Carthage in silence, as we had gone. At home, nothing had changed. The servants went their way. The bakers baked, the weavers wove. I did not see my mother at first, for she had given birth. I had, I learned, another brother, Hasdrubal, but he was with a nursemaid. My mother was confined to bed. My brother Mago seemed afraid of me. We played no more. Something had come between us. We kept to separate ways. My father was away. I felt alone.

But Silenus had been told and a new learning had begun. Day after day I was with him alone. He had instructions that I was to learn not just Latin, but also Greek, the language of command for Carthaginian armies since the generalship of the Spartan mercenary, Xanthippus.

Both were hard, but as one year passed, then another, I began to see the rigour in the first, the beauty in the second. I owe much to Silenus, that wrinkled, stooped old man who knew so much, had seen so much. And he tried to make the learning fun. We had been studying the Latin imperative. "The imperative, Hannibal, is the voice of command. Study it with care, for you are born to command. It is a clear part of speech in Latin. The Romans are a people who command clearly and simply."

But I didn't find it clear at all. I foundered on the irregular imperatives. Rather than being angry, Silenus was patient. He made up for me mnemonics – I knew already that this word was from the Greek for "remember" – and still I remember them. "*Dic* the *duc* has no *fer* and that's a *fac* – tell, lead, bear, do," the irregular Latin imperatives. And we played with little poems. I thought we were just having fun, but of course Silenus was teaching me. He was pleased, I remember, with my:

> *Puella Carthaginis ridebat*
> *Quam tigris in tergo vehebat.*
> *Externa profecta*
> *Interna revecta*
> *Sed risus in tigre manebat.*

> *There was a young lady Carthaga*
> *Who rode with a smile on a tiger.*
> *They returned from the ride*
> *With the lady inside*
> *And the smile on the face of the tiger.*

What else did I learn that shaped me? Of Alexander, great golden Alexander. As my Greek improved, Silenus brought from his chest and gave to me those treasured rolls of papyrus that were a copy of the work of Eumenes of Cardia, Alexander's *Ephemerides*, his *Journal*. We read this together many times.

We studied again and again Alexander's victories: how, at Issus, he made the Persians fight on unfavourable ground and then routed them with his cavalry, his golden armour gleaming in the sun. How, at the Hydaspes, he defeated even the great Indian elephants of King Porus or how, at Gaugamela, he showed the virtue of patience before the mortal strike. At Tyre Alexander was patient and, in the end, that great city fell for all its mighty walls.

Once my father came in when we were reading the *Ephemerides*. "Reading again, Hannibal? Silenus, I want a doer of deeds, not a reader of words." But I knew what I was reading to do and what I did not even Alexander could have done. I had none of Alexander's Macedonians. I took a mercenary army, men brought together from the corners of the earth, and held them together through fear and love. They were often hungry and unpaid, but they did not betray me. For sixteen years we fought in Italy alone.

But let my story tell itself. I am still in Carthage. I am six or seven. Silenus teaches me. I learn. Those days seem still. Each passes as the last. I sit alone with Silenus from breakfast. A slave brings us lunch. Then two hours more of learning, then my ride. An hour of instruction from Abdolonim, my father's chief groom, then freedom to gallop far.

How good Silenus was. He would marry ride and lesson with Xenophon. "You can't know too much Xenophon," he would say. "Good for your Greek and even better for the life that awaits you." So would we read from the *Peri Hippikes, On Horsemanship. "Look well at the horn of the hoof. A thick horn makes for much sounder feet than a thin one. Take care, too, to see the hoofs are high front and back, not flattened . . ."* Silenus told me that Xenophon wrote this for the instruction of his own sons, Gryllus and Diodorus. I liked to know that. I wondered what they were like, these sons. One fell at the battle of Mantinea, fighting the Thebans. "But how did he die?" I asked Silenus. He did not know. Bravely, I was sure.

So these days came and went untroubled, calm. Sometimes at night I would wonder at my solitude as I drifted into sleep. But I knew in my youth of something to come for which all this was preparation. I did not question. Then the messenger came.

I had never heard the gong before, though I passed it every day. It stood below the terrace of the great hall. Each morning, as I crossed the courtyard to my classroom, two slaves would be polishing its bronze surface, taller than a man, until it shone like a mirror. Above the crossbars of beki wood on which it hung was a great hammer, a thing as old, they said, as Carthage itself. This gong was heard as Aeneas deserted Dido, Queen of Carthage, and as she mounted her own funeral pyre in her madness and her grief. None knew who had sounded it.

11

Its sound that afternoon made my neck hairs bristle, so pure was the pitch. I was studying with Silenus. My boisterous brother Mago burst through the door. His stammer was always worse when he was excited. "H-H-H-annibal! A aa messssengggger has come!" Outside, the household was already assembling in the yard. From below the gardens in their cages, my father's elephants were trumpeting, disturbed by the gong. Hamilax was busy here and there, marshalling the folk, for all had come at the wondrous sounding of the gong, the kitchen slaves, the gardeners, the bakers, the water-carriers, all. In a corner on a makeshift bier there lay a man, his clothes torn and filthy, his beard matted with salt, his face the face of one who has made a long journey.

Standing on the steps that led to the hall, by a statue of a Cabirian called Aletes, discoverer of mines in Spain, Hamilax saw me come from my classroom, Silenus behind. Hamilax led me with him through the crowd. "We are waiting for the Elders," he said. "Word has been sent. It is as well, for the man we are to hear needs time." He left to see to the messenger. I stood where he had stood, on the steps alone, the crowd thronging about me.

When the Elders came, they merely joined me on the steps, boy though I was. But was I not Hannibal, son of Hamilcar, of the line of Barca, yes, even of Dido? I remember still the smell of Gisco, Sufet of Carthage and Chief of the Council, his sweating body reeking of frankincense and musk. He was appointed Sufet only in my father's absence for war. The folds of his neck hung down like a donkey's ears. His stomach overflowed to hide the scarlet breeches on his upper thighs. His pig's eyes glinted at me from the fat that was his face.

His right arm round the shoulders of Hamilax, the messenger limped to join us. The crowd hushed, expectant. This memory is far away, and I was but a boy. Yet if I cannot now remember exactly what he said, I remember how he said it. In a voice that faltered, he began, "Elders, people of Hamilcar, Carthaginians, I have come in haste from Hamilcar and from Sicily to tell you, to tell you . . ."

"Speak, man!" ordered Gisco angrily.

". . . that our fleet is lost."

A murmur drew across the crowd, as a wind rustles leaves. Gisco snapped the spatula of aloe that he carried to scratch his scrofulous skin. "Go on, man, go on!"

We all knew of the fleet we had sent two months ago to support my father's campaign against the Romans in Sicily. Though secure enough at his base on Mount Eryx, my father was short of supplies – and pay. His Balearic slingers were paid in women, and there had been few enough of those, cooped up as the army was with the Romans holding the rest of the island. The other troops, especially the Numidians, were paid in gold. Of that my father had none.

All this we knew from my father's regular despatches. So, at last – the Council had been most reluctant, Silenus told me – a special tax was levied. It had to be. After twenty-three years of war, our resources were spent. The trade that was our greatest wealth was much reduced for want of galleys to reach to the far shores of the Tartessians and the Oestrymnians, to the islands of the Cassiterides and its mines of tin. Rebellions on the Cyreniac frontier meant our trade in precious silphium was now a trickle. We had no troops to spare for mere marauding tribesmen. Sicily, from which we always drew so many of our slaves, was almost closed to us.

Yet the tax, largely on the merchant class, was raised and paid, a new fleet built, equipped. One hundred and fifty quinqueremes, replacing those we had lost earlier in the war at the naval battles of Mylae and Ecnomus, set sail for Sicily, laden with supplies. All this I knew, patiently explained to me by Silenus. Since then, there had been no news.

The messenger resumed. "The plan of our admiral Hanno

13

was always clear, discussed, agreed by many here. Burdened with supplies for Hamilcar, he was to avoid the Roman fleet, sail to Eryx and land his stores. Taking on board Hamilcar, your father, Hannibal" – and he raised a weak hand to gesture to me: how proud I was – "and the best of his troops to serve as marines, he was to seek out and destroy the Roman fleet.

"So was it planned, and well so. I was myself on Hanno's craft, a quartermaster, as has my family – though we are poor – served this state for – "

"Shut up, man!" shouted Gisco. "We want none of this. The fleet, man, the fleet!"

Raising his head, the man continued in a monotone that cleared and grew as his tale. "We mustered at Holy Isle, Hanno planning a final run from there to the coast of Sicily before the cursed Romans learned of our intent. But, by Melkarth, by some great doom, the Romans knew. The wind was behind us and our ships ran fair across the sea. I was on deck. Through the spray, through the early morning mist I looked for the coast of Sicily. Then the lookout cried, 'Ahead, ahead, ahead!' Above me on the poop deck I could see Hanno grasp the rail and stare. Becoming clearer by the moment and lying just off the Aegates Islands was a double-tiered crescent – of Roman ships.

"But the sea was behind us. To attack, the Romans would have had to row into a heavy sea head on. Our sails were full. Had the Romans stayed on their stations, we could have swept past them, laden as we were. And, as was right, Hanno gave the commands. The arrowhead of our fleet in tight formation tacked seawards, swerving to avoid disaster. But, but – " This time Gisco did not upbraid him. Hamilax brought water. The man drank, continued.

"But disaster came to us. Into that sea, breaking over their prows, drenching their soldiers, their galleys came, the Romans rowing at us, incredible, impossible, their oars flaying sea to foam. Against the wind, still there was only the boom, boom,

14

boom of their drums, setting the rowers' stroke. Then trumpets flamed and fired their ranks.

"In line, ordered, full against us they came. Seeing disaster, Hanno had our ship, then three more, heave to. The rest sailed on – to death. We saw, we saw" – and tears choked his voice – "we saw it all. Full ahead, ship skewered ship. Bronze beaks stripped wood, bit and bit. Oars smashed, sterns caved in. Ship after ship capsized. At first, our fleet held firm, hoping to force through. Then, one by one, they tried to slip away, but Romans grappled them. The sea was swamped with wreckage, corpses, provisioning for Hamilcar. The Roman soldiers boarded one by one our almost unarmed ships and gaffed and stabbed and smashed and killed til all the sea was shrieks and dying cries. Of our own Carthaginians, Artembares died there, though he was master of 10,000 stades and pious too to Melkarth, and Dadaces the chiliarch, Tenado and Asdrubal, Metallo the myriarch, Arabo, lord of my own clan. All are now but souls clamouring for passage across the River of Ordeal. Of our allies, the bodies of Arcteus, Adeus, Pheresseues, Pharnuchus swirl and butt against some cliff where rock-doves nest. As for Tharybis of Lyrna, death scabs his black beard red. Seisames the Mysian, he is dead, and Syennesis, Cicilian king, Ariomardus too and Matullus of Chrysa.

"I could take the orbit of the sun and not tell all and I am weak and faint. I have seen that which I would not, disaster on disaster. All is lost."

The man slumped in Hamilax's arms. Nothing stirred. Fear spread through the crowd. Gisco, to his credit, spoke out. "Go home, now, all of you. The Council will meet and declare what is to be done. Hamilax, take this man inside." Signalling for his slaves to bring his litter, Gisco was gone.

He returned later. With several other Elders, he questioned the man further. Hanno had fled with three other ships back to Holy Isle. The Romans, victorious, had not troubled to pursue them but returned to Lilybaeum. From Holy Isle, Hanno had sent two messengers by skiff – the first to us, the second to my father. He was following on to face such fate as the Elders might determine. When I asked Silenus what that might be, he would not say. I was to find out soon enough.

From that day of the messenger, my life changed. Although my normal ways were soon resumed, even Silenus was unsettled. My mother, Hamilax and the entire household were busy with preparations for what was thought to be my father's imminent return. The whole of Carthage seemed occupied with itself and the news of the disaster of the Aegates Islands. From Eschmoun's sacred grove the smoke of votive offerings rose daily in the air. The Elders, it was said, had not left the chamber of the Council, considering under the roof of Baal Hammon what was to be done.

I continued with my studies, my riding lessons, my practice under Hamilax with sword and spear, but all my teachers seemed distracted. Then I learned from Silenus who had it from Hamilax who had it from his brother Astegal, Steward to the Council, that the Council had instructed my father to reach terms with the Romans and then come home. On what basis, Astegal did not know.

Was it eight days after the coming of the messenger, nine? Silenus and I were reading Plato in the stillness of the classroom. The clamour of excited voices broke the peace. I shall always remember the point we had reached in Plato's *Republic*: "*We are each accustomed to posit some one form concerning each set of things*" – eidos hen hekaston peri hekasta ta polla in Greek: I can still remember it now – "*to which we apply the same name.*" Silenus had explained this to me in terms of the many gods of Carthage, how in their multiplicity they were the same. I was about to witness in life, not philosophy, something to which we might give many names, and of all my childhood memories this is one with which I wrestle still.

The hubbub outside was in response to a call to a general Assembly. My mother, my brother and sister, I and all those of our household of the rank of freedman slave and above were to go at once to the great public square below the Acropolis. Hanno had returned. Judgement was to be given by the Council. Following the standard of our house, a black scorpion on white, held by Hamilax, we left my father's house.

Through the narrow streets we went. As we drew nearer to the square our passage slowed, such was the press of people. My sister Sophoniba began to cry. Silenus picked her up and carried her. As we came to Byrsa, the heart of Carthage, seat of her temples and her courts and of her Council, members of the Sacred Legion lined the way.

Seeing our standard, one of them fell out and led us through the crowd. The great square was, to a young boy, vast. To the north, below the Acropolis, was the Chamber of the Council. On either side of that within the square were benches, reserved for the principal families of Carthage. There we took our place. A line of soldiers kept back the swelling crowd, leaving an area of perhaps a hundred strides clear before the Chamber of the Council.

Trumpets rang out. Slowly, with dignity, the forty Elders came out from their chamber, Gisco last, and took their seats of hammered bronze on the terrace above us. I had almost hoped to see my father, true Sufet, come after Gisco. When would my father come? Behind each chair a slave fanned his master. At the side, Astegal, High Steward of the Council, watched.

What is it, more than fifty years later, that I remember of that day? What is it that I cannot forget? I think above all the silent menace of the crowd. As Hanno was led towards us from the harbour gate, a profound and dismal silence fell. He was manacled and chained. It was a long walk from the far side of the agora to where the Elders awaited him. It was a walk life-lasting. Behind him came the Elders' servants, brandishing lashes to keep back the crowd.

17

There were too many who had lost a son, a brother, a father, a husband, a lover under Hanno's leadership. As he shambled towards the waiting Elders, in silence a thousand fingers pricked and ripped. A child tore at his cheek. A girl, who had hidden a knife under her sleeve, slashed his neck. Hands, reaching across the ropes that marked the path, tore out handfuls of his hair. Blood spurted from a wound in his thigh. They threw broken glass under his feet, burning oil, excrement and filth. None felt the lashes of the servants seeking to drive them back. Hanno fell, and as he lay a hand stretched out a red-hot poker. He screamed. Even from that press, I smelt his burning flesh. The servants turned their whips of hippopotamus hide on him, driving him on.

Crawling on his hands and knees, Hanno drew level with us, blood on his face and hands, his tunic torn and fouled, safe now from the crowd but not from judgement. Gisco stood up. He did not need to ask for silence. "Hanno, you have betrayed the sacred trust of Melkarth and Eschmoun, of Baal Hammon, Tanit. The priests have consulted the auguries, the virgins of Eschmoun the entrails of a fawn. You are condemned. Let that which is customary be done."

The howl that rose from the crowd as from one throat was not of this world. Four soldiers stepped forward. No patricians, these, but burly men, seasoned veterans who served the Council for gold and women. I saw from my place on the bench the calloused patches – we called them "carobs" – under the chin of the first that come from years of the helmet's chin-strap.

They seized Hanno, lifting him to his feet. Two held him up. The third tore his filthy tunic neck to knee. The fourth brought forward a great stake and placed it in its socket in the ground. The crowd's noise fell away as Hanno was tied, his back to us and the crowd, his bloody face to the Council, to the stake. The whoosh of the whip through the air was followed by a sound like no other, a sucking, tearing sound as the iron in the thongs of the whip tore at flesh, breaking the bones of Hanno's back. Flecks of blood and blobs of skin stained the ground around. Only with the ninth stroke, or was it the tenth, did Hanno scream.

They untied him. He fell to the ground, inert. A bucket of urine, thrown over his head, revived him. One of the veterans seized him by the hair, held up his torso to the view of the crowd. They moaned. The head of a heavy mallet glinted in the sun, fell, rose and fell again. So were broken the legs of Hanno, admiral of the fleet. The soldiers lifted down the stake. With three great nails the soldiers nailed him lying to the cross, a nail in each hand and one through both ankles. Straining now, one pulling on a rope tied to the top of the cross, they raised Hanno, crucified. As it lurched into its socket and Hanno cried out, the crowd's roar surged and swelled. His belly torn by the whips, Hanno's intestines hung and swung from the settling of the cross. It was done.

I have seen many crucifixions. I have ordered many. But the first of all things is the best and the worst. For Hanno I felt and I feel now pity. The ways of the gods I know are cruel and strange. But of many strange wonders, none is stranger than man.

That afternoon, Silenus told me to read on my own. He said nothing, but I felt the distaste of a cultivated man, a Greek, for such practices as crucifixion. "Why are you withdrawn, Silenus?" I asked.

"Get on with your work!" he snapped. But soon he rose from the table at which he was working and paced up and down the room. "Because, because . . ." he said, and I had never heard him angry before. "Because . . ." He turned sharply to his chest, drew out a scroll I had not seen before. Finding his place, he began to read, his voice trembling:

"*If the soul really is immortal, what care should be taken of her, not only in respect of the portion of time which is called life, but of eternity!*

19

There is no release from evil except the attainment of the highest virtue and wisdom . . ."

" 'The highest virtue and wisdom,' Hannibal, do you hear, do you? Now listen, listen to Plato's *Phaedo!*" And he read on:

"The way to the other world is not a straight and single path – if that were so, no guide would be needed; but there are many partings of the road, and windings . . . As for that soul which is impure or has done impure deeds . . . from that soul everyone flees and turns away; no-one will be her companion, no-one her guide, but alone she wanders in extremity of evil . . ."

"To whom does that apply, Hannibal? To Hanno, or to those who crucified him?"

I did not answer. Even now, I do not know.

The days that followed were tense. The whole of Carthage swelled with talk. My father had been instructed by the Council to reach terms of peace with Rome after twenty-four years of war. Despatches went back and forth. Through Astegal and Hamilax came the news.

We were to evacuate the whole of Sicily, swear not to attack Syracuse nor the allies of Syracuse, surrender all prisoners-of-war without ransom and pay an indemnity of 2,200 talents within twenty years. Then, we learned, the Roman commissioners had been instructed by the Senate that the indemnity should be paid within ten years. To Roman demands that all their deserters should be given up for execution and that our troops should give up their arms and pass under the yoke, my father replied that he would rather fight on. Those points the Romans conceded, winning instead an increase in the indemnity by a further 1,000 talents and the promise that we would evacuate not just Sicily, but Corsica and Sardinia as well.

Silenus was sad. "This is the end," he said to me, "of nothing. Your father has made peace because Carthage is exhausted. The Romans have made peace because they too are exhausted. But Regulus was right. There is not room for two great powers. One must be destroyed." But I thought not of such things. To me, a boy, the peace meant that my father was coming home – to stay.

We were at the harbour to meet him, I, my mother, my siblings Mago, Hasdrubal and Sophoniba, Silenus and, of course, Hamilax. None of the Elders came. There would be time enough for councils. The people had come, of course, warned of my father's return by the trumpet heralds high on the temple of Eschmoun. They would have seen his galley round the great mole and enter the commercial harbour and we heard their shouts of welcome and of joy. But we awaited Hamilcar Barca within the inner military harbour, shut off from the outer by great nail-studded gates.

One of these opened. I heard a harsh command. My father's quinquereme leapt into our sight and swept across the basin to its quay marked by two columns, the scorpion of our house on each, the horns of Ammon on their capitals. He vaulted over the thwart and was with us, taking first my mother then each of us in his arms. Only when he embraced Hamilax could I see him fully, tall and lean, a full hand taller than Hamilax, strong. It was his eyes, though, that held us all, clear, deep brown on purest white. He smiled. "Come, let us go home," he said, and led the way to the wagon waiting by the quay.

I hoped to hear it all from him in time: the fires, the legions, Eryx, Sicily, the years of battle. I hoped for time. I knew that at first he would be deep in council and seeing to affairs. But the war was over. There would be time. That was not to be. The Truceless War began.

II

MERCENARIES

Leaving Sicily, my father's orders were that our troops should return gradually to Carthage. They had not been paid for several years. Huge sums we did not have were due. I knew my father's mind, for I was with him when he admitted Gisco and other Elders who had come to our house. "I have fought for nearly seven years in Sicily," my father said, "and now you have peace. Give me mine. I must see to my own affairs. Pay the soldiers as you can. They are to trickle back, not flood."

"Pay them, Hamilcar, with what?" cried Gisco.

"Why, the jewellery you wear itself would pay a squadron, Gisco," my father joked, leaving the room. But he had every confidence in Gisco. "He may be no soldier," my father said, "but as an administrator he has no equal."

Several days later, my father left Carthage with Hamilax and four trusted slaves on a tour of his estates, his forests of oak at Zartana, his granaries at Chozeba and Tirzah, his summer house at Issachar and farms of sheep and goats at Marephath. He was to be gone for several months. We were all to wish he had not gone at all.

We became aware of the mercenaries' returning almost imperceptibly in the months my father was away. Their camp was to the city's rear upon the plain that stretched away and round the gulf to Tunis. I saw it grow as, each afternoon, I went for my ride with Abdolonim. The Ligurians had been first to return and pitch their ordered tents of skin upon the sand. Then came the Lacedaemonians, a race apart, who slept upon the ground within the ditch that they had dug. Soon the Balearics came, slingers from the Spanish isles, who formed no order like the rest but mingled, ate and slept wherever they could.

Darytians from Gaetulia next put up their shelters of dry grass and waited in the wind.

A month passed and returning Iberians set their marquees of canvas with the rest; the Gauls made shelters out of planks, the Libyans out of stones. The Negroes, Numidians and Libyans slept in trenches in the sand. The camp grew. There were 10,000 there, then 20,000 and Abdolonim would not let me near and a sense of menace grew around the camp as strong as was the reek and stench of this great host, the mercenaries of Carthage.

From the city to the camp plied traders, pedlars, women, boys. The women were of every nation on the earth, brown as dates, sallow as olives, yellow as melons, white as alabaster; women sold by sailors, seized by soldiers, stolen from desert caravans, captured at the sacking of cities, worn out by the penises and practices of many men when they were young and beaten when they were old, left to die among the donkeys and the dung. All moved and mingled in the camp, women of Cappadocia with gold plates in their hair, of Gaul with wolfskin on their breasts. Those of Cyrenaica, wreathed in violet gauze, vermilion-faced, sang songs of sadness where they sat on mats of rush. Amongst the clamour and the smell and smoke of many fires moved Lusitanians, with necklaces of sea-shell and pendulous naked breasts, gathering for fuel the droppings of the animals to be dried in a strengthening sun.

So much I could see for myself. But by the month of Eloul, in mid-summer, I began to hear from the servants and the slaves and from Silenus of merchants unpaid for their wares, of women for their services. Sellers of oil and water, tailors, moneylenders, bakers all complained of accounts ridiculed. For a sheep, the mercenaries offered the price of a pigeon; for three goats that of a pomegranate. The soldiers, it was said, had begun to drink wine, a thing forbidden on pain of execution in a Punic army. Prowlers were abroad at night and from the city there came complaints of thefts and rapes and pillagings. With the summer heat there rose a tension that afflicted all. Even Silenus found no consolation in his scrolls, in his philosophies.

Still my father was away. Still Gisco waited. I felt for the mercenaries, unpaid still, and knew that they must dream of many things that might have been and some that might yet be. One would buy a farm, one a ship, returning to their native lands with that of value from their years of war for Carthage. So did I imagine them dozing in the sun, counting up their years of service and their gear lost, their arms and shields and horses. Now, they had nothing, save their wounds and scars and grumblings. Carthage replied with barred gates and doubled watch and silence.

At last Gisco acted. I was at Khamon's Gate to see him depart in his purple litter, bunches of ostrich feathers at each corner, crystal chains and ropes of pearl swinging to the movement that it made.

Behind him went twenty dromedaries, their bags heavy with gold, the bronze bells around their necks clanging as they lurched along. Around them rode the horsemen of the Sacred Legion, armoured in golden scales, astride their snorting stallions from Hecatompylus, the plumes of their bronze Boeotian helmets soaring to the sky. Then came the clerks on donkeys, with the tablet and the abacus for reckoning what was owed. With them went Silenus, unadorned as was his way, in simple cotton shift. Last in litters came the Twelve Interpreters, skilled in desert tongues, each with parrots tattooed on both arms, their headdresses of peacock plumes swaying softly in the breeze.

That struck me at the time, that Gisco knew at least he must communicate with many men who had no common tongue. Some *dekadarchoi*, some captains, Silenus had told me, would know Punic, but he was to speak the words of Gisco to the Dorians and Spartans, the Boeotians and the other Greeks. The

Twelve would deal with the Libyans and Numidians. As for the rest, the Gauls and the men of the west beyond the Pillars of Herakles, Silenus did not know.

It had, I knew, always been a policy of Carthage to keep its army polyglot. So would insurrection be more difficult. But if this worked in war, it did otherwise in peace. The Truceless War began, as Silenus said, not from principles nor passion, but because people could not communicate. I have made it my business from that time up to this to learn the tongues of those around me.

Arriving at the mercenary camp, Gisco and his entourage were soon surrounded by men clamouring for the pay that was their due. Two heralds sounded silver horns, the noise died down and Gisco spoke, standing on a table of the clerks. First he told, Silenus said, of the Republic's gratitude to its soldiers for the service they had lent to Carthage. "We want our money, not your gratitude!" cried back someone who spoke Punic. Gisco ploughed on. Times, he said, were hard. Carthage was now poor – "But you are not!" came voices from the back – "and if a master has only three melons, is it not right that he should keep two for himself?" The indemnity to Rome was crippling. The treasury was empty, the purple fisheries exhausted, the farmland abandoned in the war producing nothing. Carthage would have to sell its silphium reserve and further tax the trading towns. "Why, only yesterday," said Gisco, "I had myself to pay for a bath-slave what a year ago would have bought me an elephant, no" – he must have thought they would appreciate his wit – "a virgin from Bithynia."

So Gisco went on. "Excuses are like arseholes," came a voice in Greek from the back of the crowd. "Everybody's got one!" Those that understood – not Gisco – laughed.

By now the crowd was thousands strong and pushing hard against the circle around Gisco formed by the the Sacred Legion. "You will be paid, all of you, in full – but in time."

Gisco paused to let first Silenus, then the Twelve translate this to the crowd. The menace grew as the words "in time" sank in and were passed in many tongues around.

"I have with me," Gisco then cried out, "a xthet of pure gold for each of you as earnest of our faith. As for you Balearics, whose pay is always women, a caravan of virgins, fattened up and rubbed with benjamin, is even now on its way from Abdera. We have commissioned galleys which will take you to your homes. You will be paid in full before you leave."

"For our horses too?"

"Yes," said Gisco mournfully, "for your horses too. Now form up lines before these clerks who will pay you each the gold and take a record of what more each of you is due."

This too was translated round the camp. Numidians from the mountains, wrapped in the skin of bears, who had been leaning forward, ominous on their clubs, and Dorians, flaxen-haired, who had begun to finger their swordbelts made of iron, now relaxed. It might, Silenus thought, have worked, for these were people who had trusted Carthage, some for generations.

But just as the mercenaries were beginning to form obedient lines, a giant Campanian stepped forward and sounded a great horn. He was beyond the horses and before the mercenaries and what he said was said so fast the harm was done before any could gainsay. He announced rapidly in six different languages, in Latin, Gaulish, Balearic, Libyan, Iberian and Greek, that he had something important to say. Since it was Greeks who were most numerous around him, he went on in Greek.

"Now hear what this man has truly said," the Campanian shouted. "He called you cowards, vermin, sons of dogs and bitches. Had you not lost for Carthage the war with Rome, she would not have to pay her indemnity to Rome so why, then, should you be paid?" Silenus tried to move to Gisco to translate this for him, but was held fast in the press. "One stater is all you will get. These clerks are here to record not what you will be paid but how you are to be punished, in the Cantabrian mines or as galley slaves. These were the true words of Gisco. Let us not take a stater. Let us take Carthage itself!"

So simply was it done. The horsemen of the Sacred Legion were pulled from their mounts, Gisco's circle drowned. Hands tore off his necklace of blue stones, his gold clasps, his heavy earrings. The dignity of Carthage was trampled in the dust.

They were all held then in a human corral, the Sufet and Silenus, the Twelve, the clerks, the high-born of the Legion. The bags of gold were brought. The Campanian – his name was Spendius – seemed in command. "What shall we do with them?" came cries. "Kill them!" said one, and "Cut off their balls!" another. "No, let's eat them . . ." Spendius held up a great axe, double-edged. Silence fell. "What we shall do" – he paused – "is keep them," he said, "as hostages, though we may have some sport with him" – and he prodded Gisco in the stomach with his axe – "first."

Silenus was a gentle man. The pain it caused him first to witness what was then done and next to recount it to the Council was a pain from which he was never to recover. Years later in Spain I found his copy of Homer's *Iliad* with this passage marked and marked again. Priam, King of Troy, is mourning for dead Hector, his greatest son, champion of Troy which now must fall, for Hector has been killed by Achilles:

γεραιὸς
ἐντυπὰς ἐν χλαίνῃ κεκαλυμμένος· ἀμφὶ δὲ πολλὴ
κόπρος ἔην κεφαλῇ τε καὶ αὐχένι τοῖο γέροντος,
τήν ῥα κυλινδόμενος καταμήσατο χερσὶν ἑῇσι.

The old man sat veiled, beaten into his cloak. Excrement lay thick on his head and neck, he was an old man, for he had been rolling in it, he had gathered it and smeared it on with his hands.

Such, I suppose, Silenus thought his sorrow and his suffering to be. Yet his was a less brutal suffering than many begun that day. First the mercenaries put Gisco in a frame of rough-hewn planks. To the board behind his neck they nailed his hands and to the one between his legs they nailed his knees. A man they called Zaracas did these things, moaning with the pleasure that this brought him. It was Spendius, though, who put out the Sufet's eyes, pushing with his great strength on the Sufet's sockets with his thumbs until both eyeballs popped. Then he bit through with his teeth the cords of both the Sufet's eyes. His tongue, Silenus said, was torn out by Zaracas, his ears cut off by a dark-skinned Libyan they knew as Mathos. Then they put his eyeballs, his ears and his tongue on a rope of pearl they tore from Gisco's litter and they placed it round the neck of Silenus of Caleacte and sent him back alone to Carthage to tell the Council of their terms.

Silenus left the Sufet living still and all his clerks and Twelve and Legionaries lying in a rubbish pit where pigs snarled for scraps. First Spendius had had them tied together, a collar of iron round each neck in the manner of the caravans of slaves that cross the trackless deserts of the south. Silenus saw the camp boys come, filthy, naked, uncircumcised and verminous and urinate upon their heads. Spendius brought the quartered azure standards of the Sufet and threw them down upon their heads.

I was in my father's hall, its floor of polished lapis-lazuli, when that night the Elders came to hear from Silenus of the mercenaries' terms. The night was dark. A grey mist filled the sea which beat against the wall of Carthage with a noise of sobs and dying breath. The Elders came into the hall bearing their sticks of narwhal horn. In mourning for the shame upon the Sufet, some had torn their robes. Others bore their beards enclosed in mauve leather bags fastened round their ears with silken blackened string.

They heard from Silenus of terms they could not meet, had

they even wanted. Outrageous sums were asked, gold and silver, mines in Spain, ten zeters too of land for every man. For their leaders they demanded in marriage virgins of the great families of Carthage. This outraged the Elders that our Punic blood should even be presumed to mix with that of barbarians. Meantime they wanted from our stores amphorae of wine and guinea fowl, mackerel and meat and spice and seasonings, all this within two days.

Baalhaan, the senior there, spoke out for all and ordered Astegal himself, High Steward of the Council, to leave that night and find Hamilcar my father. Safe for many months within their walls, the Elders of the Council could not speak for peace. So they spoke for war.

Those were oppressive days. Silenus was too weak to teach or talk. He stayed in his room, seeking solace in Euripides. The city gates were barred to all. The people of Carthage were terrified and tense, our household servants sullen and recalcitrant. There was dark talk of a holocaust, a *tophet* in our tongue, the burning alive of children to appease Melkarth and Tanit-pene-Baal. Even Tunis, our subject city just across the bay, had, we learned, revolted, its Elders opening their gates, its merchants their stores and its women their legs to the mercenaries.

Two days later, the supplies unsent, we heard the mercenaries were before the wall, just out of bow shot or of javelin. No Carthaginian would have fired, though, for this is what we saw, those many of us high and safe upon the wall. Twenty of the Sacred Legion were lined up, tied to short and sharpened stakes.

Six mercenaries approached the first. Spendius the Campanian was there, his skin gleaming with woad, his amulets of silver gleaming in the sun, and Mathos and yes, Zaracas, Silenus said. The bonds of the first Legionary were cut. Spendius and Mathos seized his legs and stretched them out. Two others took his shoulders and his arms. They lifted him up and, muscles heaving, brought him swiftly shuddering down, impaling him

29

between the legs and upwards through his guts upon the stake. Taking his shoulders from behind, the giant Spendius pushed him down again and then again, laughing a crazed laugh and each time the Sacred Legionary screamed a scream that filled the air.

It can only have been worse for the other nineteen, knowing what awaited them. I have had many men impaled. How long they live depends on many things. If the stake is long, it penetrates the heart and death is swift. If the impaled is old or frail or weak of will, their ordeal is soon ended.

The mercenaries' stakes were short, their victims young and strong in body and mind. I am then sure they were alive when, one by one, Zaracas cut their throats before us all and caught some blood of each within a bowl. By Melkarth and Eschmoun, by all the brightening stars, by moon and sun and sea, each tribe on earth has customs and has ways which, though peculiar to itself and strange to others, is no less wrong for that. Yet what Zaracas did next, no man should have done or do again.

Turning to the walls of Carthage, stepping forward to us all, he raised the bowl and moaned and drank in one great draught the blood of twenty of the Sacred Legion. Beside me, Silenus retched, turned and hurried away. Raising his head towards the sun like a stag drunk newly from a stream, Zaracas sang a weird and sickening song, a war paean, a dirge.

Baalhaan had called for catapults to fire. Too late. I stood and watched as the missiles of the catapults kicked up the empty and the blood-stained sand.

The sky was dark for days thereafter, rank with smoke, shutting out the sun. The mercenaries were burning the country villas of the rich, some no doubt of the house of Barca among them. Their numbers grew, swelled by slaves who joined them to be free. Wild bands of Nomads, dressed in white cloaks of wool with leather necklets, wooden earrings, their boots of hyena skin, came on quadrigas and joined the waxing camp.

Bandits, broken men from Cape Phiscus and the promontory of Derna, Garamantians mounted on their painted mares, Atarantes who curse the sun, locust-eating Auseans riding zebras and wild asses, Gysantes who eat lice and Zuaces, covered in ostrich feathers and masked with black veils, all these came to join the mercenary host and destroy Carthage.

The trumpet heralds signified that, once again, there were mercenaries before Khamon's Gate. Hundreds of us climbed the walls to watch. Silenus this time would not come. My brothers Mago and Hasdrubal were with me. What we saw was mercenaries digging a pit. To this they brought their prisoners, already emaciated, foul, tufts of hair torn out, and last Gisco, carried in his frame, a monstrous tiara of hippopotamus hide on his head. They had daubed unguents on his wounds, his knees, his hands, his eyes, his ears to stave off infection, keep him alive for suffering.

Into this pit were thrown the ambassadors of Carthage, but not until the legs of each were broken by bronze bars. Then came donkeys, bearing Gisco's gold. The mercenaries poured this basket by basket over the men below until they lay gleaming in the sun, all but drowned in gold. Huge Spendius reached down and took up some coins. These he stuck to an arrow-shaft smeared with tar and with his great bow of yew he shot the arrow swiftly at the city gate before him. We did not understand, until a sentry brought the arrow to Baalhaan on the wall.

The coins were not of gold, but gilded lead. Gisco had played and lost.

Discovering this duplicity seemed to change the mercenaries. Now, day by day, they marshalled and wheeled upon the plain. Their archers for practice shot at flamingoes on the lagoon. From their camp we heard no more the sound of drunken revelry but, instead, that of their smiths, forging swords and shields. Piles of lances soon were to be seen, stacked like sheaves of corn and in their pit before the walls before our eyes the Sufet of Carthage and those who had gone with him died from thirst and sun and leaden gold.

Some messengers reached the Council, passing in the night through wicket gates to bring the news of widespread insurrection. Of our subject cities, all but Utica and Hippacritae had risen up, murdered their Carthaginian garrisons and opened their gates to Spendius and Mathos, now acclaimed as joint Schalischims, Generals of the Free. The two loyal cities were beseiged, and from our walls all could see the carpenters and masons, smiths and wrights among the mercenary host prepare for seige the catapults and rams, ballistae, onagers and tollenones that would soon, we thought, be turned on Carthage.

Yet the city was impregnable, all knew that, standing within its mighty walls on its own peninsula almost surrounded on three sides by sea and on the last by a lagoon. The mercenaries might straddle the neck of land which joined the city to the continent and on which they were camped beside the river Macaras, but we would wait. We had water, food enough to wait for Hamilcar, my father, who would come and lead an army to destroy the hubris of the mercenaries.

Baalhaan, acting Sufet, grew impatient. He appointed to command one Haggith, on my mother's side a cousin of the Barcas, a merchant, pallid-skinned from hours inside at long accounts and reckonings.

The Sacred Legion was some 6,000 strong. To their number Haggith decreed all able-bodied citizens should be added. Each morning as the cocks crowed they lined up along the Mappalia for drill with lance and sword. Haggith was everywhere about the city, the arsenal, the treasury, the lighthouse, the corn bins and the cisterns, checking, ordering, disposing. He had the elephants from the city walls prepared. Their bronze breastplates were re-cast, their tusks gilded, their towers renewed and strengthened. I saw all this as each day I walked about the city and wondered: when will my father come?

Haggith was ready, his force prepared. Abdolonim was going with them, captaining a cohort, and so it was not with my father that I first saw the standard of the Barcas going off to war. The mercenaries were now divided into three armies, one beseiging Utica, one Hippacritae and the third encamped still upon the landward plain. Each, it was thought, was of some 20,000 men.

Haggith's force was only half of that. He put his trust in our elephants, knowing that my father had had none in Sicily and that the mercenaries would be unfamiliar with their lethal ways. The Council had determined that Haggith should first relieve the seige of Utica, a morning's march across the Gulf of Carthage. In Utica were galleys which we needed to bring fresh supplies and troops.

All of us who stayed behind crowded onto the wall above Khamon's Gate to see the force depart at early dawn. To reach Utica, they would first have to face the mercenary army on the plain. Haggith's army formed into one long line three deep and marched upon the mercenaries. The Sacred Legion formed the first line, the household slaves and servants, armed with slings, on the flanks. Next came the heavy infantry, their long pikes waving in the air. Amongst them were the city's freedmen, unacquainted most with war but bristling like porcupines with arms – a lance, an axe, a club, two swords. Last came the elephants in five squadrons, the camp followers in between, and flanking them on either side the Numidian cavalry on nimble short-legged garrons, the riders bearing but a shield of hide and scimitar.

They had surprise at least to help them. As they came near the mercenary camp – we could see all now in strengthening light – at Haggith's command the last line of the elephants and cavalry, he amongst them, his purple litter rocking like a ship at sea, held back. The Legion and the infantry marched on to a great sudden din of tympani and trumpets, assbone flutes and drums.

33

Action stirred across the mercenary camp like a dog fresh from water. Horns were sounded and the mercenaries came out, their slingers to the fore. They began the slaughter. Before their volleys of clay pellets and lead bullets the Legionaries fell, first one, then two, then twenty, scores. The forces were perhaps 200 strides apart when, on the run, hard at the Legion's centre, the giant Spendius in the van, a wedge-shaped syntagma of mercenaries armed with long Etruscan swords burst through the Legion's line and fell upon the freedmen and the merchants in our centre.

Encumbered by their gear, unable to go forward or go back, tripping over dead and dying, blinded by their own blood, the Legion and the infantry of Carthage fell in piles of limbs and lances before the mercenary swords. Spendius swung, as if a flail, a giant axe, and heads and arms and hands were littered on the sand. Beside me on the wall, Baalhaan groaned and turned away.

The mercenaries began to sing a song of victory, ululating through the dust and smell of blood. But then a new sound came, a searing, soaring trumpeting of elephants, a sound of madness and of rage. In one single line, Haggith himself brandishing a pike and mounted on a great bull, the sixty elephants of Carthage charged upon the press of mercenaries and our shattered troops.

The elephants' tusks were gilded, their ears painted blue, their trunks daubed with red lead. Each had a spear fitted to its chest, a sabre to its trunk, a cutlass on each tusk, circles of sharp spikes around each lower leg. Blood flowed over their great ears from the goading of their drivers who sat and screamed from towers of leather on the elephants' backs. Behind each driver rode two archers, now showering their arrows on the host, on friend and foe alike. Armoured in bronze, the elephants broke upon the battle.

Men were choked by trunks, decapitated by cutlasses and

sabres, disembowelled by tusks. Human entrails hanging on their heads and trunks and tusks, the elephants raged, trampled, hacked and gored, rearing on their hind legs, smashing men to pulp, tearing limb from limb, wheeling, turning, deadly, mad. One had a mercenary impaled on its chest's great spear, and shook as to be finished with the cadaver. The beast turned, trumpeting, possessed, back towards Carthage, ripping with its trunk parts off the body, a lower leg, a forearm, then a head, throwing them aside along its charging way.

Another, maddened by a mercenary arrow in its eye, threw off its tower and ran on bellowing to the camp, straight through the stockade wall, mowing down the tents and huts of grass, passing on from sight.

The frenzy passed, though several of the beasts ignored their drivers and stood, pounding with their feet at piles of dead, making a mush of what had once been men. The mercenaries that survived had fled.

I went out with the Sufet and his guard to greet the victors, those that lived. Then pouring from the city came the people, most with knives in their hands, flocking to have their revenge upon the mercenaries. In groups of four or five, some were still defiant and alive. These the people killed like mad dogs, from a distance stoning them. Some were stabbed and stabbed again by women, children, slaves. Haggith sought the corpse of Spendius to have, he said, the head mounted on a pole and carried on to Utica. It could not be found.

It grew hot. The people of Carthage worked with bare arms, reapers, murdering the dying. Baalhaan had rounded up the hundred or so mercenaries who, though wounded, could still stand. The elephants' work was not yet done.

The prisoners were led down to a flat place by the river. At Baalhaan's command, ten elephants followed. I did not go to watch. The screams of men and trumpeting of elephants, that was enough. Then, at first in ones and twos, and then in a black

35

crowd, the ravens came to settle on the dead and dying, pecking out by choice the eyes and exposed guts.

Haggith re-formed his force and went on to relieve Utica. His messengers brought news that the mercenaries had not opposed him. He was in the town. All was well.

But into their town the Uticans had admitted only Haggith and some few. The elephants, the army had stayed outside the walls. That night, the mercenaries returned in force, led by Mathos and, it was said, by Spendius. Not for nothing had they served with Hamilcar Barca in Sicily.

They dealt simply with the elephants. Rounding up a herd of pigs and sheep, the mercenaries covered them with pitch. They set light to the animals and drove them blazing through the dark to where the elephants were tethered. Terrified, the great beasts fled into the night, but not before they had wreaked havoc on the men about them. What the elephants began, the mercenaries finished, slaughtering many, seizing arms and gear before they stole away as they had come.

One thing they did they must have planned with care. At next daybreak by the main gate into Utica, Haggith found some forty of the elephants' drivers, lying ordered, tongues protruding, faces blue and nostrils oozing slime. Each wore round his neck a bowstring cord.

At dusk, Haggith slipped away from Utica and found in the hills the remnants of his army. Marching only at night, hiding by day in olive groves and orchards, he made his laborious way back to Carthage. Of all this he gave at least a true account to the Elders, of how at Gorza and then three times more he might have fallen on the mercenaries, but he was afraid. Perhaps his honesty won him his life. He could feel the cross that was his due. He had lost sixty elephants, 3,000 men, corn and baggage, gold and silver. He asked for poison in his shame. The Elders would decree. Then my father came.

He had been far in the interior, deep in the mountains of

Marazzana when Astegal found him. He had returned in the night, unheralded. Already the mercenaries were encamped again across the isthmus, cutting Carthage off. Hamilax it was who woke me in the very early light. "Hannibal, your father bids you go to him." Hamilax looked older, drawn.

"My father! Where?"

"He says that you will know."

Without thinking I dressed, ran from the house and to the wall and found the stone and slipped inside and climbed. He stood there, gazing out to sea. Without turning, "Am I in time, Hannibal?" he asked. I shivered in the morning chill. I did not know. "Yes!" he cried, and turned and strode across the battlement to me. "I have come in time. Carthage called and I am here. Remember that, Hannibal."

"But Father," I spluttered, "Gisco, Haggith . . ."

"I know, I know. Come and sit down." We moved to a bench in the lee of the wall.

"Is Carthage in such peril, Hannibal? Let me tell you of the Nysalles, a tribe who once inhabited deep inland the Libyan desert. The south wind dried up the water in their storage tanks. They were left with no water whatsoever. And so the Nysalles declared war on the wind and marched out to defeat it. The wind blew, and covered them with sand. They were wiped out, and now the Nasamones hold their land.

"Do you understand? The mercenaries have declared war on Carthage. They might as well have declared war on the wind. But I have much to do, and you will help me. This will be for us rehearsal for a greater war. Come."

So for the next weeks I accompanied my father everywhere as he prepared for war. The classroom was forgotten. I hardly saw Silenus or my mother or my siblings. This was learning of a different kind.

The campaign of Hamilcar Barca against the mercenaries began not in the shrill of trumpets nor the clash of arms, but at a desk, early, morning after morning. Everything was recorded, tabulated, planned, the stocks of men and arms and horses, elephants. "I cannot fight them – yet," my father often said. By the middle of each morning we were all about the city, my father kind and brusque, gentle and harsh by turns as occasion demanded.

The blacksmiths had no bronze. My father took it, for all the extravagant protests that he met, from the Elders' treasury. The armourers had no gut for bow-strings. The hair of all the city's female slaves was shorn and used instead. When that proved not enough, my father turned to freedmen's wives.

He drew 300,000 gold kikars from the Syssitia, the company of merchants, and imposed a tax of 200 gold xthets on the rich. If one refused to pay or claimed he lacked the means, his household goods were sold at public auction, my father himself a leading bidder. A thing unparalleled, he even demanded money of the priestly colleges – and got it. Who could deny a Sufet who had himself contributed 160 sets of armour, 2,000 xthets, 3,000 gommors of wheat and much else besides?

He sent Hamilax by ship – the mercenaries had no fleet at least – to Liguria for 3,000 soldiers, all to be paid a full year in advance at sixteen copper xthets a day. He reformed the Sacred Legion, those 3,000 who had returned with Haggith or remained behind as garrison, dismissing and replacing officers, forbidding wine or women, compelling them to train all day and sleep at night on the ground within the public squares.

He drilled his growing army. The infantry were given shorter swords and lighter shields and ash sarissae, lances thirteen cubits long. To the heavy cavalry of the Sacred Legion he added 800 men he picked himself from Malqua, a thing unheard of, training them relentlessly, equipping them with bows and light double-edged axes, tunics of leather and caps of weasel-skin. From even slaves and artisans he chose 300 men as slingers. His was an absolute command, and yet each week he sent accounts to the Elders.

Two months passed, three. The people grew anxious, sullen when we passed. "Barca is afraid," they said. "Barca is a quartermaster, not a general. Will he never march?" Across the plain beyond the pit where Gisco's and the others' corpses rotted, the mercenary camp was once more full and threatening. Round it now and right across the isthmus to the river ran a wall of mud and stakes, topped by thorns. At intervals along its length, the mercenaries had set up strange and chilling scarabim and sorceries, chevrons and charms. Dead eagles, human foetuses, heads of lions, strangled ravens passed their stench into the breeze.

Still my father waited and prepared. Several times he woke me in the night. Alone we slipped out of the city through the wicket by Khamon's Gate and walked west across the sand to where the river Macaras wound into the lagoon that guarded Carthage's side.

Fast and full of menace flowed the river, strong and silent through the night. We combed the banks among the marshes looking for firm ground and placing markers when we found it. I threw a branch into the water and, by the moonlight, saw it carried swift away. How could an army ford this? My father knew what I was thinking. "Tomorrow, I will show you, Hannibal."

The next evening, we climbed the western wall. The wind we call a *chthon* was blowing, relentless from the west, as it always did at certain times each month. My father pointed to the river mouth. "Now watch, Hannibal, watch!" The wind coursed over the dunes of soft and drifting sand, picking up clouds of it as it passed over the river. Gradually, the flow of water slowed. The river mouth was silting up. In growing dark, it closed. "By morning, the channel will be clear again. We will cross, Hannibal, this time next month – if the wind blows," and he smiled. "Now go and sleep, my son." I left my father standing with his plans.

The next morning my father told me to go with Hamilax and five slaves to the workshops of the carpenters, collect eighty mallets and long chisels he had ordered and take them to the yard where his elephants were being quartered and equipped. He was there before us. He had the eighty drivers of the elephants form one line four deep. "You all know what happened to the elephants before Utica. The mercenaries may try something similar again. If your elephant runs amok, kill it" – and he bent down to pick up a mallet and a chisel – "with these. You know the spot – between the ears. But strike hard and quickly, at the first sign of trouble."

I was dozing in a chair beside my father late at night. He and Hamilax were talking. I woke up at the unfamiliar name, "Naravas". "Go to him, Hamilax. Tell him to await the signal. Give him" – and my father took from out the chest before him a great ring of gold and onyx – "this." Hamilax took the ring and nodded, left the room.

"Father, who is Nava, Nara . . . ?"

"Naravas, Hannibal. Do not forget that name. Carthage has few allies, even fewer friends. He is both. You will meet him when he comes. Now, let's both go to bed."

It was the second evening of the month of Ziph. The river Macaras was silting up. My father had sound the call to arms. Suddenly Carthage was astir. Soldiers armed themselves as women wailed against their chests. Horses reared, protesting at their bits. The Elders came in litters to attend, the priests and acolytes to bless. They showered the way before the gate with pine cones, symbols that the mercenaries should be as pine trees which, once cut down, are destroyed forever.

With muffled arms in silence in the dark we passed through Khamon's Gate, my father leading on his speckled bay, I beside him on my pony. We came to the river. As had been planned,

40

half the elephants were led a hundred yards upstream into the river, their bulk checking the river's flow. The other forty formed a wall downstream to stop any men or gear swept away.

The mercenaries' campfires burned on as we crossed. We marched along the further bank and then re-crossed the river. We camped in silence on the plain behind the mercenary host. No fires were lit. Salted beef was passed. At first light by whispered word we assumed order and marched.

It was fully light when the mercenaries' sentries saw us. Their trumpets sounded. The mercenaries poured out to form one long line. With screams and shouts they ran towards us. We held formation. I had seen my father draw this in his hall with Hamilax and again with his commanders before we left Carthage, again and again and again until tempers frayed but everyone understood. Our elephants were first, light infantry and slingers in between them. Our second rank, ten strides behind, was heavy infantry, and then our third, cavalry and bowmen.

Five hundred strides before the forces would have met, my father's trumpet rang out. As one man, our army stopped, our elephants turned round and passed through the soldiers in the second row who followed in their turn. With cries of scorn – they are running away already! – the mercenaries rushed towards us, their spearmen, bowmen, slingers throwing as they came.

They met one straight and solid line, now longer than theirs. I was kept to the rear, beside my father and his trumpeters and Hamilax. Our infantry had formed syntagmata, solid and impenetrable squares with sixteen men two ranks deep on all four sides, pikes protruding, shields reaching to the ground. An elephant was stationed to the left and right of each syntagma, the heavy cavalry behind. The mercenaries broke against this wall. They were impaled upon the pikes, unable to break through, their line too thin, their men too tired by running.

Inexorably, our centre holding firm, our wings began to close. If the mercenaries also had a plan, I could not tell it. Through the dust I saw only mercenaries hacking at our syntagmata. From the elephants' towers, our bowmen shot. Above the noise there was the screaming of the elephants, some enraged by arrows in their sides, but held steady by their drivers. Before each of our syntagmata there grew a wall of dead and dying. A group of mercenaries broke away, running to the east. My father sent cavalry after them. I saw scimitars flash, the mercenaries fall.

Some were braver. A group of perhaps sixty Sicilians, clad in leather, armed only with short swords and shields, stood resolute before a syntagma. Three of them slipped beneath an elephant as it trumpeted and reared. They cut at the animal's girth until its tower fell and then, bawling, it fell too, its belly hanging from the cuts of many swords. Its dying bulk was a further wall beyond which the mercenaries could not pass as my father's slingers from behind kept up their murdering rain.

The mercenaries now were bunched, our circle closing and then closed upon them. The elephants advanced, as I had seen them under Haggith, pounding, tearing, rage released at last. We sat and waited, watching. Only Spendius and some forty with him cut their way through. Hamilax turned his horse to follow. "Let them go, Hamilax," my father said. "We'll settle with them later. Meanwhile, they can be our messengers."

At last, exhausted, the elephants withdrew. Another trumpet, and the syntagmata broke up, laying down their pikes and man to man addressing such resistance as was left. Many mercenaries just put down their arms, holding up their necks for the sword's cut. Others put their sword hilts in the sand as spikes and sheltered behind their shields. They were killed by lances from behind.

A battle is like lust. The frenzy passes. Consequence remains. The fighting was over by mid-morning, but the aftermath continued through the day. We had lost only some 600 men. Two elephants were dead. The mercenaries' losses were enormous and all that day our soldiers moved among the dead and the dying, stripping armour, collecting arms, throwing corpses onto piles.

We took 2,000 prisoners. Five hundred were taken to a stand of eucalyptus trees by the river. Hamilax saw to their disembowelling. They then were tied by their own guts to trees.

The mercenary camp was next, the huts and hovels fired, the women and campfollowers rounded up. They were marched up to the outer southern wall of Carthage. The archers took their time in killing them for sport, drawing then relaxing bows, laughing, hitting first a thigh, an arm until their victims bristled from the arrows and bled, moaning, to death.

Gisco's pit my father ordered covered with earth. By evening we were ready again to march. Alone, my father and I walked up-river to bathe in the Macaras. We came upon a trail of blood. A wounded mercenary had dragged himself away for water. We found him near the bank. Ravens had taken his eyes, but he was alive. Without a word, my father drew his sword, cut off the mercenary's head and kicked it into the river.

We marched first to Utica. The mercenaries, under Zaracas the prisoners said, had abandoned their seige. We went on to Hippocritae only to find the same. My father, Hamilax and Haggith conferred. Haggith was sent with 4,000 to beseige Tunis, held it was said by Mathos. We were to find and destroy the forces of Spendius and Zaracas and then join Haggith at Tunis.

In the months that followed we sought an enemy we could not find. There were skirmishes in plenty, alarms in the night as mercenaries attacked our pickets, then withdrew. My father remained calm. "See how well I have taught them, Hannibal! Hamilax, warn Naravas."

We followed the mercenaries into the inland hills and then the mountains. Our food grew scarce, our lice fat. My father ordered the tents of all the officers to be burned. We slept on the ground among the men. The closeness of an army is a thing of love. I found it first among the mountains of Marazzana.

For months more we marched and skirmished. We came to a plateau, ringed with peaks. "It will be here," my father said. That moonless night the dark was suddenly ablaze with light. In a ring, around, above us, burned a thousand fires. Our elephants, uneasy, trumpeted their alarm. My father simply slept.

He gave his orders in the half-light. "Beef, Hamilax, as much as they can eat, and all the dried figs too. Send me the commanders," and to them my father gave his plan. With stomachs full, our army formed into one square. The syntagmata and elephants were its outer rank all round. The cavalry and slingers were within. When the sun rose, we were ready.

They came in silence from the peaks above, very many, four or five to each of us, ordered this time, menacing. Their slingers shot. Our shields were raised. Their first charge was exploratory, by light-armed men. They lacked the heavy cavalry or elephants which could have breached our line. Our slingers killed or wounded many as they came. The next was far more serious, of heavy infantry behind high Roman shields, pressing hard upon our eastern side. A second force attacked us from the north. A third approached our southern side. Well out of shot, the mercenaries were forming for the charge in ranks upon our eastern side. They began to run, a wave of men towards us, three deep, greater by 200 strides than was our length.

In unison, our trumpets rang. My father was chewing calmly at a fig. From the east, the sun behind them, banners waving, arrow-shaped, a host of cavalry rolled towards us in a cloud of dust.

"Nar-a-vas, Nar-a-vas." Hamilax began the shout which all the ranks took up. The horsemen caught the main mercenary line, cut through it cleanly, wheeled and cut again. Of its own volition our square became a charging line and I was among them on my pony by my father in the dust and blood and noise. A bearded Gaul ran to me. In one sweep my father's sword cut off his swinging arm. His blood sprayed me. I gloried in the battle and since that day I have loved to fight and know no fear.

I still see now my father embrace Naravas when, hours later, all was done. Together they themselves cut off the arms of Spendius, using his own sword. Zaracas too we captured, wounded but alive. We saw to one elephant, its trunk cut off, its entrails hanging. Hamilax killed it with a chisel between the eyes.

We left the carnage to the lions and the vultures. Spendius, his stumps bandaged, was thrown over a horse. Zaracas was dragged behind. Late in the evening, ten days' hard march later, we came to Tunis. Approaching across the plain, we had expected to see Haggith's campfires burning. "Perhaps he has already taken the city," Hamilax said.

"Perhaps," my father replied.

In the dark, the crosses were eerie. At first light the next morning they were not that. Haggith was there, what was left of him. They had crucified him with a dagger in his mouth, having cut off his genitals, his toes and fingers. On both sides away from him there ran a line of crosses round the city wall.

My father sent a force to cut the bodies down. Fire from the walls repelled them. He sent Hamilax to Carthage for catapults. We waited. He had men scour the countryside for wool and this, soaked in pitch, was tied round rocks and stones. Then my father had all our men, Naravas' too, equipped with bows and set to making arrows, their heads daubed in pitch.

Tunis' buildings were not of stone but clay and wattle, roofed with grass. We prepared for weeks. We were ready, yet still my father waited for one more thing to be right – wind.

The catapults were set up, sixty of them. A dry wind came

45

from the south and blew all day. Before the walls in sight of all, my father had Spendius and Zaracas brought and held. His first sword-stroke cut off Spendius' head. His second cut the torso from the hips and the mercenaries on the walls of Tunis watched in silence. Zaracas he split first to the hips with one great downward swing.

Without the arms of Spendius there were still ten pieces of two men, catapulted into Tunis. That done, great braziers were lit before each troop of archers and each catapult. At one trumpet, a rain of fire fell upon Tunis. It burned for three days and nights. Four times, each of those days, my father renewed his hail of fire. He knew how much water there was in Tunis.

Irregular groups of mercenaries sought a different death. Some, on fire, jumped from the walls. Others ran from the gates. Some of these were killed. Most were captured and then crucified upon the crosses of Haggith and his men. All about the crosses and our camp sat and squawked the black and bloodied ravens.

Of course Carthage rejoiced when we returned, our bodies blackened by the smoke, our clothes fouled by the reek of burnt flesh. "Hamilcar, our saviour, Eye of Khamon," cried the people, even Baalhaan, wearing his tiara with its eight mystic tiers, an emerald shell in the middle. I slipped away. I wanted to see Silenus. I had missed him. He was not in our classroom. But a scroll was open on his desk. It was the fourteenth book of Homer's *Iliad* and, returned from the Truceless War, I read:

Ζεὺς
ἐκ νεότητος ἔδωκε καὶ ἐς γῆρας τολυπεύειν
ἀργαλέους πολέμους, ὄφρα φθιόμεσθα ἕκαστος.

The gods decreed that from youth even unto old age we should labour, fighting in arduous wars, each of us until we are dead.

46

III

SPAIN

I had never been to Melkarth's sacred shrine. I was never to go again, through the enclosure of plane trees and on through the plantings of almond trees and colocynths, cypresses and myrtles, along that path paved with black pebbles and past the cedars that were sacrosant, and up six silver steps beyond the stelae, one of emerald, one of gold.

The room was high. Cracks in the upper walls admitted fitful light. Twelve blue orbs of glossopetri stood there. Behind them I saw a great slab of roughened darkened stone, standing on its legs of lapis-lazuli. A fire of aloes and of laurel wood was brightening the dark. I stood beside my father. All was still. From anterooms came chanting in the Canaanite tongue, close, closer until the chanters lined the walls around us, men in linen mantles, coucoupha necklaces shining out. Some were naked necromancers, covered in tattoos, carrying on short sticks their fetishes and charms. Scheminiths with eight strings, kinnors which had ten, tambourines and salsalim, citharas and aulechim, simsimiya and makruna played and boomed and sang.

From a hidden door before the altar came the High Priest Achololim in white. All sound ceased. "Hamilcar, son of Hasdrubal son of Hannibal of the line and lineage of Barca and even too of Dido, why do you come to wake the serpents of Melkarth?"

"You know, Achololim, why I am come. Let it be done."

From behind, a eunuch covered me in a mantle of blood red. Two more brought a black dog. One held its head, one its feet above the fire before the stone. My father stepped forward, took a sword and with one stroke cut the dog in two. Its blood hissed on the fire. "May this fate befall you, Hannibal, son of

Hamilcar, if you break this oath," Achololim intoned. The acolytes moaned, the drums beat again.

To Achololim's right was a trough of stone. A white bullock was led there, then a black ewe, symbols of the day and night. My father cut their throats. Blood filled the trough. I moved forward and then plunged in my arms. I remember to this day the words I took from Achololim and swore.

"By the eight fires of the Cabiri, by the stars, meteors and volcanoes, by the Cave of Hadrumetum and the Passage of Ashroket, by slaughter, by all that burns, by desert, by sun, moon and earth" – yes, how I remember! – *"hialpi mer sva Melkarth, ok Eschmoun, ok hin almattki an Panit . . .* I swear by the serpents of Melkarth, by Eschmoun, by the blackness of Panit I swear this great oath of the seven hates to Rome, undying enmity to Rome, no peace to Rome, no truce with Rome, no mercy unto Rome so long as I shall live or any Roman walk upon the land or sail upon the sea. By my being, all these things I swear."

Yes, I took this hate from my father. But I have honed and whetted, refined it, made it mine. It has been the alembic of my soul.

I returned home in a litter with my father silent from the vow. Still bloody – I was not to wash until next dawn – I went with my father to the pleasure garden. Sitting on a bench of beki wood we each sought our own. A stork flew ponderously overhead and I thought of the fear of the carp in the ponds as the great bird's shadow crossed the water where they swam. So too did some strange fleeting fear pass over me and now I know that fear again for Carthage. How have I tried to save her. She will not save herself.

My father leant forward, eyes narrowed, anger in his voice. "Carthage, Hannibal, is all but spent. That which our war with the Romans did not cost us, our war with the mercenaries has. Our treasury is empty. Sicily and Malta, Sardinia, Corsica and

Ebuza, all are closed to us yet even so the cursed Romans demand their indemnity of gold.

"The Council has deliberated and decided. We will build a new Carthage – in Spain. Silenus will instruct you, but in Spain there is gold and silver, olibanum, tin and precious stones. And there, Hannibal, there I will build a new army. And then, Hannibal, then" – and his eyes burned into me as he grasped me by the shoulder – "then there is Rome." He broke off. There was only the passing of a listless wind through the trees above us and the ripples of the frightened fish on ponds.

If the Truceless War had taught me of fighting and of generalship, preparations for our departure to Spain taught me things of equal importance. Hour upon hour my father sat in his hall with Hamilax, poring over lists and maps and plans. He was to take 12,000 troops, 3,000 horse, 40 elephants. Thirty patched-up galleys were to accompany him. Then there were the miners and the weavers, goldsmiths, clerks and scriveners, carpenters, harness-menders, cooks and slaves, the body to the head. As an exercise, my father had me act as quartermaster.

With Silenus then I too drew up my plans and so passed the first months of my tenth year. How much does a man eat, a horse, an elephant? How long does a pair of boots last? How many nails do you need to build a fort? How many blacksmiths do you need to shoe 3,000 horse? Will garum keep for several months or more?

Of course I continued with my other lessons with javelin, spear, sword and horse, but my mornings were devoted to my plans. These my father would order submitted for his scrutiny sometimes in Greek, sometimes in Latin, sometimes in Punic and so I learned language as I learned logistics. I learned too from Silenus of the geography, peoples, customs, and languages of Spain.

Of the west and southern coasts we already knew much. At Tartessus, our legends told, our forefathers from Tyre had founded a great city before even Carthage. It grew rich from trade in tin but when, three centuries ago, it refused the sovereignty of Carthage, it was destroyed, its children slaughtered, its women sold into slavery. When our admiral Admago left that place, he dropped a lump of iron overboard, vowing by Eschmoun that Tartessus should never be peopled again until the iron floated to the surface. Such prisoners as were taken were stoned to death in Carthage. Admago had the head of the Tartessian leader, one Abracus, put into a skin full of human blood. "So," he said, "does one enemy of Carthage have his fill of blood." So did Carthage deal with those who dared defy her. And now?

Just down the coast from Tartessus, my great-great-grand-father Hannibal had founded a colony of Carthage at Gadez, a huge and natural harbour. Inland of that, at Medina and Sidine, were the silver mines that yielded much already and promised more. Going first to Gadez and settling us there, my father planned to subjugate or ally the tribes, raise troops, develop trade and then, north-east across the peninsula, found a city of New Carthage, Cartakhena.

Subjugate or ally. That thing too I learned from Spain and from my father. The Truceless War taught me how to deal with enemies. But in Spain I saw that another way to deal with enemies is to make them your friends.

One of the Spanish tribes of which we knew was the inland Oretanians. They dressed, Silenus told me, only in leather. So rough is their country that they eat as much as they have and never as much as they want. They have no wine, but drink only water. They have no good things at all, not even figs for dessert.

The Spain of which I learned from Silenus was full of the unexpected. A land of many kingdoms, one of its northern kings was so rich he had, or so it was said, 800 stallions and 16,000 mares, twenty for each stallion. The progeny of these mares were so swift of foot that many believed them begotten of the wind and not of any stallion. So many were the same king's hunting dogs that four large villages were exempted from taxes on condition they supplied these dogs their food.

As strange I found Silenus' telling of an eastern tribe, the Massagetians. Their leader was a woman, one Tamyris, and the whole tribe's womenfolk were warriors, unknowing of the distaff or the loom, their right breasts bared for battle. If a man of the tribe is asked who he is, he will tell you his own name and his mother's, then his grandmother's and great-grandmother's and so on. Tamyris, it was said, had once gone blind. Her doctors declared that she could be healed only by bathing her eyes in the urine of a man who had lain only with his wedded wife. She tried first her own husband's urine, but remained blind; then other men's, a great many, one after another until at last her sight was restored. Then Tamyris had all those men who had not been faithful to their wives brought together in one place and their eyes gouged out.

What else did I come to know of Spain from Silenus? Of its geography, of course, and that from the *Geographica* of the Greek scholar Eratosthenes. Silenus had met this man, years before in Athens, and he told me how he had stood entranced as Eratosthenes held forth in the agora on mathematics, on astronomy, physics, geography, on the principles of music.

What a people are these Greeks. There are no questions they do not ask and few they have not answered. When they have nothing left to talk about, they talk about talking; with nothing left to think about, they think about thinking. The cursed Romans have no will for either.

So from Eratosthenes did I learn of Spain, though with Silenus' help. His Greek was difficult to a boy. "Difficult, yes, Hannibal," Silenus said, "but how elegant!" and he proceeded to expound upon the intricacies of Eratosthenes' prose, with its anaphora, asyndeton, synesis and tmesis and other things besides. I was more interested, however, in the topography of the land to which we were soon to go.

51

My father's preparations were complete. The day of our departure was determined. Outwith the city wall the force was marshalled, wanting only its leader. The Council came to our house and, in his great hall, bade my father well. The launching of the thirty galleys was all yet to be done. That evening I went with my father to the shipyards by the harbour and against a flaming sunset amongst the imprecations of Achololim, the chanting of the acolytes, thirty of our galleys entered first the sea. He-goats were tied to the rollers on which they passed from the yard so that their keels slid blood-stained to their home. I asked my father the origins of this custom. "In better days for Carthage, Hannibal, prisoners-of-war, not goats, were so tied and the blood of men marked the launch of each new galley. Let Melkarth grant that this be so again."

The journey to Spain passed easily. We marched west along the coast, in sight of our fleet. My father rode in the van. Silenus and I, my mother and my siblings travelled in litters borne by household slaves. We passed the cities dependent still on Carthage: Cirta, Annaba and Jijiel, Tigzirt, Tapasa, Gouraya, Siga, each bringing to my father's camp gifts of earth and water, symbols of their troth. For thirty days and more we marched, until we came at last to the Pillars of Herakles on the straits of the Tyrrhenian Sea.

What a man was Herakles. The Phoenicians our progenitors, the Greeks, the Egyptians, even the Romans claimed him as their own and worshipped him as a god. When he had come as we had just done to Mount Hacho, he found it joined to Gibraltar and his passage blocked, though there was sea on either side. He simply broke the mountain down and passed on to Spain, sailing in the floating cup of Helios the sun god on a burning sea. So were born the two Pillars of Herakles between which we were to cross. And when the Alps blocked my way, I thought of this. When a door seems to be closed, go through and know not fear.

Our fleet came up. We had, I knew, no transport ships, but the crossing of the straits was effected by my father as he had planned it months before. For days back and forth to Algechiras across the straits in Spain plied the thirty galleys, laden to their thwarts with men, goods and provisionings until only we of my father's household and forty slaves were left to cross – we, and the elephants.

It was the one issue of logistics on which I had foundered completely. Neither Silenus nor Hamilax nor even the beasts' own drivers had been able to help me. None knew, it seemed, how to transport elephants across water, let alone across ten miles of sea. None could remember such a thing being done. When I asked my father how he intended to get the elephants across, he guffawed. "How, Hannibal? Why, the elephants will fly to Spain!" and then he turned away.

I should of course have known, for I had heard my father order Hamilax to take a detachment of men to the mountains behind us and fell timber for rafts. My father had them brought up to the quay. The slaves brought load upon load of earth and heaped it on the rafts until their level matched that of the pier. Then they raised walls of palms and fronds around this floating land. Two female elephants next were led along the earthern pier and onto what must have seemed to them dry land. Others followed without fear.

So, in four crossings, were the elephants of Hamilcar, captured in the forests of the Garamantes, towed on floating land to Spain. I had watched and learned. I was to use the same technique myself, to get my elephants across the Ebro and the Rhône. But I had learned, as I had before from my father and would again, that problem gives way to plan.

One other remained. Amongst my father's household was a surly Numidian, one Zetenes, a princeling son of a desert ally. We had not been far from Carthage before we learned that his father had not sent him to Hamilcar Barca from love. He was the journey's bane, complaining incessantly about the march, the heat, the flies, the food, his slaves, everything. He only wished, he said, to return home, and would not go to Spain.

We were standing, the last to embark, on the quay. The slave sent to strike the last tents approached my father and explained that Zetenes refused to leave his tent and come. I only saw my father look at Hamilax and nod. We had been at sea for some time before I noticed Zetenes' absence. My father was seeing to my mother's needs, for she had not been well. But Hamilax was standing in the stern, looking silent back to Africa. I approached him. "Where is Zetenes?" I asked. Hamilax did not turn round.

"I cut his throat," he said, and Mount Hacho soon behind me merged with a setting sun.

We went to Gadez, its huge harbour opening to the north, protected to the west by a long spit of land. A causeway had been built to join this to the mainland. Within a wall out on that narrow spit the city stood. To a boy's eyes it was like Carthage, a little Carthage. It had an agora, temples and, of course, the council chamber of the city's Elders and a court.

Even now the Romans call us savages. But many hundreds of years before Rome was even thought of, whichever of their preposterous foundation myths you believe, Carthage established a constitution. Only the Greek states have ever done the same. The Romans rule by fear outwith the law. Carthage, it is true, also ruled by fear, but fear within and of the law enshrined in constitution, and so Gadez had its council and its courts because it was of Carthage.

Our home stood, as it did in Carthage, apart from the others, at the extremity of the headland, smaller but otherwise a copy of that which we had left. Soon my life resumed the pattern it had known before the Truceless War. Mornings of study with Silenus, afternoons of riding and of practice with the javelin, spear and sword. Leaving only a small garrison and Hamilax in charge, my father marched inland. We saw him little. I had been a boy thrown into a man's world. Now I resumed the boy's, and one year turned to two.

It had always been my father's plan to build in Spain a new army and a fleet. For both he needed allies, mercenaries or both and so each month or so strangers would come to Gadez, as hostages or guest-friends, most to join the growing camp outside the city wall, beyond the causeway on the mainland, to be trained and exercised in war. So it was that first I met Maharbal, the hostage son of Kandaulo, King of the Oretanians, a people now bound in league with us.

As a prince, Maharbal had been accommodated in the city and not made to work or do anything disgraceful to his rank. My father was always careful about such things. "Always respect other people's customs, Hannibal," he used to say, "unless they are Roman ones!"

I had seen Maharbal once or twice about Gadez, his shock of fiery hair, his big-boned limbs. He had a horse tattooed upon his forehead, the sign of royal blood. Every high-born Oretanian, I knew from Silenus, claimed direct descent from their god Rhecanus the Rider. On his thigh he bore a tattooed bear, the mark of his tribe, and he seemed at bay each time I saw him sitting sullen in the sun under the eye always of a guard.

I was going to the Temple of Herakles Ammon at Silenus' behest to speak with the priests. Crossing the agora and turning up a street I came upon him playing knucklebones in the dust. I squatted down. His guard coughed, disapproving. He looked wildly over his shoulder, ignoring me. I saw the lice in his red hair, the golden gryphon round his neck on a greasy leather thong. "Take no notice of the guard," I said. "I am Hannibal, son of Hamilcar."

"I know who you are," he replied in halting Punic without looking at me, staring at his dice. Muttering a prayer to some sky-god for fives, he threw a one and four.

"Try again," I said, this time in Iberian. He threw two fives

55

then held me with his eyes that blazed, green eyes. My loneliness was eased and I was glad.

"Maharbal," I said in Punic, "when I am a man, a soldier, will you be my ally?"

"What are 'allies'?" he replied.

"Men who fight each other's enemies in sacred trust."

He stood up, looked away, communing with a power that I knew not of. He turned and, quick as thought, swept the dagger from my belt. The guard stepped forward in alarm. I motioned to him to be still. Maharbal cut, just by the base, the thumb of his right hand. He held the dagger out for me. I stood up, took it from him, cut my thumb and our hands, our bloods, our fates were joined. "I shall be your *anda*, Hannibal, your blood-brother, and you mine."

Hamilax would learn of this, I knew, and then my father. I was not afraid. "Maharbal is my friend," I said to the guard. "See that you treat him as such." Every enemy of Rome has had cause from that day until his death to thank Maharbal, prince of the Oretanians, friend of Hannibal, commander of his cavalry.

In the months that followed, we were inseparable. Maharbal joined my classes with Silenus. He learned much. He taught us much. And with horses he was inspired. Bareback, alive on snorting stallions, broody mares, Maharbal was as one with them as we raced or cantered, walked and talked on forest paths or coastal strands. I turned fourteen.

And in that year in Spain then I was given my first horse and my heart sings still with love for him. Burnt almost black by sun and wind my father had been back for several weeks, resting briefly and then planning, talking, training troops, arranging trade, his black beard streaked now white. The horse fairs were his special joy, both as a soldier and a man. His army growing, he had need of many horses. Word was sent and so each month there came to Gadez trains of tribesmen from the north and from the east, lean men in lynx-skin bonnets, their blouses loose, their trousers tied at the ankle, their black tents borne on donkeys and on mules. With some ten, with others twenty horses came, all adorned in finery for sale, plumes on their heads, nets of scarlet wool glittering with sequins on their necks.

That day my father wanted chargers for his own guard. All forenoon the dealers brought their best before him. He peered in mouths, at upturned hooves, sounded chests, felt shanks. If he was satisfied, he nodded to Abdolonim his groom who would move away and haggle with the dealer, six xthets here of gold for that horse, eight for this. Maharbal and I stood by and watched and learned. "Is that the lot?" asked my father of Abdolonim. "There is one more stallion, sir, called Peritan, for whom that man" – he gestured at a dealer – "wants thirty xthets."

"Thirty!" my father replied. "Why, the beast must draw the chariot of Eschmoun! Where is he?"

"Some fool let him slip his tether. They found him hard to catch – but here he is."

At last they led up at a careful walk a pure white stallion saving a black blaze upon his head, huge, of fourteen hands. The groom pulled him up before us. "Here, Sire," said the unctuous dealer, "is the horse called Peritan . . ." and at his name the stallion's nostrils flared, his black eyes rolled, he tried to rear his head.

"Look, Hannibal, look at *that!*" said Maharbal beside me, something close to anguish in his voice. I remember feeling sorry Silenus wasn't there to see what he had brought to me on parchment translated into flesh. I ran through the *Peri Hippikes*, as Xenophon advises, starting at the feet. The horns of Peritan's hooves were deep before and behind. He stamped, just missing the groom's foot, and his hooves made a ringing sound like a cymbal. His leg-bones were strong but lithe, his chest broad, his neck arched, as Xenophon has it, like a gamecock's. His mane was long and strong, if ill-tended, his spine well padded.

"That," said Maharbal with awe, "is the perfect horse."

My father walked around him, careful of those pawing hooves. "I like his looks. Let's see him move." Abdolonim took a step towards Peritan. He neighed like a war-trumpet and, notwithstanding the weight of the groom, forced up his massive head. The groom pulled and pulled. To the earth dripped blood. "Look at that bit they've got on him," I whispered to Maharbal. "Look at those barbs! And even that can't hold him."

"And still he's got his head up!" Maharbal replied, in his excitement lapsing into Iberian.

Abdolonim walked round to the horse's front, making soothing clicking noises. Peritan stamped and backed and rolled his eyes. Abdolonim was reaching for the mane to mount when Peritan gave a violent start, lifted the groom clean off the ground and lashed out with a furious leg, missing Abdolonim by inches.

"Enough, Abdolonim," my father snorted. "If that's the pick of the strings, let's waste no more time. I've work to do." He turned to go.

I knew. "Father," I called out, "please!" My father stopped and looked at me. "Let me try."

"Hannibal, that is a vicious horse. There's nothing worse."

"Not vicious, Father, brave. Look where they've beaten him. Look at the weals under his belly."

I held my father's gaze. I was almost his height now. "If you can ride him, he's yours," he said at last.

I walked to the horse. I did not question. "Go," I said to the groom, "away from him, away, down wind, where he can't see or even smell you. Give me the reins, slowly. Don't jerk that bit!"

What did Peritan mean, that hated name? My Iberian was growing better. Dark, I thought, or dark one. Well, this horse must have a new name. Light, not dark. "Belleus," I said in Punic, "Belleus!" and his ears pricked up. I eased the rein gently, gently. He raked a forefoot, restless. I ran my left hand down his glistening neck, then to his headstall, easing off the bit. "Belleus, Belleus, Light One!" I whispered in his ear and he strained forward, wanting, I knew, to be gone from there.

"Soon," I said, "soon," reaching to my full height high up to his mane. He took quick steps forward, I ran with him and gained momentum, then I leapt. We galloped through the salt flats where flocks of wildfowl rose and fled away.

When we returned, my father was waiting in the sun. I swung off, cavalry style, across the neck. "Thank you, Father, thank you for my horse. I call him Belleus, the Light One."

I turned fifteen. My voice broke. Down formed on my chin and on my cheeks. It was time to kill my first man. It should by custom have been done with my father, on campaign. But he was away when reports began to reach us of trouble in the eastern hills. Brigands of the Basetan tribe were harrying our settlements, raping, looting, threatening our mines. Hamilax had no choice. Taking sixty chosen men from the garrison my father had left, he rode out at dawn.

For four days I tracked them, waiting. Belleus knew, and went gently on his way. The first day was the hardest, across the miles of salt flats landward of Gadez. There was no cover. I had to stay so far back that, many times, I almost lost Hamilax and his men. At noon on the fifth day, I presented myself. Hamilax would not send me back now. Besides, what was left of the meat that I had brought to eat was rank and high. I should have taken black bread and cheese instead, but when I stole into the kitchens before I left I took what I could find.

Hamilax and his men had dismounted for the noon meal in a grove of oaks. I simply rode in, men reaching for their javelins until they recognised me. Hamilax was sitting eating on a rock. "Good day to you, Hamilax," I said.

"Hannibal!" and his bread stuck in his throat. I slipped off Belleus and led him past Hamilax to the stream to drink.

Hamilax took me roughly by the shoulder. "Why are you here, and how, Hannibal? Are you mad?"

"No," I replied, taking his hand off me, "I am come of age. I have followed you because the time has come for me to take my man – "

"The time has come, Hannibal," he interrupted, "to take you home. I am about a man's work, not a boy's. And if any harm came to you, your father would have me crucified."

"And if, as will be, I succeed, you will be honoured. Anyway, you have no choice."

Afterwards, back in Gadez, Hamilax recounted all this to Silenus. What convinced my father's Steward was, Silenus said to me, my eyes. Hamilax had, he said, only seen such eyes before through helmet-slits in battle.

His plan was simple. Amongst his force was a local tribesman whose village was not far. Hamilax intended, he explained to me as we rode, to go there, conceal his force and wait for the Basetans to attack the village. "What if they don't?" I asked.

"Ah, then my plans will change," replied Hamilax wryly, and kicked on his horse.

The hill-top village was called Vekher. Built of brown stone as if part of the outcrop itself, above a broken hillside backing to a gorge, it was no different to many I had seen in the hills on the ride from Gadez. Across its open side there ran a palisade of boulders and of thorn behind which small and wiry ponies snapped and grazed before the simple houses blocked their way. Goats and sheep moved upon the hill and would be brought within the wall at dusk. A goat-boy's piping called. No, it was no different. But it was here that I became a man.

I slept beside Hamilax in the headman's hut after a meal of goat and figs and rancid watery wine. I woke and all was still. I wonder still why I woke and went outside: was it some sixth sense, or the prompting of some god? In truth, I think it was the many fleas that were the richest part of Vekher's hospitality. The fates of many men have turned on less.

The moon was nearly full. I climbed a tall crag, the village look-out, worn by many feet. At first, I was not sure. I think I knew the Basetans were there before I saw them, a creeping shadow of a column of some fifty men on horseback in the valley road below, but climbing up the hill.

I woke Hamilax. He too climbed the crag and saw. "Good, Hannibal. Now wake the men. Tell them to make no noise." When we were gathered on the beaten earth within the circle of the village huts, Hamilax gave his orders. We would wait, mounted, inside the palisade. When the brigands had come through its gate of thorn, Hamilax would sound a horn. Five men would seal the gate. None were to escape. "And do not trouble me," he said in the same flat voice he always used, "with prisoners."

The first streak of dawn was touching the hills and growing gold when we heard their horses. I felt my javelins and my sword and Belleus quivered under me. Grey shapes growing clearer rode in laughing, confident of cattle and of women. We sat still, concealed against the rough-hewn wall. Then the horn rang out. We charged.

At first there was only confusion. Men milled among the bawling cattle and the villagers of Vekher yelled and screamed and showered friend and foe alike with stones. A horse veered across me, a javelin in its neck and then I saw him, to my left, on a piebald horse which wheeled and shied. His war-cap was of black and greasy leather, his corselet of some hide or other, stained with wine and sweat. In the soft light of the dawn I saw his eyes were blue, his beard blond, his face freckled. He noticed me. He checked his horse and frowned, drew back his heavy spear.

I poised my javelin, kicked Belleus forward. There was a dark mark on the corselet's hide, just above the heart, and as I charged I threw, reaching for my second javelin, winding the throwing-thong as the first struck home. His spear passed harmless by me. So did I become a man one morning in Vekher.

There was a second man, as I turned Belleus from our charge upon the first. I caught him in the neck with my second javelin just as he raised his spear. Then there was the smell of blood and cattle dung and crushed grass before the cackling women of the village moved among the dead or dying, finishing our work.

We buried our six dead and formed our column to go home. I took my former place towards the rear. From the van, Hamilax called "Hannibal!" and waved me forward to join him. He said nothing more. That was enough. So did a boy who had left Gadez alone return a man, leading his first force.

Silenus was at the gate. We had been away twelve days. My father had returned meanwhile to a household, Silenus said, in panic. Where had I gone? I was to leave Belleus to a groom, wash and change and go at once to my father in his hall. Hamilax had gone to him straightaway. So he will know, I thought.

I knocked, standing in a clean and beltless *chiton*. "Come in," my father called. He was sitting at the far end of the hall, by a brazier for the autumn chill, with Hamilax, the table by them covered with maps. He stood up. We looked at each other, down the hall. "Hamilax, leave us," my father ordered. Saying nothing, Hamilax went through a side door.

My father walked to a chest in the corner. The belt was of soft leather. Six emeralds and six rubies gleamed in the evening light. The clasp of silver was a scorpion, symbol of our house. My father held it out. "The sword-belt of a Barca, Hannibal, and a man. Take it with a father's pride."

He led me, belted, to the fire and to a chair. We talked until the fire was low, the household still in sleep. I think a slave brought food and drink. We talked first of my killing. "No, I was not afraid. It was all so clear. I felt" – and I struggled for the words – "I felt a peace, a purpose. In some way, I was not there." He was silent.

"Was it," he asked at last, "was it – like lightning?"

I remembered the power. "Yes, it was."

"Then you are a Barca, Hannibal!" and we laughed, for our family name means just that. And then we talked of Spain. Or rather he talked. I learned of his plans, progress with the native tribes, the numbers of his new army and his fleet. He showed me his many maps. "Here, Hannibal, here!" and he pointed to a promontory on the eastern coast. "Here we will build Carta-khena." The hand with which he pointed lacked two fingers. I wanted to ask him when he had lost them. I never did.

He talked on. Cartakhena was to be a base for trade, yes, but for Rome. "To march on Rome itself, Father?" I asked.

"Of course!" he replied quickly, animated. "Pyrrhus did it. So shall I – or rather we, Hannibal, now you are a man." He smiled.

"Who was Pyrrhus?"

"Pyrrhus? You don't know about Pyrrhus? What has Silenus been teaching you? The wonderings of the Greeks, I suppose! Well, study Pyrrhus with more care than Plato from now. Pyrrhus . . ."

Through the night until the dawn I heard of Pyrrhus, King of Epirus at twenty-two, a brilliant general and strategist who fought in full-scale battle aged thirteen when Alexander's former generals were ranged against each other. My father's interest was in Pyrrhus' invasion, in 280, of Italy. At Heraclea, he beat the Romans. "Whipped them, Hannibal! Not once, but twice, the second time at Asculum!" my father said, pacing round the room in his excitement then drawing for me what he thought was Pyrrhus' battle order.

It was Silenus, days later, who filled in the details that my father chose to forget. Yes, Pyrrhus won a second time at Asculum, but at such cost to his own army that the phrase "Pyrrhic victory" was born. And though he marched on Rome, their Senate, persuaded by the eloquence of the blind and aged

Appius Claudius, refused to negotiate at all so long as foreign troops remained on their soil. Pyrrhus had won two battles, but he could not win the war.

I now accompanied my father everywhere – except, my brother Mago said jealously, to the latrines. My hours with Silenus were reduced, my hours at arms drill and horsemanship increased, invariably at my father's side. He always found the time for practice. "You can only ask of men what you can do yourself, Hannibal," he said one afternoon when I grew weary of practice with the javelin. "Now throw again."

If it was to my birth I owe my hate of Rome, it is to those years in Spain I owe my ability to act upon that hate. They were largely years of peace. The native tribes were quiet for the most part, allied or crushed, throughout the southern part of Spain. My father's concerns were trade, his army and his fleet. We travelled far, establishing ports south and east along the coast at Belo, at Carteia and at Baria to serve our mines inland. Our galleys back and forth to Carthage plied.

I do not know why my father so favoured me above my brothers, Mago and Hasdrubal. I was his eldest child and therefore heir and close to him in looks. Mago had a stutter and was weak. Hasdrubal was always at his books. "Your brother is a scholar, not a man," said my father once when he asked for Hasdrubal to be called for javelin practice and was told he was with Silenus, reading. That would never have excused me.

Yet both my brothers tried. I remember that early morning in Gadez. I had got up before the household was awake. I often did, to walk, to look, to think. From the courtyard I heard grunting, the clash of wood on wood. In a disused stable I found my brothers sparring with mock swords and shields. I watched. They only saw me when they paused. They were embarrassed. "W-w-we were only p-p-rac – " stuttered Mago, out of breath.

"Only *playing*, he means," said Hasdrubal, looking at his feet.

"Then play like this instead," I said, moving to them, picking up a staff. "Your footwork is all wrong. A swordsman starts with his feet . . ." Whenever I could from that day on I helped them and they learned. My father never knew. Perhaps he never noticed how his younger sons were changing as they grew.

I hardly saw my sister Sophoniba and my mother. There was no time for women in those years. I knew of course of the brothels in Gadez, the whoring of the soldiers and the sailors. Maharbal once asked me to join him, but I never knew desire until I knew Similce. There were whispers. None dared them to my face. Though Maharbal was my friend, he was no more, no Hephaistion to Alexander.

There was another Hasdrubal in my life then, a nephew of Gisco. When my father was still fighting the mercenaries, he had been sent to Spain by the Council of Elders to ensure a steady supply of silver. I had heard talk of him, and his fortress at the mouth of the river Guadiakth to the north-west, down which the galleys brought their riches. I always wanted to see this river, running wide and green, they said, deep inland. I asked my father once if I could go, when one of Hasdrubal's galleys put in at Gadez on its way back there from Carthage. "The Guadiakth, Hannibal? The west?" He was angry. "No. Like me, look north and east" – his eyes narrowed – "to Rome. You are a Barca. Remember your vow." Rome, Rome, burned into me.

My father had met Hasdrubal several times, I knew, during our first years in Spain when he was much away. As I turned sixteen, letters between them became more frequent. By then I was encouraged to read all my father's correspondence. When I could, I discussed its content with my brothers and with Silenus. Hasdrubal's importance was growing, for his influence in Carthage was great, first by birth and now by money. It was his galleys which brought to Carthage the gold and silver with which we paid the Roman indemnity.

It was from these letters I learned that Hasdrubal was keeping for himself a full third of all that passed through his hands. My father, also sending the produce of the mines in his control to Carthage, was keeping only an eighth. Yet the cost of maintaining his growing army – now 20,000 foot and 5,000 horse – let alone his fleet of now eighty galleys was huge. Our lands in Africa, despoiled by the mercenaries, were still yielding nothing. On the contrary, letters from Abdolonim, left in charge in Carthage, always ended with requests for money and the lines of worry on my father's face grew deep.

So came Hasdrubal to Gadez to discuss, as my father's letter of invitation ran, "matters of mutual interest". I disliked him from the first, the ostentation, the vulgarity. Not with one trireme did he sail into our harbour, but with six quinqueremes, lavishly equipped with matching sails of black and prows of beaten gold. On my father's orders, Hamilax was at the dock to meet him. From the wall above I saw him borne towards us in a litter, one he had brought himself. At my father's hall he even had his slaves announce him and he swaggered through the doors.

Hasdrubal was a bear of a man. His hair was black and long and ringed, his forehead low, his eyes set deep and small above a huge splayed nose that seemed to spread across his pursy cheeks. His mouth was small and pink, absurdly delicate, all but lost in the mass of beard that, like his hair, was oiled and ringed. Heavy earrings stretched his earlobes, tinkling as he walked and his great stomach swayed above his belt towards us. There was an energy about him, though, an animal's energy. He was a man, I felt, of great desires. I was to find out of what kind.

He embraced my father, nodded at me, ignored Hamilax. Wine was brought and figs. Hasdrubal took before he was offered. The slaves withdrew. "So, Hamilcar Barca, we meet again." His voice was deep and growling. "And this must be your eldest whelp," he said, looking at me as he chewed a fig.

He spat out the seeds, looked again at my father. "And what can we do for each other?"

"You are direct at least, Hasdrubal," my father replied with a smile.

"Pah! This is no council in Carthage. Speak." And as Hasdrubal chewed and spat and drank, my father offered him my sister.

"How much?" Hasdrubal asked. My father named a huge sum of gold as dowry. Hasdrubal reached for the flagon of wine, poured a little into his empty goblet, sat back and belched.

"And a quarter share of the two new mines at Medina that I have developed." Hasdrubal poured more wine into his cup. There was silence in the room.

At last, "Fill my cup, Hamilcar, fill it and I will take your Sophoniba," said Hasdrubal.

"Now you speak plain, Hasdrubal. What more do you want?"

"I want," he said, taking another fig, "your African estate at Zartana."

Hamilax rose in his chair. "Sire!" he exclaimed. My father held up his hand. Hamilax settled back. It was a huge price. Not only were the many oak trees invaluable, but the estate stood on a main caravan route to the south. And it had been Barca land, I knew, since the foundation of Carthage.

Perhaps it was a fair exchange. My father was buying influence in Carthage and alliance in Spain. Sophoniba was barely fourteen, Hasdrubal almost thirty yet he had never married. An economic alliance. "And, Hannibal," my father told me later, "one that guards our backs in Carthage. See the many letters," and he pointed to a chest, "questioning what we are doing here. They say still that Carthage should look south and leave the north and west to Rome, that we will anger Rome. Why, like Pothet" – I had a parrot of that name – "they sing only one song! Well, they will be more circumspect when Hasdrubal becomes my son-in-law."

Perhaps my father had no choice. Perhaps I was angry because I had, I confess, thought of Maharbal for my sister. It was time we bound ourselves to Spain by more than arms or money.

Hasdrubal left the next morning, to return when the moon was full. The wedding feast disgusted me, the drunkenness, the gorging. I have never understood inebriation. The ways of life are dark and strange enough without clouding even more our understanding.

I left as soon as was decent, but not before I saw Hasdrubal paw and grope my little frightened sister, his fat fingers opening her bodice before all and dropping down a pomegranate. His right hand followed to retrieve it, his left raising up her skirt and sweat dropped from his leering face to glisten in his beard. I suppose he had her that night, grinding his great belly in and out and up and down. Perhaps she interested him for that long at least.

I never saw Sophoniba again. She never bore a child. She died of a fever, high in Hasdrubal's acropolis above the Guadiakth, or so some said. Others claimed that Hasdrubal had stuffed her for his pleasure with ripe plums and then his penis, causing an infection of her womb. I see again now, as I write, my sister's suffering face that night of her wedding. There have been so many wrongs.

I never talked to my father of these things. I think Silenus knew, for he gave me the day after the wedding a copy of that work from which he had read after Hanno's crucifixion – Plato's *Phaedo* – and in the time I had available I struggled to understand. He said rather gruffly that he thought my Greek was up to it now. "*We make the nearest approach to knowledge,*" says Socrates when he is about to drink the hemlock that is his sentence, "*when we have the least possible intercourse with the body*

but keep ourselves pure until the hour when God himself releases us."
This I have tried to do. If I have failed, may Sophoniba, and
many, forgive me.

The sense of the marriage was plain and in that, I admit, my
father was right. Its fruits kept us busy. Double the trade, double
the fleet and, crucially, double the news. There was not a port
on the seas where Hasdrubal the Handsome, as he was ironically
known, did not have his spies, his ears and voices. My father
joked that Hasdrubal knew what was happening before it had
happened. He made no joke, however, of the news that the
Romans had annexed Sardinia. They had, reported Hasdrubal,
asked the "permission" of the Carthaginian Senate first. What
my father called derisively the "Peace Party" had agreed.

The loss of Sardinia prompted my father to an action for
which he was in any case of a mind. "Damn them!" he cried
when he had read Hasdrubal's despatch. "But I am ready.
Hannibal, go and tell the commanders that the time has
come. We will move now. We march east. We will found
Cartakhena, expand in Spain. And then, Hannibal, then . . ."
He did not have to finish his sentence. Then, Rome.

But the Romans came first to Hamilcar. Again, somehow
Hasdrubal had news of the embassy and so we were prepared.
"Remember this, Hannibal," my father said. "My daughter –
yes, and Zartana – for such information. I would have given
more. Swords and information: the perfect symbiosis."

We were prepared. Our military camps were moved inland,
our war galleys sent to the Guadiakth. The boom across the
inner harbour was removed. The Romans would see a place of
merchants, not of war. And then my father too went inland. I
was to receive the embassy alone. I did ask why. "Because,
Hannibal, the only Romans I can bear to see are dead ones. And
I will take Hamilax with me too, in case his sword hand starts to
itch. Tell them your father, the great Hamilcar Barca, has
become a miner. They might even believe you! And you

can practise your Latin!" Slapping me on the back, he was gone.

The Romans believed the forlorn and lonely son of Hamilcar, perhaps because they wanted to. They had, I knew, enough troubles with wars in Illyria and Gaul to look for more. They did not even disembark. I walked, unarmed, on board the galley of the envoys. They sat at ease on couches, drinking wine. I cannot now recall even their names. They hardly even spoke, but had some boy read what their masters had to say. "*Senatus populusque Romanus Hamilcari Barcino salutem dicit . . .*" It went on and on. I followed most of it. What were we Carthaginians doing in Spain? Was Hamilcar Barca raising and training an army, contrary to the wishes of the Carthaginian Senate? Would we adhere to the treaty? "*Velut vos apud Sardiniam?* As you have in Sardinia?" I interrupted, ignored. When the boy eventually shut up, as a slave fanned the sweating envoys I simply told them my father was away at the mines working so that Carthage could pay her tribute to Rome. In Spain we would stay until the tribute had been paid. With nothing else to say, I left.

They rowed in a desultory fashion round the harbour for an hour. If they were hoping for evidence of war, they must have been disappointed. The next Romans I saw were in battle. They had less of my time than those envoys.

The Romans make a mockery, I know, of "Punic faith". Yet they it was who broke the early treaties between Rome and Carthage. They it was, not the Carthaginians, who built their state on deceit and theft and war and brutal conquest, destroying the Latins, the Etruscans, the Samnites, the Sabines, the Senones, the Umbrians, the Lucanians and other peoples whose name is now but a memory.

My father came back and asked for my account of the embassy. "I told them the truth, Father, that we were here in order to pay their tribute."

He laughed. "You are a proper Barca, Hannibal. My father Hasdrubal, when he was Sufet of Carthage, once called on one of the Elders, Khalanim. He was told by a slave 'Khalanim is not at home,' although my father knew perfectly well that he was. When Khalanim returned the visit, my father called out: 'Not at home.' Khalanim recognised his voice and said so. 'That's rich,' replied my father. 'I believed your slave, and yet now you won't believe me!' Well, I'm pleased the Romans believed I wasn't at home. Their manners have improved since I saw them last in Sicily."

The next day, we marched. I never saw Gadez again. Hasdrubal was at Cartakhena before us, having gone as he preferred by ship. He had set up camp and begun work on the walls. He never wasted time, Hasdrubal, whatever his desires.

I saw at once the sense behind my father's plan to build a city there, and a port. It was as natural a harbour as any, almost as good as Gadez or even Carthage itself, sheltered behind a headland. From there, the whole of the east and north of Spain was open to us. Our galleys could reach Carthage even faster. The Balearic Isles were within sight on a clear day and there my father planned to go to raise more slingers for his army.

We had been at Cartakhena only a few days. War was far from our minds. Water was, and walls, and streets and building, all the making of a town, when under oar, its torn sails flapping, trailing gear across its thwarts, one blackened galley came to port. My father had sent six, exploring up the coast.

The few survivors told a sorry tale. They had anchored in the mouth of a river, two days' sailing to the north, before a town we knew as Heliche. Foragers sent ashore had not returned. The man in charge, from Nabeul in Africa, sent more. They too did not return. Instead of sailing away, the galleys waited.

"Waited?" exclaimed my father. "For what?"

He got no answer. Those that had waited did. Fire arrows at dusk. Only the one galley escaped.

"Vettonians, no doubt," Hasdrubal remarked.

"We march at dawn," my father answered.

So we marched, 1,000 foot and 500 horse, to teach the Vettonians the power of Carthage. Hasdrubal remained to see to works at Cartakhena. Our scouts reported nothing on our way, but smoke signals preceded us on the hills. We came to Heliche, a miserable town of clay and wood but straddling a steep rise above the river.

I must tell this quickly. Tears rise in my eyes, for fear that I have failed him who so loved me. Across the hill before the town there was a line of oxen and of carts, yes oxen and carts. Belleus snorted, pawed the ground. I looked at my father, questioning. He dismounted. I followed. He gave his orders quickly, clearly. "Four rams ready at the rear. Crescent line, two deep, cavalry on the wings. *Synapismos*, locked shield order. Frontal assault." We had rehearsed such manoeuvres many times in Gadez. Up to the gates, covered by our shields. Raise shields. Ramming detail. In.

The unexpected. "Always expect the unexpected," was one of my father's favourite saws. Should I have known, when my father did not? We were advancing in close order up the hill. Then trundling, rushing down the hill towards us, suddenly ablaze, the carts and maddened oxen came, bursting through our line. Our men were broken into muddled groups. Theirs streamed towards us from the gate, a horde of screaming men with targes, cutlasses.

I was separated from my father, with me nine or ten of our Numidians. I took the first Vettonian on my spear, the second through the belly with my sword and they were all around me. I cut and thrust and fell, struck on my helmet, and saw a cutlass raised above me, blue eyes, smell. His head, cut off, fell on me and it was my father, straddled over me, lance and sword and shield. "Regroup!" he yelled, "Regroup!" and others came and he took me with his left arm, spearing with his right, and was dragging me down the hill when a spear caught him in the side and my father's blood ran down my face and still he dragged me down.

Our cavalry came, drove off the Vettonians. I lay with my bleeding father on the ground, then rose, head reeling. "Take command!" he said, "Command!" and I left him with his groom, led our re-united men and did as he had planned. Their frenzy spent, their stratagem failed, resistance in the town was weak and we worked butchery, not war, before I fired the town.

As heat and cinders from that fire blew down on us, I sat beside my father on the ground. He was weak when I returned. His eyes wandered, searching. He focused. "Is it done, Hanni-bal?" a whisper and yet strong. I nodded and my eyes filled with tears, as they do now, and I was not eighteen but a boy who wakens in the night and is afraid. He drifted from me as the sun burned and the kites wheeled overhead. His body arched with pain. His left hand, the one without two fingers, seized my arm. He raised his head and held my eyes. "Rome, Hannibal, Rome!" he said to me, death rattle in his throat, and he who was my father died.

IV

COMMAND

I have lived long, five and sixty years, and sometimes now I cannot bear the pith of it. My past mists round me, swallowing that which I have been.

I cling to many places I have seen, etched upon my memory. Sometimes I sit now when my hand can write no more and my spirit is on fire and these too many places pass before me, like ships slow sailing down the Hellespont. The square of Hanno's crucifixion, mountain passes, plains of pebble or of grass; wastes of snow, sky-spearing mountains, foothills flower-banked, blossomed valleys, marshes, rivers, seas.

And that hillside before Heliche. I remember every stone, feel still the death-hold of my father's hand upon my arm. It is all chance. Chance should be a god. The beat of the wing of a dragonfly, light-lifting, is not more swift than is the fate of man.

Belleus walked and cantered back to Cartakhena without the rein, for my arms were round my dead father, steadying him stinking as we rode. Death. The cloying, rich, sweet and sickening, sticking, stinking smell of death. Through the night, not stopping, back we rode.

They came out to meet us, Hasdrubal mounted for once, and Hamilax, my brothers, Silenus. Rolling came the keening of the women and again I hear it, rolling on through time.

Everyone can master grief except for he who has it. Hasdrubal's did not stop him ensuring his succession to my father. From the tent where I had gone I heard the soldiers' acclamation. He would no doubt already have sent to Carthage for the Elders' approval. I did not care.

They had taken my father's body away. Hamilax would see it was prepared. I lay in my tent, unwashed, crusted with my

74

father's blood and neither sleep nor tears would come. Maharbal was with me. "You must eat, Hannibal," he said. Flies buzzed, lethargic in the heat.

"I'm not hungry," I replied.

"Then drink at least." He brought the pitcher. I drank. "Amongst my people," Maharbal said softly, "it is the custom to mourn at birth and rejoice at death. When a child is born, its family gather round and sorrow at the suffering it must endure. When someone dies, we bury him rejoicing that he has escaped the miseries of life."

"Miseries?" I mumbled. I sat up. "What of the glories, Maharbal? I mourn for the glories that were within my father's grasp. Now he is only a name."

"All good things must be paid for, Hannibal," Maharbal said at last, "before or after."

It was Hasdrubal who roused me. Blunt, direct, bursting in. "Hannibal, get up. You're needed. There's the funeral to organise, the pyre. I've too much else to do," and so I saw to the passing of my father.

Hamilax had placed my father's body, washed and dressed in his gold armour, on a bier in the middle of the parade ground. When I came out, squinting from the sun, the troops were gathered round it in their thousands. Maharbal had Belleus ready, his saddlecloth of black, a black plume in his mane and three times I rode around the bier amid the thronging chant of lamentation. Hamilax's bath-slave approached. "My master told me to prepare a bath for you to wash away your blood. It is ready."

And I cried out, "No! No water shall come near me until I have laid my father on a burning pyre and heaped a death mound over him and cut my hair for him. I will know no second sorrow like this while I am still one of the living. Maharbal, have the heralds sound. Begin the feast."

And so around the bier were driven many oxen, sheep and

bleating goats and swine to be slaughtered and roasted for the memory of Hamilcar. Each man ate his fill as I sat alone throughout upon my horse before the body of my father, though many bade me join them. The body. Always the demands of the body. Most lives are to be found in food and sex and drink and all the small indulgences of life.

The feasting done at last, the wood was brought. To a pyre of fifty cubits' breadth I carried in my arms the body of my father, his armour glowing in the fading sun. I placed beside it two-handled jars of oil and incense, honey, myrrh. My father's hunting dogs were brought. Hamilax had the knife. I cut their throats and laid them down beside him. With the same knife, I cut my hair and laid it on my father's chest. Then came my brother Mago and then Hasdrubal, Hamilax and Hasdrubal the Handsome and then the captains of the syntagmata and horse; for hours they came until the stars were bright. All too cut their hair and covered up the corpse.

"Do we have any prisoners?" I asked Hasdrubal, standing by the pyre.

"Eighty-five at present." He was always a master of detail.

"Any Vettonians?"

"Some, from the last skirmish before your father" – he checked himself – "was, ah, killed."

A skirmish? Is that all he thought? I was too tired to care. "Bring twenty of them here." In the dark by torch-light I cut their throats, unthinking, taking them by the hair. My brothers threw the bodies onto the pyre until the knife slipped in my bloody hand. There were three left. "Tie them living to the pyre." Hamilax nodded. "Then light it."

All night the pyre crackled and soared, the priests droned their chants. For a while the Vettonians screamed. My brother Hasdrubal began to cry. "Cry somewhere else," I told him. And when the dawn star rose and saffron-mantled light coloured the sea, it was enough. "Bring wine," I said to Hamilax beside me.

Many jars were brought. In turn, we each poured wine on the smouldering pyre until the fire was still. Then we took up the bones of Hamilcar my father and placed them in a golden urn and prayed to Melkarth that he should go well to Mithra.

We built a grave mound for him, on a bluff above the sea. I brought the urn and saw the men had dug the cist on a south-east line to point to Carthage. "Re-form the cist," I ordered. "Make it lie north-east."

Someone, was it Maharbal or Hamilax, asked why. "Because the bones of Hamilcar must point," I said, "to Rome."

I went then to the beach and in the lee of a rock lay down and slept at last a deep and dreamless sleep. There is no greater medicine. So often has it healed me. Now this blessing does not come. I lie sweating through the night, turning over many things.

Maharbal was beside me when I woke. "Hasdrubal wants to see you," he said and he walked with me back in silence. I washed, I remember, and the bath was red, red with my father's blood, the Vettonians', and I saw that suddenly and leapt out, upturning the bath over my couch and chest and clothes. The slave was frightened. Maharbal wrapped me in a cotton gown. "Burn all this," he told the slave. He took me by the arm and led me to see Hasdrubal.

His tent was huge and fine. He lay on a couch. A fair-skinned girl was massaging his feet. She must have cost him. "Wine?" he asked. I shook my head. "Come, sit." I shook my head again. "All right, Hannibal, I have taken overall command. I expect confirmation from Carthage shortly." He reached out an arm. A cup-slave sitting by the couch filled a goblet of wine, handed it to him. The slave had, I saw, no legs. So it was true, what I had heard, that Hasdrubal the Handsome had the legs of many of his body-slaves cut off.

"Why do you do this?" I asked him, pointing to the slave. It seemed hugely important.

He sipped, looking at me. "Slaves without legs, Hannibal, cannot run away."

The death of my father, his funeral and slaves without legs. Everything muddled in my mind. "Are you listening, Hannibal? My slaves are my concern. Yours is the army. I want you to take command. Report to me weekly. I have trade and politics and" – he leant forward quickly, slipped a hand up the slave girl's shift – "and other things to see to." Silence, Hasdrubal pawing the girl. "Well," he roared, "do you accept?"

I nodded, turned and left.

Command? This meant little. I was born for this. It was natural. The army. For what? I walked to the stable yards. I wanted to see Belleus. Why did Hasdrubal want an army? Did he hate Rome? I asked the same questions aloud to Maharbal, walking beside me in the sun. "These things will become clear in time," he said. Then in ones and twos, tens and twenties, hundreds came the men blocking our way, surrounding us, chanting, chanting, "Hann-i-bal, Hann-i-bal!" and the tears ran down my face.

For many months I simply worked, from the moment I awoke until late at night. I slept only to work again and here was born the perfection of my army that so many times defeated Rome. So was there a justice to my grief. The death of Hamilcar gave birth to the perfect army. Let this be my father's true memorial.

It is normal now, what we achieved. Even here in Bithynia I found the local troops adapted to the ways that I first developed. I. I should say Maharbal and I. It seems so simple now.

Two or three months after my father's death, we were on exercise in the hills to the west of Cartakhena on a sodden winter's day with 1,000 horse, 3,000 foot. We were dis- mounted, as usual waiting for the infantry to come up. A keen troop leader, a coarse-featured Lusitanian, came up to me with some request or other. But as he spoke, a curious thing happened. His mouth opened wide. His eyes bulged. He swayed and gurgled blood and fell forward towards me. There was an arrow in the back of his neck.

A shower of arrows whistled down, coming from behind a crag. "Shields!" I shouted, as arrows struck quivering in the ground or rang on iron helmets. The screams of the wounded pierced the din of the alarmed men and horses as I moved to Belleus. "First three troops, mount. Other two, coral and hold position!" I shouted. In a V we galloped up the ridge, arrows pinging off our shields and horses' armour. We drove them off, of course, some hardy band of tribesmen from the north. But it was difficult and dangerous, for they withdrew in good close order, forming a hedge with their long lances and a marching barrier with their shields. Our javelins thrown, there was little we could do but let them go. We needed infantry, not cavalry, and ours was far behind.

We returned to the troops we had left, this time posting roving scouts and not just pickets. Maharbal and I were sitting by a fire that smoked and billowed in the rain. The troop commanders reported. We had lost thirty men and sixteen horses, the tribesmen only two of their number. I took this badly. Just another minor skirmish, one amongst hundreds that I have forgotten. But it niggled. "We outnumbered them, Maharbal. They couldn't do us much harm once we were mounted, but nor we them once they'd formed that hedge. Cavalry and infantry. Stalemate."

Maharbal poked the fire with a stick. "It needn't be."

"What do you mean?"

"Why not make the infantry cavalry and the cavalry infantry?" he said, looking up. "Two in one."

Why not, indeed. "Why not!" I shouted, leaping up and clapping Maharbal on the shoulder in the Spanish rain. So was born the first great innovation of Hannibal, the hammer of his army.

It took a long time. A cavalryman had always carried just a small shield, two javelins and one long dagger that was no use for offence. He was armoured – a breastplate, helmet, greaves – as was his horse. The cavalryman's art was to throw his javelins at the gallop, rising up to do so, whole weight on the thighs. Javelins thrown, he was useless, and had to return to his lines for more.

My father had formed several squadrons of lighter cavalry, known as peltasts from the Greek *pelte* for a light shield. Neither they nor their garrons wore armour and they carried only sling or bow and their small shield. These I did not try to change, but hone, perfect in accuracy of shot.

We started with just one troop, 300 men. We gave them wooden swords. For weeks we trained them, day after day. They were surly. It did not go well. One noon-break Maharbal came up, sweating from his teaching, even in the winter cold. "There's going to be trouble, Hannibal. The men are restless. They have had enough. They say they will leave when their term is up – if not before."

I should have explained, not merely ordered. I was young. I have learned since then. I was sitting, my back against the barrack wall, with a view over the drill ground and its rows of straw soldiers for my horsemen-infantry to attack with the sword. "Send them over, Maharbal," I said.

"What, all of them? The whole troop?"

"Yes, you *anda*, yes."

I walked out to meet them. Mostly big-boned, fair-haired northern Celtiberians, that troop, bow-legged men who could ride almost before they could walk. They were surprised when I addressed them in their own tongue. "Sit down," I said and I did too. "Maharbal tells me that you are unhappy," I began, cross-legged on the ground. No-one returned my gaze. "Well?" I asked gently.

A wizened, grizzled man, his blond beard greying, spoke up

from near the front. "Hannibal, I served your father first in Sicily. I came to his standard when I learned that he had come to Spain, for I was proud to serve the Barca" – men about him murmured their agreement – "but as a cavalryman, not" – he spat – "a mule." I knew their word for infantry, mule. "Fourteen years in all it is that I have stood for Carthage. And now this." He held up his wooden sword. Men nodded, muttered their support.

"What's your name?" I asked.

"I am Castello, a *dekadarchos*, appointed by your father." A file leader, no less. Yet another reform of my father's, splitting the troop into thirty files of ten on the Greek model, a veteran in command of each, and suddenly I was in the room in Gadez with him, his arms about me when I had killed my man and I needed him and he was dead.

"Castello, why do you serve Carthage?" I asked calmly, mind forced back.

The men fell silent, puzzled. "For five gold xthets a term," someone shouted from the back. Yes, they were paid well, and on time. Hasdrubal the Handsome saw to that.

"Is that all? Is that the only reason you serve?" I shouted back. "Castello, is it?"

His blue eyes faced me squarely. Silence. "I, I – I know nothing else. And, and" – now firmly – "I am proud to be a *dekadarchos* of Carthage. In my village, I have respect."

"And if you could be more proud, what then?" I stood up. "Listen to me, all of you." And so I told them, of my vow, of my father's dying words, then of the way that I would do it. A new army, a marvel of the world, a revolution in the art of war, disciplined and trained to perfection, mobile, invincible, bound to march and defeat Rome and end its tyranny. "You will be the first of these new soldiers, the first and the best. There will be pay, yes, and booty, spoils, but there will be a glory that time will not age. Your children's children will hear tell of how you marched with Hannibal, son of Hamilcar, and won. This is my dream," I said. "Will you join me?"

Castello came up first to kneel before me, hands crossed in fealty across his chest as is the Spanish way. One after another they came, in silence, leaving me to resume their practice with the sword. I had won my first victory.

Maharbal told me later that my speech had moved many of those seasoned men to tears. I had not noticed. I can explain what I said, but not why it worked. Yes, Silenus had taught me well the laws of rhetoric, the variants of pitch and clause and tone and voice and gesture. But there have been many better orators than Hannibal.

I too took up again my wooden sword. But first I had the trumpet sound to still those Spaniards at their drill. "Celtiberians," I shouted as loudly as I could and all the followers and harness-menders, the barrack cooks, the sentries too could hear, "I thank you. You shall be from now my Guard and fight with me in the foremost ranks for Carthage. Castello, you will be its colonel, its *loxarchos*. My Hammer Guard, I salute you. Now, the cross-stroke . . ." The rest was drowned in cheers.

We did it. In three months I had my troop as adept with the sword as I was myself. They were growing stale with practice. One day I called Castello to me. I had learned to share to lead. "So much for the sword, Castello. What about the lance?"

He paused for a moment, then, with a smile of blackened, broken teeth: "I'd rather be a true mule, I suppose, than just a donkey!" We developed a holster so that each horse could also carry a lance.

I can still recall the hours and hours of experiment it took to get the holster right, to find the perfect length for the lance: not so short as to be useless against a normal infantry lance, and not so long as to affect the horse's mobility, nor catch the files when the troop was in close order. And finally, a larger shield. Not one of a true mule. We tried that. Too heavy not to affect the javelin-throw, even I had to admit. But larger nonetheless.

So I had my Hammer Guard and Carthage the nucleus of a new army. Hybrids indeed. Cavalry one moment, infantry the next and all that summer still we drilled and exercised until I had twelve troops trained, then twenty.

Hasdrubal had followed my reforms with guarded interest. He never, I admit, complained about the cost. He just showed me his accounts at each of our meetings – weekly, as he had promised at the start, unless he was away. I thought – and talked – throughout that time of little more than the army. I was little interested in Carthage, policy or trade. Hasdrubal seemed content to let it go at that, until one windless afternoon he came to the parade ground.

He was hugely fat by now. Eight slaves it took to bear his litter, caparisoned in silk and chains of gold and gems, and put it down beside me. The curtain opened. He was eating nuts. "Still playing at soldiers, Hannibal?"

"I'm pleased to see not all your slaves lack legs," I gave him back.

He was amused. "So, the whelp has learnt to bite as well as bark! Hannibal, what is all this for? On what are we – or rather you – spending almost a full quarter of our revenues?"

"I am preparing an expensive present."

"For whom?" he asked. Another nut shell landed at my feet.

"*Senatui populoque Romano, Hannibalis Barcinus gratiam refert,*" I began.

"Speak Punic, blast you!" He had no time for other tongues, did Hasdrubal the Handsome, nor for books and Greeks and tutors. "I am, like a true son of Carthage, a trader, not a scholar," he told me once. "And what does that make me?" He only laughed.

"Hannibal returns the Roman compliment. I am going to march on Rome."

Hasdrubal stopped chewing. His eyes sank into his swelling

flesh. "So a report to the Council along these lines, eh?" He changed his deep voice to a singsong. "To the High Sufet, Light of Baal, and the illustrious Council of the Elders of Carthage, Hasdrubal sends greetings. Your Spanish army, now some – how many have you got now, Hannibal?"

"Thirty-five thousand," I replied, "including six re-trained."

"Some 35,000 strong – I won't bore them with your mumbo-jumbo about re-training – is now able under the command of Hannibal, son of Hamilcar, properly to guard our trade routes. This may seem a large force for the purpose, but the local tribesmen are recalcitrant and fierce and we are about to continue our expansion north to mines of iron and of silver." He resumed his normal growl. "Something like that, eh, Hannibal?"

"Say what you like. What's your cut now, by the way?"

He guffawed. "Enough, Hannibal, enough. Anyway, it's time you got off exercise and into action. See this," he said, unrolling a map.

A fat finger pointed north and west. A town marked as Majrit, a river a little south of a town marked as Tago. Hasdrubal's sweat dropped onto the scroll. "I want it. All of it. And don't forget" – he laughed again – "to come back. And, by the way, your mother's dead." He drew the curtain. The nut shells cracked under my feet as I turned away.

"And, by the way, your mother's dead." The mother that we had left in Gadez, the mother that I never knew. I could not even remember what she looked like. I remembered her making Mago watch the maiming of Regulus, little more. There was no time. And anyway a part of me still shrinks that I was born of human flesh. They say there is no greater pain than childbirth. In pain my mother bore me, but the pain of childbirth passes. My pain has not eased but grown. Hannibal would have been better born not of woman, but of stone.

I saw Silenus before we left. I had hardly seen him since

Gadez. He had in any case more fertile ground to till in my brothers, Hasdrubal especially. I had, I thought, learned all he had to teach me. I was wrong. Only now do I know how little I know. That's what Socrates said at his trial, charged with claiming to be the wisest man in the world. "I admit to that," he said, "but only because I know how little I know."

I went to say goodbye to him, no more. "Remember Epaminondas, and Jason," Silenus said, a private but a pointed joke, and reached out to me his hand.

"And you, Gisco?" I replied.

"That I prefer to forget, Hannibal. Forgetfulness is an art too much ignored. I ask for you that you will never need it." I need it now, but know not where it is to be found.

I was nineteen, almost twenty. Two years I was away. We quelled and ordered the land on Hasdrubal's map. I remember the night alarms, the puny hill-top forts, the ease with which my Hammers crushed the tribes who sought to block our way, enveloping them as cavalry, then dismounting, penetrating, killing as infantry. First learn from others, as I had, then learn for yourself, and that is what I did when I conquered that huge part of Spain.

I started with myself, sleeping on the ground with the men, eating what they ate, wearing what they wore, fighting as they fought. The first village that we took, Maharbal cleared the headman's house for me. I refused. "I prefer the ground I know to fleas I don't," I joked, but that was not the reason. I was preparing. We had bad water, and my bowels screeched and ran as did the men's. I found a touch of vinegar the answer. And then the men drank less water, too, no more than they needed and provisioning was easier.

Then I turned to the cavalry, training, exercising until each horse would obey touch, not sound. Commands in battle shouted or spoken are often lost in the noise. As a general, I have always preferred signs and mirrors; as a horseman, touch.

We practised in the hills of Spain the cavalry feint and the wheel, the charge and mock retreat. Maharbal's idea, that one, to keep your strongest horses in each squadron in reserve and have them charge when the enemy is drawn on by the mock retreat.

I learned and learned. We had been having trouble with the horses' feet. We were in deep hills of flinty stone. Belleus was lame, like hundreds of our horses. The *Hipparchikos* of Xenophon, his treatise on the Cavalry Commander. I did not have the text with me. But I remembered. *"For hardening horses' feet, throw down some stones and curry the horse on these and make him stand on them . . ."* Or something like that. I remembered the strange verb, *psexein*, to curry, wear away, rub down. We had no such word in Punic. I suppose our horsemen had always worked on softer ground, on desert sand. Anyway, it worked. All our lame horses were picketed on lines of stones, not grass, until their feet healed – and hardened.

I used my Hammer troops less and less to put down the native tribes. They were a hammer to crack a nut, indeed. The peltasts stung them instead, and then I used my infantry. They were trained in both the delta-wedge and the diamond. These were the traditional forms of infantry offence, and good ones, easily adapted to defence.

I had studied both in theory with Silenus. I had seen both in practice with my father. Both of course were Greek. The first, named after the Δ shape of the capital Greek letter *delta*, was introduced by the Theban general Epaminondas. Using it, and a novel slanting attack by the left wing, he had inflicted on the great Spartan army at Leuctra a crushing defeat.

The diamond form for infantry, the *rhombos*, was developed by Jason, tyrant of Pherae in Thessaly. I never liked it much. It was too static. The delta was more flexible. I taught it on that campaign to fly, or so the men joked. It occurred to me when I was watching two of our infantry companies attack four groups of Spaniards, loosely bunched. They were making a poor job of it, holding to their formation as they had been trained, because the Spaniards, as they usually do, were rushing here and there.

"Spread out," I shouted to myself. "Encircle them!" Of course they just ploughed on and got there in the end, but I knew. I drew it for them afterwards in the dust. "If the sides and rear of each delta had just swung outwards," I said, "like" – like what? – "like, like a bird's wings, rising from its sides . . ." And so we had another innovation, known by the command "Fly!" There are many dead who can attest its efficacy.

We tried it on that campaign in all its variants. "Flying" to form a straight front, a crescent, an inverted V, to each its own clear command. A general is only as good as his communication. We developed many things which are now normal in war. What I called the "refuse", by right or left flank, for example.

I had noticed that in a frontal infantry advance, both opposing lines tend to slant to the right, as each man instinctively seeks the protection of the shield of the man on his right – the shield is carried on the left arm. So it is left flanks, not centres or rights, that usually clash first.

The "refuse" means breaking off the rightward slant and sending your right wing left to break the enemy's centre. It takes timing. In Spain I thought of it, developed it and practised it. I combined it with the well-known *anastrophe*, the wheeling-back, when the files about-turn, march to the rear and take up their position behind the centre or the other flank, doubling its depth and strength. So refuse with your right flank or your left, wheel it back, reform the delta and send its doubled strength driving through.

It gladdens me to write of these things. I took the best of the past and added the best of myself. I made an army that was never defeated because, until what I had made was copied, what I made was best. It was a far cry from what was expected of a Carthaginian army. Until my father's time, that had relied on the shock charge of the elephants alone. Our infantry was poorly drilled, expected largely to mop up after the elephants. That was enough for the wars that Carthage fought in Africa.

Some day, perhaps, a learned Greek like Silenus will record the history of generalship and warfare. They may record some of the many other things that Hannibal began. I am as proud of my system for breaking cavalry horses as I am of my refuse and I learned this too on my Majrit campaign when we had many captured horses to train.

Belleus' belly when first I saw him bore witness to the usual method of breaking a horse. "Rareying", it is called, brutalising it should be. I had put Castello in charge of breaking a new group of twenty captured colts, dappled greys, almost wild. As was the custom, Castello had them coralled, each with a halter and a barbed bit. I went to watch him at his work one morning.

The grooms were prodding, hitting the most stubborn colts with long wooden poles to accustom them to touch. They cursed and sweated. Castello yelled. The dust was thick. There was a smell of fear, a sense of hate.

Horses are like men. They must do willingly that which they are trained to do or they will not do it well. I walked away and sat under a thorn tree. How could this be done differently? We had to tame the horses' spirits, but not break them. I walked back to Castello. "Stop this!" I ordered. "There must be a better way." One by one the grooms stopped, the colts moved to the far side of the coral, the dust settled.

Castello was beside me at the fence. "What do you have in mind?" A fair enough question. I didn't know. As we waited, he swung the rope he held.

"Give me your rope, Castello." I vaulted into the coral as the colts reared and shied away. Tame, not break. I approached them gently.

"Watch out!" someone cried; "You'll be trampled!" another.

I held up a hand for silence, eyes fixed on one great beast which did not move away but stood and pawed the ground, blood dripping from its mouth. "I will not hurt you, colt," I whispered and his ears pricked up, "I will not." I moved up to him, took off his bloody bit, rubbed his sweating side. He reared up before me, hooves crashing at my feet.

"You are a brave man, Hannibal," Castello said after. No. I just was not afraid.

I took the halter, looped on the rope and gently, slowly, talking all the time, I turned the colt's head and tied the rope to its tail. Many have asked me how I thought of this. I didn't. The best of our actions come to us through a kind of madness, provided it is of the gods. Round and round we walked together, quietly. I signalled to Castello to come.

He took the first colt. With another length of rope, I did the same again and in an hour we had all twenty colts galvayned. "Now leave them be," I said. "Come and eat." We left the colts turning round and round. When we came back, they were all still. "Leave them so each morning for a week," I told Castello. "Then you can train them."

We returned to Cartakhena, more slowly than we had gone. I had 600 hostages, 3,000 prisoners for the mines and, at Hasdrubal's request, another 400 who were to become galley-slaves. I had enlisted many new troops.

Hasdrubal had been busy. From his regular despatches to me I knew that he had been pressing on with building. I don't know what I had expected, but it was certainly not what I found.

I had left a town of mud and tents and half-built walls, what I had supposed was just another trading post for Carthage. I returned to a city of stone upon a hill, surrounded by a huge and gated wall, and below that a large and bustling harbour with a new breakwater stretching into the sea.

I rode through the western gate with Maharbal alone,

leaving the rest outside on the plain below, Castello in command. "How has he done this?" asked Maharbal in awe. I did not answer. I had only seen its like in Carthage as a boy. On we rode along the cobbled streets faced with houses and with shops of new-cut stone, across the market-places, upwards to the citadel. Some stopped and stared at us as we passed. There was no welcome here. A builder's cart blocked the street. Sweating Negro slaves unloaded beams and blocks of stone and sacks of lime under the whip of a hook-nosed Assyrian. "I will tell them to let us pass," Maharbal said.

"No. We'll wait."

"Since when does Hannibal attend a carter?"

"Maharbal, we'll wait."

And wait we did on fretting horses in the narrow street amid the smell of sweat and dung. What was Hasdrubal doing? This was a great city, the seat of a potentate, a king. King of what? Of course, the more so since my campaign, King of Spain.

Across his marbled hall, Hasdrubal's eyes were almost sunk in fat when I looked at him, lying on a couch. A mincing eunuch had led us there, across a fountained courtyard, along still corridors where our footsteps rang in silence. There were perhaps twenty boys and young men about him in the room, some playing games of dice or chess. Their hair was ringed and perfumed and I did not have to guess which way round he used them.

"So, the conquering hero comes," Hasdrubal growled to the room at large, "and with his" – he sneered at the word – "companion." Maharbal stiffened beside me. Hasdrubal's fancy boys sniggered.

"You too, Hasdrubal, have been busy, I see," I retorted, "in more ways than one. Now let's talk. Clear the room."

From his couch across the room his eyes bored into me. But people have always obeyed my commands. With remarkable agility for someone of his bulk, he was suddenly on his feet. He clapped his hands. Haughtily, his bedboys left.

"And that wretched creature too," I said, crossing the room, pointing to the legless cup-slave by his couch.

Hasdrubal guffawed. "But Hannibal, I have improved on many things since you went away. He no longer has a tongue! But since you would be alone, then get rid of him," a podgy finger raised at Maharbal. I simply spread out the fingers of my left hand by my side. So often had we used and practised silent orders in the field. Maharbal's footsteps died away.

"Some wine, some food?" Hasdrubal the Handsome asked.

"No, but I would like to sit down."

He gestured to a couch of satin, its brocades of gold. I walked to two stools by a brazier in the corner and sat on one. Surprisingly, he followed. "Now," he began, and for two hours we talked alone.

His income – I should say ours – was staggering. The mines were proving far richer than even Hasdrubal had hoped. "Do the Elders know this?" I asked him.

"They know what they need know. The Roman tribute is being paid."

"What of the rest?"

"The rest, Hannibal, you see about you. And I want more. I want" – he unrolled a map of the whole Spanish peninsula – "I want all this. I want you to get it for me."

I said nothing.

"And you, Hannibal, what do you want?" From far below the sounds of the city reached us through the silence and I heard again my father's dying words. "Me? I want – " I swallowed, looked right at him. "I want only Rome."

"Then give me Spain, and then take what you want. Now, what further forces do you need?" We talked of horses and of troops, of forges, provisions, of all the mundanities of war.

"You should know of certain, certain, ah, problems,

91

Hannibal." Hasdrubal pronounced the word with delicate distaste. "But you may safely leave them to me."

"No doubt," I said. "But what are they?"

"One is called Carthage, and the other Rome. There are certain, certain" – again that fastidiousness – "elements in Carthage who dislike what I, what *we* are doing here. I am kept well informed, of course, but the peace party in Carthage is growing. There is even talk, for example, that you and your army should be recalled."

"Recalled! But . . ." I expostulated.

"Let me finish – recalled and sent to conquer south in Africa, leaving the north and west to Rome."

Hasdrubal gestured. Pushing himself along with one hand, holding a goblet of wine in the other, the legless mute grotesque came up and then withdrew. Hasdrubal drank deeply. "The Romans are behind much of this. They want a new treaty – once the indemnity is paid in full, of course – under which we will withdraw from Spain. That is why I am going tomorrow to Saguntum."

"But Saguntum is – "

"A day's sail north, the most prosperous town on the seaboard. I am going to meet an embassy from Rome."

"To say what?"

"To say sweet nothings, to win more time, why" – and he put his head back and bellowed with laughter – "to soothe the Romans' fevered brows. And then, Hannibal, I shall do the same with the Elders. So will I get what I want, Spain. What you do with your army afterwards is up to you. Do we have an understanding?"

"I will come with you to Saguntum."

"No. I don't need a warlike Adonis with me. Besides, I already have an engagement for you as my, ah, as my – representative. A banquet in my honour given by some Spanish chiefs. Tomorrow at sunset."

Maharbal was waiting for me in the courtyard. Two grooms brought up our horses. I was mounting Belleus by the gate when I heard the sound from round the corner of the wall. I slipped off Belleus, following the noise. It came from the midden for Hasdrubal's household by his palace wall. On the pile, still in its afterbirth, its little limbs struggling in filth, a new-born baby mewled. I called for the grooms. "Whose child is this?" They would not meet my eyes. "Are you dumb? Tell me!"

"The child is my master's," one mumbled, shuffling his feet, "by one of his favoured slave girls."

"But why does she not nurse it?" Maharbal asked.

"My master forbade it, lest it spoil her breasts."

I felt sick, turned away, fought the anger rising. Maharbal reached into his tunic and took from his purse a golden xthet. "This is no death for any humankind," he said to the groom. "At least kill the creature," handing over the coin.

My mind was full of many things when I rode out next afternoon to the Spanish banquet. I took only Maharbal with me and six of my Hammer Guard. Hasdrubal had urged me take a full squadron, but I have always disliked ostentation. My clothes were clean but simple, plain cotton. Hannibal has never worn insignia of rank or jewels or baubles. I had shaved, tied back my hair, no more.

The village was an hour's ride inland. Hasdrubal must have told them to expect me, not him, for there were outriders to greet me with the usual platitudes in halting Punic: "Hail, mighty Hannibal, great son of the great Hamilcar, Light of Carthage, Conqueror of Majrit . . ." In crisp Iberian, I told them to shut up.

Within the banquet tent the six chiefs came up and gave to me their oath of fealty. I had many of their men among my army, Turdetanians mostly, although these chiefs were proud to rule their parts of that whole. They are interminably interested in their own genealogy, Spaniards. They are all related to each other and, eventually, to their gods. I was always careful to respect and exploit such ties within my army. A troop, a squadron, a syntagma is better bound by blood than any other bond.

I was growing restive at the endless courses, oysters, mussels, cockles and limpets, then thrushes on beds of asparagus, then turbot and hake and gilt, bream and sole, then pigeons stuffed with ortolans and ortolans stuffed with nightingales and boar and duck, restive at the carousing, the empty noisiness, the feigned friendship of it all. Then she came in, at the far end of the tent from me, to the sound of music which slowly hushed the din.

Similce, that was her name, the drunken chief beside me said. Graceful as roebuck, delicate as reed, gentle as gossamer she glided, trembled to the dance and all fell silent to the magic that she made. I saw her tapering hands, the curvings of her breasts and hips, her mouth so finely wrought below the reaching cheekbones, the delicate nose. Her beauty slowed my breath and caught my soul.

Nearer she came, nearer. As she arched and sinuated before our table, I saw the tiny hairs upon her forearms. From my bowels, with all my being, I wanted to touch and lick, protect them. I was twenty-one and there had come to me the miracle of love. In that first sight of her there was all the erotic sensuality of innocence, so much stronger than the carnality of adulthood.

Even now, tears blind me as I think of these things. Tears for all the things that were, and for all the things that might have been. I rode back to Cartakhena in all the soaring lightness that is love.

V

WAR

There was much to do, as love stirred and coursed through me. An army is more work at peace than it is at war. There were men to quarter and train, latrines to build, stables, provisionings, promotions, complaints, commands. With Hasdrubal away in Saguntum, there were the mine and galley slaves I had brought back with me to order and to place.

Three days after the banquet, I heard from Hasdrubal. He had allocated me quarters in the city, a fine house of stone. I preferred to be among my men. The sounds and smells of armies, these I know. So Hasdrubal's eunuch found me in my tent down on the plain, studying my commanders' reports. I opened the despatch at once, Hasdrubal's hand as ever clear and strong.

"To Hannibal Barca, Hasdrubal's Captain General, greetings. I am comfortable here. The wine is excellent, vintage Falernian, which I have always much enjoyed. The women are agreeable enough for my comfort, although my hosts had not known that, as I age, I have come to prefer them younger and younger. There is something very pleasing in destroying pubescent virginity. It is the innocence, I think, the power to corrupt innocence I so enjoy. And now, I hear, a girl has cracked the iron that I thought there was in Hannibal for heart!" "Damn you," I shouted loud and my guard came in, alarmed. I waved him away. How did Hasdrubal know that which was so new to me, that which was unsaid? His spies, everywhere.

I read on. "I hope to have the pleasure of the girl's company. I do not normally involve myself with others' meat, but I hear she is a gazelle, and uncircumcised to boot. Anyway, enough of this. You should know that I am about to sign a treaty. That is

95

something I have not done before. You will not like its terms. But then, you need not keep them, at least not for too long. I will seek your counsel" – Hasdrubal seek my counsel? – "on these matters when, in a day or two, I return. My hosts have promised me – I gave them gentle hints – a boy or two from the Greek cities of Ionia. And as you know, I am a true servant of love. I have always regarded pederasty as the triumph of oral education. You should try it." He signed the letter "Your brother-in-law, Hasdrubal."

I heard a cough. Hasdrubal's eunuch had come in. "Do you wish me to take a reply?" he asked.

"Get out," I said quietly. "And if you value your life, never bring to Hannibal again a letter from your master."

It was the fourth day after the banquet. I woke earlier then normal, when the light is weightless and the world is new and the heart sings. I have always been a creature of the morning. I lit an oil lamp, used the same tablet Hasdrubal had sent me, quickly smoothing from the wax his filth. "To Fuano, Chief among the Turdetanians" – that I had learned on the night was her father's name – "Hannibal Barca sends greetings."

I wrote fast, stylus cutting lightly in the wax as it does now, for I am glad of this and its memory runs clear. "I wish to take as my wife Similce your daughter. I want no dowry, only her. Send me your answer by him who bears this." Nothing more. I have always tried to be direct. That is best.

Maharbal's tent was next to mine. I woke him with a touch. "*Anda?*" he asked in puzzled half-sleep.

"Take this to Fuano. Wait for his reply," I said, putting the sealed tablet on his chest. I had no need to tell him what it said.

Of course Fuano accepted. He was honoured, he said. I don't know what men thought of me in those days. It never occurred to me to care. But to a Spanish chiefling, here was a match indeed. I did wonder as I worked and waited through the day what my father would have wished. He would have considered the strategic implications, I am sure. They were sound enough. Certainly, my Spanish soldiers never failed me. Would my father have asked me if I loved her? I do not know. He had so little time for love.

I left all the arrangements for the wedding to Maharbal. The ceremony was to take place in six weeks, in the month of Zif, when the moon was full and all the constellations favourable. The astrologers and priests had so ordained. Maharbal wisely meant to invite as many Spanish chiefs as were allied to us or might be.

He was busy. So was I. Hasdrubal returned. I knew before his eunuch came, a different one this time, for the sounding drums that marked his rowers' strokes on that windless day reached me on the parade ground where I was training six new *dekadarchoi*.

"My master bids you come to him."

My javelin flew true, piercing at the throat the man of straw a hundred strides before me. The throat. The weak point in armour. I did not just plan how to kill Romans, but where. "Match that," I said to the *dekadarchoi*. "Tell your master," without turning round, "that he knows where to find me," and I corrected the hold on the javelin thong of the man about to throw.

Hasdrubal came, of course, sweating even in his litter and I broke away from training with a curt "carry on" to the men.

"And how is your young filly?" he began.

"Tell me about this treaty," brusque, I ordered.

"That tone of voice is better suited to those savages," he said, pointing to the men.

"Those 'savages' are better men than – " No, no. That's what he wanted. It amused him. I reached into the litter into the smell of his sweat and musk and gripped his right forearm, squeezing through the fat to bone. "Tell me about the treaty."

"Let go of my arm."

I did, but I had won.

"Oh, that," he said breezily. "It is simple. Even you will understand." I ignored that. "I have agreed with the Romans to limit our, our, ah, *activities*, to south of the river Ebro. You know of it, of course." Of course, I knew of the Ebro, the great sweeping, sinuous river cutting off the northern part of Spain that became Gaul. A river I intended to cross only once.

"Anything else?"

"Oh yes, we have agreed to leave each other's Spanish allies in peace. And that means – "

"Yes, I know, that means Saguntum."

"I want it left alone, Hannibal, is that clear?"

"But it's well south of the Ebro!" I exclaimed.

He was suddenly angry. "Do you take me for one of your slingers? I know better than you where Saguntum is. Haven't I just been there! But it's an important Roman trading post. And they're a maritime lot, those Saguntines. Hardly any land. They won't bother us. Besides, it has for me certain, certain charms" – he pronounced the word meticulously, longingly – "and I should like to extend my knowledge of Saguntum as it is, not as a smoking ruin."

I turned away.

I had to understand. It is hard enough when one is old to comprehend the complex. There was no-one to help me. I could see the advantages of such a treaty. More time. I had so much more to do, to prepare before, before . . .

"I will of course tell the Elders of this," Hasdrubal broke in, "stressing how anxious I am to accommodate Rome. What I will not tell them is this," and he clapped his hands.

From behind the litter came a man I had not seen before, barefoot but entirely dressed in trousers, blouse and tunic of white cotton of the same kind that was wrapped round and round his head. There was a quiet dignity about him, a sense of peace I liked at once. He stood at ease beside the open curtains of Hasdrubal's litter, black eyes staring at the middle distance, high cheekbones, broad nose, narrow mouth, clean-shaven. And he was tall, a hand more than me, and as he breathed, mouth closed, I saw his nostrils slowly flare and sink.

"This, Hannibal, is Bostar, an Egyptian and a map-maker. I bought him in Saguntum. He came highly recommended. Ninety-five gold xthets I had to pay. Are you worth that, Bostar?" Bostar stood silent. Hasdrubal's voice softened to a menacing drawl. "For your sake, you better be. Now show him."

Bostar was holding six tight rolls of papyrus. He unrolled one. I gasped. Here was a map indeed, coloured and beautifully drawn, showing the mountains, rivers, valleys, towns of Spain north of Majrit. "Where did you get this?" I asked him in Punic.

"I drew it."

I looked at him incredulously. My father would have given up a syntagma for less.

Bostar did not return my gaze. "I have travelled far."

"Where did you learn to speak our tongue?"

Again, impassive. "I know many tongues. I have travelled far."

"Hannibal, that is what I want," said Hasdrubal, pointing to the map.

"But not this?" I said ironically, pointing in my turn north of the Ebro.

"Not so far, Hannibal, not so fast. I have won you time. Use it." He waved Bostar away. "Give me what I want, and then do as you please." And he snapped the curtain closed.

It is not enough to say that fear or love or hate or anger motivate a man. Yes, I see that Hasdrubal was driven by greed and lust for power, but what gave birth to these? I sought to destroy Rome from hate that came to me as a Barca, from centuries of enmity to Rome, but where did it begin? To everything there must be a cause. G was caused by F and F by E and E by D and so on, however complex each cause may be, but is infinite regression possible? Something must guide all.

There was no time then for such thoughts as these. I planned the northern campaign. There were some strong towns of stone. I needed seige equipment. I had it made, immersing myself in ensuring that we used only the hardest types of wood for the frames of the catapults that we called in Punic "onagers", that all the works for them and for the giant slings that we called "scorpions", all the levers, pulleys, capstans, treadwheels, pivots, that all these were made from the purest brass. To protect them from fire, I had great curtains of thick rope made for them, to be soaked in water before use. We experimented, perfected. The day I was to wed drew close.

We were married in the open air, as I had wished it, in the morning. From my tent, long before dawn, I heard the excited voices, movements of the soldiers coming early to secure a place to see – the whole army had been given the day off. That and the feast for them were my idea and Maharbal's. Free brothels was Hasdrubal's gift. He had wanted, I learned from Maharbal, a ceremony in the temple of Melkarth at Gadez. I wished to marry as I was, a soldier, among my own kind now my father was dead, soldiers. That is what I did.

In the middle of the parade ground, the priests had prepared a circle of seven white stones, covering the ground with precious stones, jaspers, sapphires, chalcedonies, emeralds, chrysolytes, beryls, topazes, chrysoprases, jacinths, amethysts, sardonyxes. Hasdrubal's treasury was rich indeed. No wonder, I thought when I saw this from my tent, that he wanted more of Spain. I have never had a body-slave. Only Maharbal was with me as I bathed and shaved, tied back my hair, put on a simple full-length *chiton* of white linen, double-lined but unadorned, and a new pair of Spanish sandals.

"Hasdrubal has sent these for you," Maharbal said, opening a casket from which shone pure gold and silver earrings, bracelets, necklaces, bangles, armlets, rings.

"At least he hasn't offered me his belly," I laughed.

"Someone should benefit, I suppose," Maharbal said.

"Divide it all, *anda*, amongst the *dekadarchoi*. But leave Hasdrubal his paunch."

I took up last my sword-belt, slipped my scabbard from its loops, put on the belt my father gave me, stepped into the strengthening sun. "Oi-ee, oi-ee, oi-ee" rang thrice 20,000 voices, so many men I could not see their end, as I walked to the circle, to wait there.

I knew Similce would enter walking backwards, guided by her father, behind me, veiled. We were to stand, facing in opposite directions, right arms side by side so that they and we might be joined. I only saw before me, ringing the sacred circle, bearded Spanish chieftains in the woollen skirts they liked to wear. My kinsmen, now, I thought.

I had seen Similce only once, at that banquet when she danced. I had never spoken to her, never heard her voice. It did not matter. Socrates speaks of the beauty of thought and imagination exercising a deeper enchantment than the beauty of form. I knew that she was coming when the crowd fell silent and the chiefs before me drew themselves up tall. I heard first her footfall, light as raindrop on the stones, then her father's, crunching, then the other six witnesses behind, Maharbal, Fuano's brother, Silenus and my brothers. Then I smelt her, gentle as the warming winds of early summer, sweet as cinammon, soft as flower petals, a smell at which my being tingled, soared.

The priests intoned and chanted, the Carthaginian, then the Spaniard, a man in dress dyed deepest woad and ostrich feathers. "Raise your arms!" he called. The priest of Melkarth tied our right thumbs together with a lace of leather. The Spaniard bound our arms together, winding seven times around them

101

silken sash, in silence nothing marred. A wheaten cake, next, broken in two halves, one to my mouth, one under her veil to hers. I heard the whoosh of sword beyond me, bullock bellow and the splashing of its blood. Seven times for seven planets, seven senses passed the priests, painting seven stones with blood. "By fire!" together running now with seven torches the priests shouted as the drums deep throbbed, "By water!" panting round and sprinkling from golden bowls, their magic symbols shining in the sun, "Let this be done!"

As when rivers, running down the mountains in the winter, throw together, angry, at the meeting of their streams their weighted waters, and then from far away a shepherd on the high hills hears it, rolling through the air, so was the sound of cheering then that day when I was young in Spain when Similce became my wife.

Fuano undid first the lace and then the silken sash and turned his daughter round beside me, raising up her veil. I looked at her and I remember now that look, a thing I cherish like the thought of Mithra, a thing from before time began. In an arching eye, a swelling nostril, a tightening of the mouth within her smile, I saw all the beauty and the delicacy that there can be in man. In that look there came to us a knowing that time has not wearied, that will not grow old.

The sash re-tied around our waists, we walked oblivious together out of the circle along a long avenue of people cheering, touching us, towards the bridal tent. I think I had been worried about what was to come, what was supposed to come. I had seen the preparations for the bridal bed. It seemed so laboured, the need to produce a bloody sheet.

I kissed her on the corner of her top lip in that cool and silent tent and she trembled as a willow in the wind. She reached a hand out to the back of my neck and ran her fingers up and down, more an oscillation than a touch. I felt a swelling wanting in strange and in new parts of me that yet was all of me, a prickling, warm rushing from my belly to my feet, exploding in my head, in my beginning and my end. Her hands were on my back and on my buttocks as I found hers, softer skin than silk, smoother than gold, rising to her breasts, those breasts I licked and nuzzled, pulling her nipples gently upwards with my lips. She raised my *chiton* over me, I hers. I cupped her breasts in my hands, until then hands of rein and sword and death, and there was nothing beyond us to mar the shuddering music that we made.

Still standing up, I entered her, clear fluid from my dripping penis on our feet. She made no sound. Her nails dug into me. We fell back joined, back onto the bed and my life was no longer only mine but to be between her and all wounds and hurt. Our two clays were broken, mixed with water. As she arched, convulsed, towards me, we were fired, one body and one mind. When I came to her, it was from beyond some far and secret place of wakened space, and she drew my seed into her body and her being.

It was so quick, so urgent that first time, yet so long a journey I have never made. I rose up from her, a new man.

We were left alone. Fuano came in to take away the sheet. We heard the cheers, smiled shyly. We were brought food and drink but of what kind, it did not matter. For two days we touched and slept and talked, explored each other's bodies and each other's minds.

We spoke sometimes in Punic, sometimes in Iberian or a mixture of both. She asked me, I remember, in that soft and lilting voice to tell her as I kept a hand upon her throat – I loved to feel its resonating vibrance as she talked – of the worst in my life.

"My father's death at Heliche," I answered without hesitation.

"And the best?" The best? I asked myself. Belleus, Maharbal, my first man? "You, you are the best thing I have known, Similce."

Sitting gently up, her firm and tender, naked, tapering breasts before me, she kissed my head.

She asked me, I remember, of the future. "I shall destroy Rome," I said.

"And then be master of the world?"

"For that, I don't know, Similce. I must destroy Rome, that is all."

"Why?"

Why? I had never questioned. "Because, because – Because I was born to it. Because I am vowed to it. Because my father raised me for it. Because the Romans will destroy Carthage, and Spain, Similce, and Spain, unless I first destroy them."

We were silent for a long time. "Is that all?" she asked softly.

"It is all I know."

"It is enough. I will help you, Hannibal," she said, and she put my head between her breasts and we lay back and slept.

The third day after our wedding we re-joined the world. There were presents to examine, though I had told Maharbal to let it be known that I lacked for nothing and wanted less. Yet we found a large tent full of gifts. "We must acknowledge them, Hannibal," Similce said, "or we will offend many." Silenus was there, writing down an inventory of the rugs and cauldrons, jewels and swords, armour, plate.

"You have made an old man very happy," he said to us. "May you live long, and be faithful to the good in each other."

"What would you do with all this, Silenus?" I asked him, indicating the rows and piles of gifts.

"Send it to Gadez, to the temple of Melkarth," Silenus replied. Good counsel. I looked at Similce.

She nodded. "No-one will take offence at that, not even my relations. They may not share your gods, but they respect them."

"There are, though, two presents you might wish to see, Hannibal," Silenus said.

He turned, shuffled to a corner of the tent, returned with two scrolls. "The first of these is from me, the second from Bostar." I carefully unrolled the first from its rounded staff of beki wood, recognising at once Silenus' own hand, each Greek character clearly formed, leaning in harmony forwards as he had taught me. The vellum was of the finest, flawless kid skin and I thought, but this must have cost him – I didn't know. I realised with shame I didn't know how much things cost, nor how much Silenus was paid, nor, since my father had died, who paid him. I vowed that this would change. Many years' savings, at least, I thought and then I read aloud those lovely lines I knew from Homer's *Odyssey*, when Odysseus says to the princess Nausikaa:

οὐ μὲν γὰρ τοῦ γε κρεῖσσον καὶ ἄρειον,
ἢ ὅθ ὁμοφρονέοντε νοήμασιν οἶκον ἔχητον
ἀνὴρ ἠδὲ γυνή· πόλλ' ἄλγεα δυσμενέεσσι,
χάρματα δ' εὐμενέτῃσι·

"What does it mean, Hannibal?" Similce asked. Of course, she had no Greek. In a quavering voice Silenus declaimed in perfect Iberian: *"For there is nothing better, no nor finer, than when a man and woman of like mind live together as man and wife, a joy to their friends and a plague to those who hate them,"* and there were tears on the cheeks of this old man who, I knew then, loved me.

There was a second passage on the scroll, this time of prose, and I recognised, from lessons long ago it seemed, the soaring periods of Plato, his *Symposium*, I thought. This time I translated, if haltingly, as I read the Greek:

"Our desire for another, to re-unite our original nature, to make one out of two, to heal the state of man, this is an ancient desire, implanted in us. Separated, with one side only, like a flat fish,

each of us is but a half-man, always looking for the other half . . .
Human nature was originally one, and we were a whole, and the
desire and pursuit of the whole is called love.

The tears were mine when I had finished. Silenus smiled and
said, "Not bad – someone taught you middling well, but wasn't
're-unite' a bit clumsy for '*synarmozein*'?" Then he laughed and I
moved forwards, taking him in my arms. "But there is Bostar's
gift as well," Silenus said into my shoulder, stepping back,
handing a second scroll to Similce. Again, perfect vellum, the
staff this time capped with gold. Similce unrolled it. It was
blank, completely blank. "What does this mean?" I asked
Silenus.

"You must ask the man who made it," he replied.

"I will. Where is he?"

"I'll get him," and Silenus stepped outside. They returned
soon, together, the man who had guided much of my past, the
man who was to guide much of my future.

"What is this, Bostar?" I asked.

"I am a map-maker. It is a map."

"What sort of map is blank?" I retorted.

Looking past us, standing straight, "It is a map of life," he
said. From anyone else, I would not have borne this sophistry.
From Bostar, this was no prank. "Show me your right palm," he
said. I held it out. He looked long. "And yours?" looking at
Similce. Longer still he looked intent at hers. "It is as well the
map is blank. It may be we can fill it. Be sure the gift is well-
intentioned." He bowed, and was gone.

On the fourth day I resumed the old. But when I woke up in
the early light it was hard to leave Similce's curves, her smell, her
skin the patina of shells. She turned softly on her side and bore
the day to me, immured in a glass wall of sleep. She brought her
midnight secrets to the green-eyed world and to me. Only the
trumpets of reveille broke that spell and I was up and dressed,

106

outside the tent before I knew that she was with me. "What are you – "

She put a hand on mine. "I am your wife. Let me come."

I looked at her and smiled. By each other's sides we went to Maharbal.

The day was hot and gruelling. A tour first of the camp and then, as was my custom, each and every commander's report delivered to me personally. Similce sat throughout them all, listening intently. Then we walked about the exercise and parade grounds of that enormous army. So many of our troops were Spanish. If they served me from some respect or Hasdrubal for money, there was for me with Similce a new and warming welcome. Only when Maharbal needed to urinate was there any awkwardness. "I have seen that before, you know," was all she said. She herself squatted where she stood and, under her *chiton*, piddled.

There was trouble with the elephants. Of the sixty, all but two cows had some fungus of the feet. The head driver was brought before us, head bowed, afraid. He didn't know how this had happened nor what to do, having tried, he said, all his salves.

"Salves?" Similce asked. "You have been treating rot with salves?" The man shifted uneasily before us. "Hannibal, let me see to this." I felt Maharbal glance at me. "I know how to cure foot-rot. The feet must be washed in a solution of vinegar, water and thyme, then kept dry – not salved." And she went off with the head driver, who was I suppose torn between astonishment and relief. When we left on campaign three days later, eight of the elephants had recovered enough to come.

It was Similce's willingness to treat the elephants that first made me think of taking her with me on the northern campaign. Then there was her grasp of logistics. That evening, after we had eaten, I was working through my standard plans for the campaign: amounts of fodder, bolts for my new onager seige engines, all that sort of thing, now second nature to me. "May I see, Hannibal?" she asked and she came to sit on my knee and, my arms around her, began looking through the plans.

"Two hundred brass cauldrons? And four wagons just to carry them. Then eight oxen to pull the wagons and then them to feed." She turned and looked at me, furrowing her brows.

"Soldiers must be fed, Similce," I replied, "and they fight better if their food is hot." Including cooks and followers, I was taking 20,000 men on this campaign. "At a hundred men per cauldron, I need 200. It's as simple as that."

Similce stood up and paced across the tent. "But amongst my people" – she smiled – "*our* people, we take no cauldrons on the march."

"Then how do you cook?"

"We put the meat of the slaughtered animals in their own intestines, then we bake them in an earthern oven or simmer them above the fire. The stomach of a sheep makes an ideal cauldron."

"But does it work?"

"Tomorrow, I will show you," she said with a laugh and she did. So there came about another of the innovations of Hannibal, another step towards the lightest, fastest army that the world has ever seen, an army of essentials, completely honed to war.

I had Similce educate Hamilax and he in turn the chief campaign cooks in the technique. I remember thanking Similce when, even light as we were, we foundered in the high Alps and the pack mules were stuck in the snow. I was pulling on their halters myself and the men were losing heart and I said, "At least there are no cauldron wagons to pull," and the men laughed and tried again.

So she came on that campaign. It was as well, or that which happened would have done when I was powerless to stop it.

Hasdrubal had asked to see me the afternoon before we were to leave. "And bring your bride," his message ran, carried by a different eunuch this time. "I hear she has a head for military matters." I took Maharbal too. Again the palace, more sumptuous now by far, and the great hall and the simpering acolytes, but the four of us sat down directly at a table on its own. Hasdrubal produced his maps. I was explaining my concern about the untried seige equipment – "You probably want to try it first against me here, Hannibal!" Hasdrubal quipped – when there was a banging at the door and Hamilax came in, breathless.

"A fire, Hannibal, a fire in the stores!"

Without thinking, I was up and halfway down the marbled hall, Maharbal I sensed behind, when I remembered Similce and turned but she raised a hand to me and called, "I will get on with these," pointing to the maps, and smiled and I was gone.

Hamilax must have told the groom to get our horses ready, for Belleus was in the courtyard. I vaulted on, gave him his head and we galloped through the streets and out the gate and down the hill across the plain to camp and we were almost there and I could see and smell the flames and smoke and I was looking round for Castello and then a giant hand, a wall, I do not know, it stopped me and I reined in Belleus in full flight and he reared and snorted but we were turning in the air. "You go, Maharbal, go on!" I shouted as he passed me. With all my being, I was going back. I dropped the reins and hugged Belleus' neck and it was like that first time when I rode him, and he knew.

I was off Belleus, panting in the dust, and past the fountains before I heard Similce's scream cut short. I burst through the door and he had her against the wall. I saw, I think, her *chiton* torn, the cloth forced in her mouth, and his left hand ricking up his *chiton* for the thrust and in his right hand, gleaming in the light, the dagger at her throat. Then he turned his head and saw me drawing out my sword. Running, I screamed, the rage consuming, and he saw that there was death in my eyes. I saw his great cock flapping as he pushed Similce away and moved so quickly. I ran to her. She was sobbing, sliding down the wall but she pointed and I saw that Hasdrubal was making for a door across the room. Only just, I beat him to the door and blocked it with my body and he backed away before me and I raised my sword to point at his groin. He started to speak, "Ha – ", but he stopped when he saw that I was going to kill him. Back he went, until a table meant that he could back away no more. Sweat was running down his face. I saw his pock-marked skin, the drooping mouth, the fleshy nose, and I drew back my sword arm for the thrust and then a hand was on my arm and it was Maharbal. "No, *anda*, no."

So many times in my life has one moment lasted, all other times subsumed within those few. Hasdrubal, eyes closed, stood fat and smelling there before my sword point at his belly. What governs actions? Without looking, I passed back my sword to Maharbal and swept my left knee up into Hasdrubal's groin. We left him moaning on the floor and Similce came with me from that place, shaking under my arm. "I should have suspected, when his people left the room," was all she said.

We left the next morning at dawn. The fire was a matter of no consequence. We lost only a hay shed. We said nothing more of what had passed at Hasdrubal's. We never did. Only three, or was it four nights later in silence Similce came to my bed – we shared a tent but not a bed on campaign – and then we healed that hurt with the great wonder that is love.

With Similce around them, the Spanish troops fought and worked as I had never seen them. My new heavy cavalry were invincible. Sometimes, to rest them, we used the elephants instead, the elephants from whom the tribesmen simply ran. I noticed how, even more than men, horses that were not used to them as ours were terrified of elephants. To make that effect even greater, I had bells made and hung around the elephants' necks. Roaring, screaming, ringing as they charged, their trunks held upright, daubed with woad, vermilion, there was neither man nor horse which did not flee.

I sent Maharbal wheeling to the north-east with half the force while I continued from the south. I learned and learned. One town refused surrender. With a sigh, I ordered up the seige engines. I have never liked seiges, the waiting, the sallies, the mining. It is a job for artisans, not soldiers. Bostar was with me when I went to find out why one of the axles on our only helepolis, a huge, many-storeyed mobile tower from which our men would climb the town's walls, had snapped. "How long to fix it?" I remember asking the officer in charge.

"Two days, once we have the wood." Of course we didn't have the wood, at least not the right wood, so the man explained. I swore impatiently.

"Silver wins cities, Hannibal," Bostar said quietly at my side.

I let him see to it. "Take whatever money you need from the chest in my tent."

That night, the town's gates were opened. One syntagma did the rest. The next morning I had the town razed to the ground. The fitter men I had sent back to Cartakhena for mine or galley slaves. The rest I had beheaded. Bostar may have shown me that silver wins cities. So, I knew already, does fear and that spreads faster than fire. There was no more resistance to us in that part of Spain.

Bostar had been shading on his maps the ground that we had conquered as we did so. Little remained. Maharbal's daily despatches were routine. There had been none from Hasdrubal when a courier came with a despatch from Cartakhena. "If it comes from Hasdrubal the Handsome, you may take it back again," I said.

"It comes from Hamilax, your Steward," the man replied.

I opened it at once. It was brief.

"Hannibal, Hasdrubal was murdered this morning. You

should return at once. Your true servant as your father's, Hamilax."

"How long have you ridden?" I asked the man. Always see to your men.

"Three days and nights, changing horses," he replied. I called the guard.

"See this man is fed and rested – and paid. Then send me Bostar and Castello."

I gave the despatch to Similce. She read it quickly, said nothing, but reached for some clothes. "We leave at once, I imagine."

"We?" I meant to say she should stay, but she rode as well as any trooper. "Yes, we leave at once." To Castello and Bostar when they came I gave the news. "Castello, I leave you in command. I will take only four of the Hammer Guard with me. Bostar, ride to Maharbal. Tell him to join me in Cartakhena."

With that, we were about to leave when in came another courier. I knew the hand of Silenus at once. "Hannibal," I read, "take care. All is not what it seems. Come with all haste, but hasten slowly when you arrive." Typical Silenus, I thought: a neat oxymoron, the juxtaposition of opposites. I just hastened.

Cartakhena was still and sullen. Doors were closed and barred as we passed up the hill. Only Silenus and Hamilax met us at the palace. "Tell me!" I asked them dismounting.

"Not here," Silenus replied. "There are ears everywhere."

We came to Hasdrubal's hall. "No," I said. We entered a smaller room on the other side of the passage, closed the door. "Well?" I asked.

Hamilax began: "Hasdrubal was murdered by one of his fancy – " He broke off, looked at the ground.

"One of his *erastai*," Silenus supplied the more delicate Greek noun.

"Where?" I asked.

"In the latrines. He was found with his throat cut, a lavatory

112

sponge in his mouth," growled Hamilax distastefully. Fitting, I thought.

"The boy who did it has confessed. He had been spurned, he claimed." More words than I had heard from Hamilax for years.

"Where are the troops I left behind?"

"Awaiting orders at the camp," Hamilax replied.

"Go and summon them, the whole syntagma. I want them in the square. Then bring the boy there, and the rest of Hasdrubal's – friends" – I chose the word carefully – "for execution."

"But there is no charge against them!" Silenus protested. "They may be innocent!" and I felt the gulf between the Greek world and my own. I was, I am a Barca, a Carthaginian.

"Silenus," I said quietly, "a Carthaginian commander has been murdered. I will respond in our ways, not yours. On your way, Hamilax," and with that rebuke one of the few remaining links to my childhood was gone.

"Then it seems that I have taught you nothing," Silenus said. "But listen to me now," and then he coughed a deep and racking cough and Similce moved to him and led him to a couch over by the window. Recovering his breath, he said in Punic, "I must speak in Greek."

"But we are alone," I interjected and those sad wise eyes met mine and he said in Greek, "Hannibal, you have still so much to learn." Then he told me.

He believed Hasdrubal's death was no petty murder, but an assassination.

"Arranged by whom?" I exclaimed.

"By those in Carthage who would make peace with Rome, those who fear this new empire here and those, Hannibal, who would next kill you."

"How do you know these things?" I asked astonished.

"You have shut your eyes to many things, Hannibal, since your father died. I have lived here quietly, teaching your brothers, reading, writing, listening, watching. People take me for a failed old man. They do not guard their tongues before me. And I have my eyes. Just after Hasdrubal's body was found, I saw a galley slip out from the harbour."

"And it sailed?"

"It set sail south, Hannibal, for Carthage." Carthage. I had not been there for, what, thirteen years.

Similce put a hand on my arm. Of course, she had no Greek. I began in Iberian: "Silenus says that Hasdrubal . . ." Her hand now pressing on my arm, I looked back at Silenus, saw him pointing to the door, a finger on his lips. I drew the dagger from my side, tiptoed to the door and pulled it open to see the back of someone fleeing fast away. "I will see that you are guarded, night and day, Silenus. Now come with us," and we went out from that palace to wait in the silent agora for what was to come.

It was a good troop I had left behind. They had deployed in perfect order round the square. "Is the boy in the dungeons, Hamilax?" He nodded. "Leave him there. Bring the rest of Hasdrubal's catamites." We watched the stakes being prepared.

Silenus said: "Hannibal, I cannot watch this. May I go?"

"You may, Silenus. And thank you." I motioned two of the soldiers to go with him. I understood. "If he dies, so will you," I told the soldiers as they fell out.

"Summon a general assembly!" I ordered the troop captain. "I want all the townspeople here to watch. Similce, I am going to see what the murderer knows. I think you would do better to stay here."

The boy was shivering in the dampness of his cell, his silk *chiton* torn and bloody. "Who paid you?" I asked him softly. He shook his head, again and again, his black eyes darting.

They took his toe-nails first. "Who paid you?" Nothing. I had no time. With the red-hot pokers at the soles of his feet, his screams took on a new intensity. "Muffle him," I said. "Now break his legs, then his fingers, slowly." Still nothing. It was the

114

burning needles through his nipples that did it. I asked him a third time, when his left breast was still unmutilated, and he nodded. I took the cloth from his mouth, leant over him. I just made it out. "Bom-il-ca-ar," he whispered, and then he died.

There were twenty-three others like him. When I returned to the square, all was ready, each of them roped to a stake, and several thousand people stood there, silent, waiting. "This is what is done to those who betray Carthage!" I shouted and the walls returned my words. Or had Carthage betrayed Carthage? Who was Bomilcar? I had, Silenus was right, still so much to learn. But however much I loathed him, Hasdrubal's murder could not go unavenged. I nodded to the captain. It was done.

The purpose to which the next twenty years of my life was given turned on the following days. Maharbal had come. The campaign was complete. Castello was leading back the army. By the time they returned, we were ready.

I learned from Silenus as much as he knew of Bomilcar, Sufet of Carthage and my father's cousin, how he had been building up his own trading empire in the south and resuming Carthage's ancient trade in tin with the Casserides. "But that is a Roman route – or was!" I exclaimed.

"*Akribos,*" said Silenus in Greek in his excitement, "exactly. Bomilcar has been, it is said, even to Rome. It seems to be agreed: Rome will have the Tyrrhenian Sea and Carthage only Africa. Carthage is to withdraw from Spain completely. There is enough money in Hasdrubal's treasury to pay off the Roman tribute and be gone."

The despatch came to me from the Council of Elders the next day. It was written in old proto-Punic, a language I had not seen or used for years. I had to ask Hamilax to translate it. I sensed his sadness that this should have been necessary. What was I becoming, who? "To Hannibal Barca, Captain General to the late Hasdrubal, the Sufet and the Council of Elders of Carthage commands: apprehend and punish accordingly those responsible for the murder of Hasdrubal; remove all goods, gold, silver and precious stones, all coins from the treasuries of Hasdrubal in Guadiakth, Gadez and Cartakhena and embark those under escort at once for Carthage; then embark as many of our army" – *our* army? I had Hamilax repeat it – "as you have galleys for, disband the rest and return yourself to Carthage."

I had promised my father always to answer Carthage when she called. But how long before the Romans wanted Africa too? Who were these Elders from, it seemed, a world long ago, Elders lying to me? Seeing old Silenus opposite me as we sat in silence, I remembered one of the paradoxes he had taught me. Epimenides the Cretan says: All Cretans are liars. If he is telling the truth, he is lying. If he is lying, he is telling the truth. Words are fickle, as are those who use them.

I had Maharbal go and fetch Castello. Those two were there, Similce, Hamilax and Silenus, when, standing in the doorway of my tent, my back to them, my eyes seeing beyond me the army first my father and then I had made, I said: "We march in six days on Saguntum."

So did Hannibal answer Carthage when she called. I did have Hasdrubal's treasuries stripped, all my army paid a year in advance, the many remaining wagons under guard entrusted quietly to Fuano who would take them, Similce said, to secret caves high in his arid hills. The camp rang with the sounds of preparation. Loud they must have been, the trumpets of alarm from the harbour, to reach me talking to *dekadarchoi*.

I mounted Belleus at once. I saw the Roman galleys clearly, four of them, coming under oar. I was there to meet them on the quay, I and my Hammer Guard, the whole 1,000 of them, for I had given orders as I rode. It was fortunate that we had been slaughtering oxen that day for a last meal in camp. There was blood ample for my purposes.

Meticulous in order did the files of my Guard surround me as I waited on the quay. They were brave men to disembark at all, those Romans, to a quayside on which my Guardsmen dripped with blood, blood on their shields, their arms, their armour, drying, deepening in the sun. My second look at Romans. Four walked down the gangplank of the first galley, in white togas, men of middle age and olive skin. "Hannibal, you have received your orders from Carthage?" the tallest asked me in Latin.

"*Habeo etiam*, I have indeed," I replied.

"Then we have come for earth and water, symbols that this town and what you have unjustly conquered of Spain now owe fealty to Rome."

I am not sure I understood the last part. My Latin was to improve. But "earth and water," these I recognised. "You will have your earth and water. Castello," I said in Punic, pointing at the first two men, "drop these two down the palace well." As they were led away, a third began to speak and I caught "Monstrous . . . sacred envoys . . ." My sword at his throat silenced him. "Go now, thankful that you live. Tell your Senate of the earth and water Rome receives from Hannibal." I waited, watching, as they rowed away.

Saguntum was no easy matter. The seige lasted several months. Its walls were high and strong and, built on rock, could not be undermined. Though we blockaded its harbour, they had it seemed ample stores and water. A deserter took twenty xthets of gold and promised to open a gate, but never did. I tried fire arrows, as my father at Tunis, but Saguntum was rich, the houses built of stone. Helepoleis seemed our only chance of scaling the walls in force. I had two more built. The Saguntines rained fire arrows and burning oil on them. I had them covered in hides and all three stood at last secure up the east wall, though they had to be guarded night and day against arson. We began to build onto them the final storey that would allow us over the walls.

Then, one evening as I was making my customary inspection,

I saw something I did not understand. The Saguntines were pouring bucket upon bucket of water over the helepoleis.

We found out why the next morning. With over a hundred soldiers on each helepolis and the same number again of carpenters, laboriously building the final storey under the cover of the soldiers' shields, the great machines were heavy. "Look out!" I heard the cry and slowly, ponderously, the sodden ground beneath the tollenones began to slip away. I lost over eighty men when one of the machines fell over. The other two were leaning useless off the wall.

If I had ever thought to treat Saguntum gently, I did no more. It was three weeks of dangerous, exacting work to build secure platforms of wood and stone for each of the machines. Morale was low. There was fever in the camp. I let it be known that the men could pillage as they wished when the city fell. I had hoped to be back in Cartakhena by now.

At last, we were ready. Two hours after dark three syntagmata with muffled arms approached each helepolis. The top storey of each could hold only twenty men. I asked for sixty volunteers to be first over the wall. I am proud to this day that as one, all the men stepped forwards.

Perhaps we had been seen. Perhaps the Saguntines kept a strong force on the wall. Be that as it may, the ground was quickly littered with the bodies of my men, dead and dying, thrown back before enough could join them as, onto the waiting troops, stones and arrows, missiles fell. "*Synapismos, locked shield order!*" I remember ordering. But almost imperceptibly, our line began to creep back from the volleys raining down. I was standing and I knew I must not fail and it was like Vekher again and sword in hand I ran up to a helepolis and pushed my way through, past the waiting soldiers, up the stairs among the smell of pitch and sweat and I was on the wall, a sword cut parried, then a lance. I thrust and killed and blocked another death-stroke with my shield and called out "Bar-ca,

Barc-ca!" and then I jumped, down into Saguntum.

Two Saguntines broke my fall. Rolling up and to my feet, dazed, I took the first one with a cross cut, swinging left to right, the second slashing back across the throat and there were very many at me but then I heard the "Barca!" call and others joined me. One was Maharbal, but otherwise I knew only dark shapes, ringing iron, the sweet smell of blood. The stabbing, swinging, blocking rhythm came, the fighting and it was in such a frenzy that Saguntum fell to Hannibal.

I sensed Similce's anger as she bathed me at dawn the following morning of men's blood and mine. I had a deep gash on my left side, another on my right thigh. My first wounds. I had felt neither as I fought. Now they throbbed and shrieked.

Similce was applying poultices, rather too briskly. I took her wrist, stopping her. "My father taught me never to ask soldiers to do what you can't or won't do yourself."

"But it was madness! You might have been killed."

"I should have been killed. But the madness saved me. I will know when I am to die." She looked away. She did not understand. "I am sorry, Similce. It's beyond me, too. I just know."

Maharbal came in. He looked drawn, thin. He had a cut across his neck at which I stared. He raised a hand to cover it, embarrassed. "I was a little late with the parry," he said with a smile. "But Hannibal, you shouldn't have done that."

"You too!" I gave him back. "You shouldn't have followed!"

"Followed? I was pushed! You should have seen the scramble once you jumped – men climbing over each other after you!"

The sack took a week. I needed forty wagons alone for the gold and silver from the treasury. I kept eight chests of gold, but sent the rest to Fuano in secret. The spoils of the town, the vases, plate, jewels I had loaded onto galleys and sent to

119

Carthage. That would give them pause for thought. I sent Silenus with the booty. "As your emissary?" he asked, "or as a hostage?"

"As my eyes and ears," I replied. Hamilax asked to go too. I agreed.

"Thank you. The Barcas will have one friend more in Carthage," he said.

The Saguntines and their town took longer. With the onagers and scorpions, the battering rams, I began to destroy the city walls, tipping the rubble into the harbour. I loaded the fitter prisoners onto the twenty galleys I had left and sent them too to Carthage. Some 1,200 remained, it may have been more. A hundred I had crucified on crosses spaced around what had been the city wall. Each cross had a board on which I had written, in Punic and in Latin, "So die those who defy Hannibal." I had a great pit dug for the rest. I had thought to use the elephants. But then the first winter rains began, and with them that cold wind from the north-west that we call in Punic *mezzar-ifoullousen,* "that which plucks the fowls". That would do my work for me. Some might survive as living witnesses to Hannibal.

Slow was our return to Cartakhena, laden as my soldiers were with spoils. When we had been back for two days, I sent for Castello. "Leave the Hammer Guard here, but to all the other troops give leave of a month. Let them take home their spoils, and bid their families farewell. In one month's time, we march."

"But that will be winter, Hannibal!" Castello exclaimed. "No-one marches in the winter."

"Exactly, Castello, exactly. So we will surprise them."

"Them? There are no longer any hostile tribes in Spain. Who are 'them'?"

"Castello, in one month's time we march." I looked away. I was at Heliche, the death rattle in my father's throat. "In one month's time we march on Rome."

Castello looked at me strangely. His eyes fell away, thumb and index finger of his left hand twisting at his grizzled beard. For the time it takes to eat an apple, the time it takes to kill ten men, he stood silent. I have never demanded obedience from my men. I have simply assumed it. Castello's voice was subdued when he spoke. "But that will be war. You will declare war on Rome, Hannibal?"

"No, Castello, no."

I took the three paces to my chest, brought from it a despatch that I had received the day before from Silenus in Carthage, the despatch I had discussed through the night with Bostar, Maharbal and Similce. I held it up. "The Romans sent an embassy of four senators, no less, to Carthage. They protested at my treatment of their envoys here and, of course, at our sacking of Saguntum. In short, Castello, Rome has declared war on Carthage."

VI

MARCH

In battle when you kill a man, easily, it is no more than that which comes of practice. That we were able to leave Cartakhena within a month, this was too. For my whole life, I had been preparing, spirit, body, mind.

The Romans would expect me to winter in Cartakhena. I would disappoint them, and Bomilcar and those at Carthage who would expect the same. The Romans doubtless would retaliate for Saguntum – in the spring. An initial naval attack on Cartakhena, I imagined. They were welcome to explore Hasdrubal's city. There would be nothing there. As for my camp, it would be gone.

I wrote to the Elders, explaining a little of my intentions. I quoted Regulus' saying to them: "*Summa sedes non capit duos.*" I thought it would be good for their Latin. "I intend," I said, "to give that power to Carthage." And I meant to show them my full intentions by my actions.

I had other reasons to begin the march. I wanted to rehearse marching in the cold and wet, examining as we moved north the lessons that would teach us. I had reservations about some of my troops. The full army now was over 90,000, with 12,000 horse. It had grown too fast since the two campaigns to the north. It was well paid and disciplined, but untested in anything more than a skirmish. If there were to be desertions, I wanted them before I reached Italy. There were too many company commanders, let alone men, I knew little and trusted less.

I felt of my army as I had when Silenus many years before had introduced me to the *Ethics* of Aristotle. There was something there beyond my grasp, fluttering just beyond my reach. I remember discussing with Silenus Aristotle's views on the question: what is the Good for man? and then reading the sentence: "*We call an object pursued for its own sake more final than one pursued because of something else . . . and happiness more than anything else is thought to be just such an end . . . something perfect and self-sufficient.*" I remember feeling of it as of many passages that there was some great truth there, but one I could not comprehend. Philosophy I have left to others. My army I could and would understand.

Besides, I wanted to leave a force behind me in Spain and send another to Carthage. Spain the Romans would be certain to invade, and Africa, by way of Sicily, no doubt. Which troops should I leave, and under whose command? These things would become clear in time. That is what I gave them.

The month we had in Cartakhena I devoted largely to the issue of supplies. My intended route was clear. Only by crossing the Alps could I surprise the Romans. It had to be possible. There would be nothing to eat. We would carry what we would need.

Salted fish, black bread and fruit cakes, these were what Similce advised and day upon day I had my Numidians, well used to these things, drying and salting fish under great awnings, shelter from the lashing rains that had begun. Every fishing boat up and down the coast brought their last catches of the season to the harbour. They were well paid. I did not lack for money, thanks to Hasdrubal.

The men of Cappadocia made the best dry bread, of millet, wheat and barley. Soon I had six stores of it, then eight. "How long will this keep?" I asked the *dekadarchos* in charge. "As long as the life of a man," he replied. That should do, I thought. As for the cakes of dried fruit, on these Similce worked tirelessly. She had chosen her own platoon of helpers from the Spaniards who had not taken leave. There were many jokes in camp about "Similce's soldiers". I saw no harm in that. These men fought and died as much for Similce as for me.

Making my usual rounds with Maharbal, I watched her once, stirring great cauldrons of raisins. Suddenly, she clutched her middle, doubled up in pain. I caught her from behind, just as she was falling back on her haunches to the ground. I carried her to our tent, laid her gently down and still she held her belly in her pain and outside in the rain I heard the coughs and concerned whispers of the many who had followed. I stroked that lovely face, smoothing away the strands of hair that lay across her cheeks. "What is it, Similce?" I think I managed at last. "Do you feel a fever?"

She smiled, reached out for my hand. "Hannibal, in six months we" – a cough, another stab of pain – "we will have a child."

Joy rose in me from my stomach, bursting to my brain and then came shame that I had not guessed and hope and fear and love, all jumbled, tumbling around. "You didn't tell me," half-question, half-statement.

"I was waiting."

"For what?"

"For," she said, squeezing my hand, "for the march to begin." She tried to sit up. "You will take me, Hannibal, won't you?" So many thoughts and feelings surged and boomed within me.

"Yes, Similce, yes," I said at last. I did it for love, for need. What else was there? I had no home, no base, no family where I could leave her. "Yes."

For I had heard from Carthage, six despatches, seven, each increasingly blunt, but written at least in common Punic. "The Council forbids you to attack Rome. Anyway, you have no fleet large enough. Your actions provoked the declaration of war. Your actions now can end it . . ." So, or something like that, ran the first. I sent a flippant reply. I wouldn't have used a fleet to get to Italy, even if I'd had one. "Though not all my soldiers can swim," I wrote, "they can all fly."

124

The third or fourth despatch grew desperate. "Since you have ignored our orders, the Council has decreed your lands and property, your goods and chattels forfeit. . ." I showed that one to my brothers. Hasdrubal simply shrugged. Mago said: "I – I'm w-with you, H-Hanni-ibal." They were better brothers than I had deserved.

Two different despatches came by another hand, one from Hamilax, one from Silenus. Both said much the same: that although Bomilcar controlled the majority, not a few mistrusted him. We still had many friends. If I could win a victory over Rome, Bomilcar would be overruled. I thought as much already. And I would win. But meanwhile, Carthage was hardly a place where I could send my wife and child.

The news of Similce's pregnancy spread fast. An easy purpose grew among the men, strong as was the life within my wife. Those were happy days in Cartakhena. I remember lying, my head on Similce's softly swelling belly, listening to the beating of a new heart; sleeping beside her, deep in enquiry and reconciliation with the day just gone, waking to know peace.

I sent out many men, that last month in Cartakhena, each with clear instructions, questions to be answered, some by ship, some on horse. Some returned, as planned, before we left and others met me on our march and so it was that I knew what to expect on that long march to Rome. I even tried diplomacy, sending men to those southern Gaulish tribes that were I knew disaffected with Rome. "Tell them," I told my men, "that Saguntum too was allied to Rome. And it is now as if it had never been." I thought this would persuade them to join me. In fact, they opposed me. The only diplomacy that has ever worked for me is that of the sword.

Those reporting on the lie of the land I sent straight to Bostar, he of many maps. Bostar had by then a staff of six, four Cyreniacs, and two Sicilian Greeks, Epicydes and Hippocrates. These two were natives of Syracuse, but both of families with old ties to Carthage. They fled from Sicily when my father left. They had no time for Hiero, King of Syracuse, and his friendship with Rome. I spent much time with them. Both had been to Italy. I asked questions, learned.

And I spent more and more time with Bostar. "If only I could have a map of Italy," I said to him one day when I had looked at maps of northern Spain and Gaul so long that I could draw them now. "For that I would pay almost any price."

He smiled, a rare thing. "You will need more than a map of Italy, Hannibal. That I can give you, free. But the map you need is of the Roman mind and character. That is a map without price."

"Italy?" I exclaimed. "You have a map of Italy?"

Bostar was silent, still. He had after all answered that question already.

"How did you come by it?"

"Perhaps it is now time you knew something of Bostar, Hannibal. Our ways have, it seems, converged." In a dull monotone, a we sat together by his brazier, he began. "Many think me an Egyptian. They think me many things. But I was born a Bithynian of Chalcedon, and my father was High Priest of our god – "

"Your priests could marry?" I interrupted. He looked at me, and looked away. I did not interrupt again.

" – of our god Rheaxthus the Shaker, under Zipoetes our King. Before I learned to walk I was being taught of many things and tongues. The King was away." He frowned. A trembling of memory crossed his face.

"The pirates took us by surprise, raiding from the morning mist our temple precincts on the shore. They killed my father, all the priests. They took the gold and jewels. They found me in the library, alone. I was twelve. One held a dagger to my throat as they ransacked the room. 'There is nothing here of value to you,' I said in their tongue, Paphlagonian. 'So, you speak our language, boy!' a tall and bearded one said, coming up to me. 'What others do you speak?' I told him. I was not afraid. 'Besides Bithynian, Anatolian, Thracian, Galatian and Greek. I am learning Punic too, and Latin. Those are my texts that you are pulling from their racks.' That amused them. Their swords dropped. 'And do you read and write as well as speak?' the man who seemed their leader said. 'I do.' I did, well, though my Thracian is weak now. The tongue is almost dead. 'Take him to the ship,' the tall one ordered. 'Learning is a thing of value,' he sneered, trampling on a scroll.

"He saw though that I came to no harm. His name was Azeth. He sold me to a Syrian merchant at Dyrrhacium, one Shadrack, with whom for sixteen years I sailed the Inner and the Outer Seas, passing three times up the Hellespont. I translated and I kept accounts and, yes, I began to draw maps. By caravan we travelled, from Colchis down to Hierosolyma, then north and west through Dacia to Sarmizegetusa. Many are the places and the peoples I have seen, and many the mysteries of the Goths and of the Jews, as we traded furs and corn and Hyperborean amber in the north, faience and alabaster, ivory and purple in the south.

"Then Shadrack died. We were in Dalmatia. His widow sold me to a Roman, another merchant, one Publius Aponius, for whom for many years I kept records and correspondence and travelled far through Italy, for garum was his trade. Rich, Aponius retired to a villa deep inland in Umbria where, he said, he would be far from the smell of fish. He was a kindly man. What, he asked me, could he do for me, short of buying me my freedom? I wanted, I replied, to read and write and draw maps. I had seen too much of life and of the folly that is man to worry for the freedom of my body. The freedom of the mind, Hannibal, that no-one can sell or buy. And as for travel, I have learned that the greatest journey a man can make is the journey inside his own head."

127

He leant forward, I remember, stoking up the brazier, alone with himself as no other I have known. In the same level voice, he resumed.

"Aponius had, he said, the ideal post. His nephew Caius Sempronius was Roman *ambactus*, envoy in Saguntum and seeking an *amanuensis*, a secretary. I had been once to Saguntum. It was a Greek town, Hannibal, not Roman. I had liked its air. I went again. But Sempronius preferred the pleasures of Bacchus and of Venus to those of Calliope and Melpomene. He grudged me even the money for tablets, let alone vellum. Then Hasdrubal came. In the course of a drunken banquet, I believe, I was sold. The rest you know."

The brazier needed fuel. I drew my cloak about me in the cold. Bostar sat as he had throughout, looking far away, and still now after forty years I can see the lines I saw then, the high cheekbones and forehead, arching nose, the eyebrows delicate and black. How old was he? I never asked. I heard a cough behind, Maharbal's I knew. I was needed, somewhere else. "We will continue this, Bostar," I said. "When we march, you will ride with me. I want from you that map of the Roman mind. Maharbal, get Bostar a good horse."

The moon was turning. The new month of Chodesh was nigh. Steadily the men who had taken leave returned. Similce was well again. The wagons, weapons, provisions, everything was ready. It was time. But first I called a general assembly of my troops, choosing for it a natural bowl in the hills some miles from our camp. I wanted as many of our host as possible to hear me and they packed the hillside, reaching far beyond. From dawn until the middle of the day they came, company by company. I remember wishing that the cheer they sent up when Similce joined me might be heard in Rome.

I had decided to speak in Greek, my army's common tongue. All the more reason to be simple, clear. What I had to say would be translated into many tongues and passed far beyond the reach of my voice. "Soldiers of Carthage," I began, "what you have heard as rumour, now hear from me. To-morrow, we begin our march on Rome." Silence, complete silence. The silence of so many is an awesome thing.

"You have all been paid, a full year in advance. But I do not want you to come for money. Our march is for justice. Rome has declared war on Carthage. They demand that we withdraw from Spain. In that, we shall oblige them." That brought some muted laughter. "They demand too the surrender of my person and that of Similce, my wife." That brought anger, indignation, as I had thought. "Would you have us grace a Roman triumph?" Shouts now, protests. Silenus' instructions had been good, so long ago. We had been reading Demosthenes, the great Athenian orator. 'The good orator never speaks at an audience, Hannibal, he speaks *with* them, as a man playing a lute.'

I played on. "And what does Rome offer in return? Why, peace, the Roman peace. There are many of you here from northern Spain, from Sicily, Sardinia who have known the Roman peace, your wives and daughters sold into slavery, your temples and your villages destroyed.

"There is not room for Rome and for Carthage. One must fall. Together, we will make it Rome, for you are the greatest army that the world has ever known. Thereafter you may live with Carthage as your ally, as your friend. Come with me, then, and with Similce. The way will not be easy, but you will return rich beyond your dreams – rich and free, free to live without the tyranny that is Rome. Soldiers of Carthage, prepare now to march."

We walked out of the bowl, Similce and I, with Castello and Maharbal behind and slowly first, then building, growing, came the sound of sword and dagger hafts and pommels, spear shafts hammering on shields, the sound of approbation. "Have the Romans really demanded that we be given up to them,

Hannibal?" Similce asked as she climbed on board the wagon that would take her slowly back to camp.

"No," I smiled. "I was only playing the lute, as Silenus taught me. But they would demand that, if they had any sense. I said so, Similce, because I am not the only man who would die for you."

It rained a steady rain the day that we broke camp, the heavy drizzle billowing at times from wind we call an *imbat*, coming from the sea. Still I sat on Belleus, only Maharbal and my brothers with me, as my army passed before us, moving north. The Balearic slingers had the van, mounted on their tiny nimble garrons, their legs trailing on the ground. Next came the heavy cavalry, 200 squadrons each the same, their lances holstered, their horses clanking from the armour that they wore. Then my elephants, eighty of them, their grey skin blackening in the rain, their drivers swaying, lurching as the great beasts moved.

Behind them came the wagons in their hundreds, laden with tents and skins and foodstuffs, weapons, stores and then for hours there passed my infantry, marching in their squares. Most were Spanish. I had tried to have them uniformly equipped, each bearing in a pack upon his back a second cloak, a second pair of boots, a plate, a cup and each man had a file for sharpening his sword and spear. Over their packs when marching hung their new long shields, most of fine-grained beki wood, some of hammered bronze, and bronze too were their helmets and their breastplates, glistening in the rain. All wore greaves of iron on both legs, sword and scabbard swinging on their left hips, short daggers on their right, and their long lance points bristled above them as they marched.

After the Spaniards came the men of many nations. I saw my Paricanians and Pactyans, shaggy hill-men from Numidia, each carrying a wooden club, studded with iron, stepping in their high fawnskin boots, their strange headdresses of horses' scalps, with ears and manes attached. They wore long woollen cloaks they knew as *zeira*, defence they said against the sharpest cold.

And still they passed, Concanians who fed by opening the veins of horses for their food, Arbacians whose weapon is the flying dart, Cerretani whose ancestors had fought for Herakles, Gallacians from the dark forests of the west, warriors black-skinned from Lake Tritonis where the Maiden Warrior, Melkarth's daughter, stepped first upon the earth, Autololes so fleet of foot they could outlast a swollen river, it was said, on they came until the plain was darkening in dusk.

At last we turned to follow. At Maharbal's signal came the thousand of my Hammer Guard, their horses black, their armour man and horse of blackened bronze, their swords the truest smiths could make, and in their middle on a light-sprung cart came Similce my wife, and on each side of her, Bostar uncomfortable in one, a wagon pulled by four horses, in both of which there lay chests of gold.

It was as I had expected, that first month of travelling. The rains grew heavier. Each muddy mile seemed like three. The elephants' feet made sounds like smacking kisses as they moved. The soldiers' swinging swords chafed their wet sides as if they had been naked.

I used the time. I looked and listened, saw the strengths and weaknesses of my troops, which would grumble, which complain, thinking, planning. Each day I had Bostar ride with me a while. I asked him what he knew of the Roman army. "Enough," he said, "enough." Of course I knew something of it from my father. If he had lived, he would have told me more. "Tell me, Bostar, what you know." And he began.

"Do you know what '*legio*, legion' means in Latin, Hannibal?"

"Yes: a *selection*, a *choosing*. Why do you ask?"

"Because unlike your army, Hannibal, Rome is made up of citizens who have been *chosen* to serve. It is to them an honour, a

131

privilege to fight for Rome, to defend their state and homes. Have you considered that?"

"They will still feel a sword thrust, just as any man," I said.

Bostar simply nodded, almost imperceptibly. He continued. "Its other great strength is in the backbone of its army, those men who are paid to serve, the long-service centurions, two to each *manipulus*."

"'*Manipulus*?'" I asked. "I do not know this word." Bostar explained. The Roman legion, he said, is divided into ten cohorts and each cohort into three maniples: the first of 120 *hastati*, younger men armed with javelin, sword and lance, the second of the same number and arms but of *principes*, slightly older men, and the third, sixty in number, the *triarii*, veterans armed with pike and sword.

"My father said their battle order is like a chequerboard. How is this?" I asked.

"Because each maniple of *hastati* is drawn up in twelve files, ten men deep. Between each is a space equal to the length of each maniple. The *principes* form a second line, but they face the spaces between the *hastati*. The *triarii* in turn face the spaces between the maniples of *principes*. Hence what your father rightly called a chequerboard."

"Let me draw what I think you mean," I said. From just a touch of one knee, Belleus stopped. I slipped off him and drew with my finger in the mud at my feet:

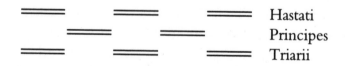

"Like that?" I asked Bostar, looking up. He had not dismounted. Horsemanship was never one of his strengths.

"Yes, just like that."

132

"So the second and third lines can movely quickly to reinforce or replace the first?"

"They can. They do. What the *hastati* cannot accomplish, the *principes* usually do. They are the flower of the Roman army."

"And if their charge also fails?"

"Then they simply retreat, filtering through the line of the *triarii*. Those steady veterans kneel on their right knees, sheltering behind their shields, and stick their spear butts in the ground, the points obliquely forward."

"Like a hedge?"

"Like a hedge, Hannibal, a deadly hedge that does not yield. Hence the Roman saying: 'It has come to the *triarii*.'"

"I see." I re-mounted. "Thank you, Bostar. I will think about this," and I rode off to see Similce.

Think I did. This system demanded frontal attack. If we refused that? It needed space, space for each legionary to fight, space for the maniples' formation. If we denied them that? Such were the matters I turned over and over in my mind as we marched. When I was satisfied, I asked Bostar more. I sought the views of Epicydes and Hippocrates on these things. I discussed what I learned with Maharbal and Castello and with my brothers. I discovered to my pleasure that Hasdrubal had an impressive grasp of military theory.

Passing up and down the long column that my army made I felt certain my great advantage over any Roman legion still lay in my cavalry. Rome's was unlikely to have changed since my father fought it, since Bostar, Epicydes and Hippocrates learned of it. Only a *turma*, thirty mounted men, armed with lance and darts was attached to each cohort and these were farmers, not horsemen. Each legion, then, had only 300 cavalry, I knew, among its 4,200 men – the legionaries and the 1,200 *velites*, skirmishers, light infantry armed only with a small round shield and darts. My mounted peltasts, I was sure, would be more than a match for them.

To each legion was attached a reserve of auxiliary troops, drawn from the towns and cities of what the Romans called their confederacy. These were the *extraordinarii*, usually 200 horsemen and 800 infantry.

I pressed Bostar on his understanding of the way the Romans fought. "It seems so rigid, Bostar, inflexible!"

"Perhaps, but it is lethal. Their *velites* and cavalry first harass the enemy, drawing him to battle while their infantry draw up. At a trumpeted command, the light troops withdraw between the maniples, whose last ranks then move up to close the gaps in the line. Nothing is left to chance. The *hastati* advance at a walk. Another trumpet and, at fifty strides from the enemy, they break into a run. At thirty strides and trumpet blast, they throw their *pila*, heavy javelins. You have never faced a *pilum*, Hannibal."

A statement, not a question. "No, but I know of them. That is why my heavy cavalry and infantry now all have the long shield."

"The *pilum* is designed for shields, Hannibal. The Romans developed it for use against the Etruscans and their shields. With the weight of its long wooden shaft behind it, its long iron tip can easily penetrate a shield – and armour, as many enemies of Rome have found. And because the iron is thin, the *pilum* buckles on impact. You cannot throw it back – as you can with your javelins, Hannibal."

"And after the *pila*, the sword?"

Bostar nodded slowly. He looked away, over the sodden plain, rain dripping from his eyebrows. "I know all this from a Roman centurion, retired after twenty-two years. Spurius Ligustinus was his name. He had a small inn on the road to Capua, where I often stayed. He taught me much, for he was glad to talk. He called what happened next the 'reaping'."

"And if the *hastati* fail, then the *principes* do the same?"

"They do. More trumpets, then the second wave. Few have withstood the *principes*."

134

"Pyrrhus did," I ventured.

"Pyrrhus, Hannibal, was a pirate, an adventurer, nothing more. And if you lose as many men as Pyrrhus, you will not live for long."

"I will not fight as Pyrrhus did," I said. "Thank you, Bostar," and I rode away. I began to hold conferences with all my company commanders once each evening we had camped. From what Bostar had told me, the Roman army was a machine. Machines like galleys or seige engines need commands. "Always look for the trumpeters and kill them," I told the commanders, at first to looks of bewilderment or even derision, until I explained, and again and again we went over our system of silent signals. My other plans I kept to myself.

We marched on through northern Spain. I dealt with all the petty orders and decisions of an army on the march. And I talked and talked with Bostar and the others. There were strategic weaknesses in the Roman army, I argued, particularly in their system of command. Their generals were consuls, politicians, not soldiers. And besides, they changed every year, so terrified were the Romans of producing a military dictator. Each year saw two new consuls appointed, each consul commanding two legions. There was no continuity of command. When Hannibal's army fought, it was as one body and one mind.

"The Romans may well be terrified of dictatorship, Hannibal," said Bostar. "But remember that their republic was dearly bought. Dictatorship may be the only thing they fear. Much have I travelled. I have known nothing like these Romans."

"Surely they bleed, Bostar, like any men," I said in jest.

Black pools were the eyes he turned on me, hinting at a heaven far and fatherless, a deep water. "It may be that you will defeat them, Hannibal. That I do not know. But they are as enduring as the grass. As many as the stars in the sky, as sand in the sea will the Romans prove themselves to be. If you destroy a legion, Hannibal, they will raise another, and another and again so long as there are enough of them alive. There is in them a stubbornness I do not think the world has seen before. Do you know of the seige of Veii?"

I did not.

He told me. "Veii, Hannibal, was a city which defied Rome. You know how the Romans drove the Etruscans, an ancient civilisation, from Italy?" I nodded. Silenus had told me, long ago, but I had not heard of Veii. "For ten years Veii, last of the important Etruscan cities, withstood the Roman seige, until the Romans captured an Etruscan augur, a soothsayer. He told them that the city would never fall until the waters of the lake around it, Lake Albanus, found their way to the sea. This was impossible. Veii stood miles inland.

"The Romans built a tunnel, Hannibal, a huge labour, for the length your army marches in a day. Down it the waters of Lake Albanus flowed into the river Anio, and then into the Tiber, and so to the sea. Veii fell. Such are the people you are determined to destroy. They are immutable as rock. They will never surrender, never give in."

We rode on in silence. "The opportunity to surrender, Bostar, is one thing I do not intend to give them."

We were two days from the river Ebro. Decisions had formed in me, as steadily as there was growing in Similce our child. I called Maharbal and Castello, Hasdrubal and Mago to my tent that night. "Name the two best company commanders," I said.

Without hesitation, Hasdrubal spoke out first: "Ezena the Numidian and Rurio the Celtiberian."

"Why?" I asked him.

"Because they are both incisive and careful. They understand both cavalry and infantry, and they have the respect of the men."

"I agree," said Castello.

"And so do I!" added Maharbal with a laugh.

I stood up to give my orders. "As of now, they are both promoted *loxarchos*, colonel. Maharbal, see that they are paid accordingly. Tell Ezena to choose three syntagmata of Africans and Rurio six of Spaniards. They leave tomorrow."

"Leave?" growled Castello. "But – "

Maharbal spoke out. "Spanish troops to Africa, African to Spain: a further twist of loyalty."

"Rurio leaves, Castello, for Cartakhena, and from there to Carthage. I have sent word to Bomilcar for galleys."

"You've asked Bomilcar for galleys?" Hasdrubal interrupted, incredulous. "But he won't – "

"Bomilcar will hardly refuse the offer of trained troops," I said.

"E-especia-al-ly ones who have been paid!" Mago got out.

We all chuckled. I carried on. "Ezena will go to what little we left of Carteia and make his base there. He is to ensure our hold on Spain, protect our rear and keep our lines of communication open. But he is to be only second-in-command."

Maharbal, Castello, Hasdrubal and Mago all looked away. Who would I leave behind? My brothers were sitting together. I took the two steps across the ground to them, squatted down. "Hasdrubal, Mago. I leave you in joint command."

Mago would not meet my eyes. He sat, twisting his fingers. Hasdrubal reached out and took me by the forearms. We stood up together. He was only a little shorter than me now. He released his hold, put his hands on my shoulders. Holding my eyes, he said: "Hannibal, we will not fail you."

"I know," I said, "I know," and broke away. "Maharbal" – I was brisk now – "leave my brothers 2,000 cavalry."

"The ones who – "

He didn't need to finish. "Yes, those ones." We all knew. Those who were only very good. Had we not trained with them for months, seeing them manage their horse only with the knee and heel and gallop at the Hanging Man, a stuffed figure

137

rolling down a slope towards them on a wheeled trolley, and draw their javelins as they rode and hit the dummy in the throat at a hundred strides and all this at full speed? A cavalryman who could manage this eight times out of ten was only very good.

"Hasdrubal, Mago, keep them practising. I want regular reports."

"We, we'll use the Car- the C-cartakhena skiffs for that," said Mago, still not looking up. "Our news will r-r-reach you first in G-gaul. I have it p-p-lanned."

No-one spoke. "You knew?" I asked him.

He looked up at me at last. "Y-yes, I knew." Suddenly, we were in each other's arms.

I half-turned from that hug, leaving one arm around my brother's shoulders. "I'm leaving you twenty of the elephants, the younger ones. You must hold Spain for us. Any questions?"

Castello coughed and sneezed and cursed. There was much of that illness among us from the wet and cold. Similce had prescribed the juice of lemons in the drinking water. "Hannibal, that is 24,500 men. That leaves us only – "

"That leaves us 68,500 – twenty-seven syntagmata – 10,000 horse and sixty elephants. That, Castello, will suffice."

It was a solemn parting the next dawn. I kept it short. "I will send for you," I told my brothers, "from Rome!" On Belleus, I took the van. I did not look back. We had climbed the crest of a hill and were descending before the hammering of spear shafts on shields from the army we had left behind grew faint and died away.

We took six days to cross the swelling Ebro by raft and ford. There was only one mishap. One bull elephant, about to board its raft of floating earth with its driver on its back, went suddenly, unaccountably berserk, turning maddened back upon the troops behind it, waiting to cross. They ran for their lives. Three were too slow. A fourth was picked up by the beast which tore off and threw away one of the soldier's legs before its driver used his mallet and his chisel and the elephant fell ponderously to earth, lying twitching, trunk still flailing in its death throes, steaming in the mud and blood. The driver was trapped in the fall. Both his legs were broken, white bone protruding from dark skin. I slit his throat. It was a kindness.

The nights were long by now, our days of marching short. We were passing through the region known as Catalunya. I was expecting trouble. Two of my emissaries had not returned at all. Three who had brought the same message: the main tribe of Catalunya, the Illergetians, had no cause to love Rome. Had not their Gaulish brethren to the north felt the Roman fist? But nor had they any love for Carthage. They had kept their lands as long as the memory of man. They were their own men, and so would remain. We would not pass. I could not leave an enemy at my back.

Subduing the Illergetians took two weary months. They would not be drawn into battle. They harassed my lines, driving off pack animals, picking off men, raiding us by night. My infantry could not defeat an enemy who only plagued them with arrows, and then rode away. They were brilliant bowmen, that I own. I began to question my dislike of that weapon. My heavy cavalry fared better, killing ten here, five there. My standing orders were to crucify any Illergetians captured alive. We killed a few that way, but thereafter they fought only to the death, or took their own lives, crying to dark gods. They had no towns, only scant villages, empty by the time we found them. This was a hard nomadic tribe, as itinerant, it seemed, as were the sheep and goats they set such store by. I studied our maps, questioned our scouts minutely. They were herders. I would herd them.

I divided the army into three, leaving 2,000 Spanish infantry to guard a proper palisaded camp. There was something there I wanted to protect, my wife. Of Bostar, Epicydes and Hippo-crates I ordered a full inventory of our stores, weapons and supplies.

Maharbal I sent speeding to the north, with orders to turn only with the Pirineos at his back. West went Castello, as far as the hills we knew as the Llena which ran south from the Pirineos. I turned east with my Hammer Guard, towards the sea, leaving the infantry with orders to follow for five days and then turn north-west.

In bands of eighty and a hundred we saw them on their shaggy ponies, always on the next hill, distant as deer on receding horizons, but always moving west before us. I pushed myself and my men to new limits. We lit no fires, shivered in the rain, rode with the owl and creatures of the night, ate only the dry rations we had drawn. Soaked first in water, the dry bread and salted fish sufficed to sustain man. I have never demanded any more of food. A week passed, two, and then we turned. First Maharbal's scouts, then Castello's met me. The trap was set.

There is a river in the heart of Catalunya that we knew as the Ter. Grassy plains reach away from it, and beyond them are hills. To the Ter we drove the Illergetians, and at a grey dawn there we found them, having ridden through the night. We held the hills. The ground was perfect for what I had planned.

They were brave, those Illergetians, perhaps 10,000 of them. As the light grew, they saw us, encircling them. We moved down to the plain, but out of shot. The Illergetians formed a circle, five and six men deep, their women, children, ponies in the middle.

I have been a fair man, according to my own deserts. I sent only three syntagmata of Spanish infantry forward, the rawest, 7,500 men. Our elephants were at camp. I would not have used them anyway. Fighting hand to hand, a dummy run for Roman battle, this is what I sought. At first the Illergetians kept good order, firing volley on volley of arrows at my soldiers as they came and hundreds fell. What would a volley of Roman *pila* do, I wondered?

I had two troops of slingers respond, concentrating their fire on where the archers stood. The stone is every bit as lethal as the arrow. It does not have the same range, but stones do not have to be made. The largest Illergetian quiver, I noted, contained twenty arrows. My Balearics each carried in their leather pouches at least fifty stones, the size of marbles. And bows had to be strung. Many of my slingers were proud to own and use the slings of their grandfathers. My army had to remain mobile, as self-sufficient as possible. No, I would not try the bow on Rome.

Sixty strides before the forces would have met, the Gaulish horns rang out, a haunting sound of sorrow running far along the hills. Belleus, snorting, shifted under me. My left hand lightly on his neck made still. That was the sign of silence. "You will hear that again before we are at Rome," I whispered to him, leaning down.

I would have done the same, I think, rushed out to meet my death. In twos and threes the Illergetians broke, and ran and threw themselves at our marching shields. Some broke up the files awhile, swinging with their cutlasses, fending with the targe, but on went the syntagmata, leaving behind them dead and dying. The Illergetians rallied to their children and their women and my soldiers broke upon that line, the shield in parry, then the sword to belly. If soldiers of the first file fell, those of the second cut and thrust and then the third. It is a thing of practice, killing well, and there was much of it that morning until only three groups of Illergetians remained at bay, with them huddled women, children, ponies.

My syntagmata paused, re-grouped. I saw the *hemiloxarchos* in charge break rank and walk behind his troop, shield reversed, held by the rim – our signal for orders. "Maharbal," I said. "Ride down. Have all the women and the children killed, then the men, in that order. But take ten men alive. Have them tied to ponies, and let them go."

Ten men telling of the destruction of the Illergetians at the hands of Hannibal would instil terror into many. I wanted no more rebellious tribes. Two syntagmata wheeled, surrounded the surviving men while the third cut and thrust and swung at the women and the children. We waited until it was done. We left the bodies to the vultures and the carrion and the worms.

No-one opposed our crossing of the Pireneos. The Romans would have tried, no doubt, if they had known. We were in the hills, the tree-line was breaking when the messenger was signalled from the east. A Ligurian, he had come from Hamilax by ship to Rosas, found Hasdrubal and Mago, learned of our route. "The Romans have appointed their new consuls for the year. Tiberius Sempronius Longus has Sicily for his province. He will sail there in the spring. He has ordered, it is said, a great mustering of galleys at Ostia." So, Sicily again. From Sicily, they would sail to Carthage. I must hurry, I thought.

"And the Romans' second consul?" I asked.

"He has been given Spain."

A double-pronged attack, then. But my brothers could hold the Romans, at least until they found they were needed not in Spain, but in Italy. And there was one more thing to try. Revolt in southern Gaul. What was the tribe there? Yes, the Boii. I would send gold to the Boii and see if the Romans still were as hot for Spain with the Boii in revolt.

"And the second consul's name?"

"His name is Publius Cornelius Scipio."

"Scipio? I know that name," I said, but my mind was already on other things. Only as I lay down to sleep that night did I remember. My father had told me of a Scipio, a Lucius Cornelius Scipio, a Roman admiral in our first war against Rome. This new consul Scipio must be his son. So, another family tradition, I thought as I fell asleep.

I sent the messenger away, well paid, with silver for the captain of the galley who would take him back across the winter seas. I gave him also four bags of gold for the Boii. "Tell them there will be more, when I arrive."

"When you arrive? You will cross the Alps, Hannibal?" the man asked, astonished.

I smiled. "From the Boii, do not go to Carthage. Go and wait for me in Rome."

We were six days in the Pireneos, strange and sullen hills of slag and grey where stunted pine trees drew upon a thin and bitter soil. We followed an old trade track, well known to Carthaginians since the time of my forefathers, the Phoenicians of Tyre. There was little snow, there on the east, and I knew a sense of peace. Up and down the column I rode each day, planning, thinking, talking with the men. I had the slingers hunt the mountain goats and we fed on meat each night. Similce's stomach cauldrons worked. She too was busy when we camped, despite the growing child, seeing to those wounded by the Illergetians, or sick, or lame, and making potions for them from her stock of herbs and powders. How they loved my wife, those many men of my army. How did I.

I was with Similce, riding in her wagon, talking in the middle of the morning when Belleus' whinny – he was tethered to the wagon – told me Maharbal was coming. "*Aegherghi!*" he shouted in Punic, excited: "Romans!"

We galloped to the head of the column. I too saw them on the foothills to the west of us, perhaps a half-hour's ride away, six of them against the skyline, from their helmets and their gear, Roman scouts. I knew the orders Maharbal expected. "We will let them be," I said quietly to him.

It was one of the few times he questioned me. "You want the Romans to know where we are?" he asked incredulously.

I looked at him, his flushed face, as true a friend as any man could have. "I want the Romans to *think* they know where we are, *anda*. When they come for us, we will be gone."

We pressed on through bitter days of cold and driving rain,

keeping as close as possible to the coast, but passing inland of the treacherous marshes and lagoons that lay there. And inland of the many trading posts that had once owed fealty to Carthage – Narxhonect, Agthes, Seute. No longer did our merchants sail the seas, that is what I thought, and these places were but memories of a greatness that had gone. It would, I vowed, return.

Each day of marching was the same. I watched and listened, thought. I heard the cheers when I had the word passed that the next day we would make camp for two weeks, near a town called Illiberan, and rest. That is not something I have ever wanted. But we would soon cross the Rhône. There was equipment to order and prepare, plans to be laid and orders given. And I was worried.

We were close to the territory of a large Gaulish tribe known to us as the Volcae. Their lands extended far east of the Rhône. I had sent two emissaries to them before even we had left Cartakhena, then more, eight in all. None had returned. If the Volcae were to oppose our crossing, that would not be easy. And I needed them as allies, not as foes, for something else that I had planned. I hoped still for my emissaries' return.

So we waited, rested. We built a proper camp, our first, dug latrines, erected kitchens. Similce demanded that I also had baths built. "Baths?" I asked. "You may have been in a wagon, but we have had baths every day, Similce, baths of rain."

She threw her herb bag at me, I remember, and the memory cheers me. "Do you want your men to scratch when they meet the Romans, Hannibal, or fight?" she gave me back.

I knew what she meant – lice. We all had them. "But soldiers always have lice," I said.

"Hannibal, sometimes you can be so stubborn! Leave it to me."

I did. Under awnings she had deep pits dug and lined with flags, then filled with water to universal consternation in the camp. "No-one will go in there," I said when I saw them. "They'll freeze to death!"

"Not when I've finished. Go back to your lists."

She commandeered eight wagons, and sent them into Illiberan for casks of vinegar. Then she had tall bonfires made and lit into which she had many rocks thrown. It was the talk of the camp. We all laughed and joked. Seething, cracking with heat, the rocks were tipped into Similce's baths, then the vinegar, then barrels of water steeped in thyme. File after file, the men jumped in and splashed and laughed and shrieked, the men who were marching with Hannibal on Rome.

Maharbal came with me to join in. "I hope the water's still warm," he said, as he stripped.

"If the Romans could see me now!" I laughed as, shivering in the wind, I jumped to kill my lice.

I found Similce sewing in her tent when I had finished, her rounding belly, swelling breasts so clearly shadowed in the light of her lamp. "We will do the same tomorrow, and the next day, Hannibal, until" – my lips caressed her on the forehead – "until all the men are de-loused" – and I nosed then the nape of her neck, deep in the smell of her, my tongue seeking out each little hair – "but perhaps I need more thyme and vinegar" – weaker now, my fingers gliding on her face, tracing her nose, her cheekbones, round her eyes – "they kill the lice, you know" – until my mouth on hers silenced her. We made love longingly, love around us, love between us, and inside her the life that we had made.

I could wait no longer for news of the Volcae. I had a despatch from my brothers, earlier than I had expected. All was quiet in Spain, but they had news of the Romans preparing to land a fleet at Emporiae, on the north-east coast. "We are planning a reception for them," my brothers wrote.

I had to hurry. We would fight the Volcae if we must. We

marched on, the men in good heart, and we came near the Rhône. We threaded through the marshes by the river, I and Maharbal, Castello and sixteen of the Hammer Guard. We saw them clearly, waiting on the farther bank, the Volcae in that dusk, their horses' nostrils steaming, behind those the fires gleaming, and in the half-light the strange helmets and the susurrating babel of the Gauls, their forces stretching out beyond my vision which, returning, saw one shape and then another which I knew at once were of those men that I had sent, now dead and dessicated totems on a river that the Volcae meant I was not to cross.

I knew the following morning what to do even as I was waking up. I dressed quickly, went to Castello's tent. He was stirring under his blanket of bear skin. "Castello, draw two syntagmata of infantry, take your pick, and dry rations for two days," I said, squatting down by where he lay. All my men were used to clear and abrupt orders. "March west first. The Volcae musn't see you. Then strike up the river for a half-day's forced march. Cross it, and – "

Castello laughed, his deep growling laugh. "I know," he said, "and catch the Volcae in the rear! I like the sound of this work, Hannibal!" and he was up and quickly putting on his greaves, his breastplate.

"I will need two days to build rafts and make ready," I said. "When you are in position, signal me. Smoke or mirror, according to the weather. We will be waiting." I saw his shield, sheeted with bronze, in the corner. "One more thing, Castello. Leave that," I said, pointing to his shield, "behind. Draw a shield of pure wood, and all your men. They will support you as you enjoy your swim across the river."

"It won't be as warm as Similce's baths!" was all he said. A light touch to his shoulder, and I was gone.

We saw his signal, smoke. The first detachments of my men were halfway across the river on their rafts, the horses swimming. In a mass the Gauls were waiting, shouting, brandishing their weapons, beginning to fire off arrows, when in perfect *synapismos* and in silence came Castello's two syntagmata marching down the rise towards the Volcae who turned, astonished, then bunched and rushed towards Castello's force.

He kept locked-order, presenting the narrowest of fronts to the Gauls. Not a third of them were able to engage my men. The Volcae were a herd of milling cattle when at just the right time both my syntagmata "flew", encircling the Gauls.

Many escaped as I sat still on Belleus watching from a bluff. Castello's line was only two deep, too thin to prevent some Volcae breaking through. "Shall I get some cavalry across and after them?" Maharbal beside me asked.

"No, *anda*. Let them live to tell their neighbours what happened when they sought to oppose Hannibal."

Someone certainly had told the Boii when, two weeks later, ten of their chiefs came to offer me alliance. That and the gold, perhaps, had worked. They had revolted, engaging the Roman garrisons at Stradella and Tortona. I consulted Bostar's maps. A plan was forming in my mind.

We were two days crossing the Rhône, the elephants in the same way my father had used to bring his to Spain. I took the greatest care with Similce, for she was very heavy now with child. For her Castello's men had brought a proper boat, taken from the Volcae. She said that she could become quite attached to sailing.

I had sent Maharbal and 500 Numidian cavalry on ahead to reconnoitre, west I told him, and southwards down the Rhône. He was gone four days. I was with Bostar in the evening when he came back, he but only half his cavalry. He was exhausted, filthy, dried blood on his armour when he came in, blurting: "Romans, Hannibal, a Roman army!"

I made him sit and tell me slowly.

He had met the force of Roman cavalry by chance, in a valley to the south. Their engagement was short, but bloody, inconclusive. The Romans broke off. He followed, down the river. "Ships, Hannibal, very many, anchored in the river mouth. A camp. But I dared go no closer. Then we rode. I had to leave our wounded. My horse foundered. I, I – " and then Maharbal fainted where he sat.

Our camp was struck within three hours. We marched through that night, guided by the fitful stars, and on, due east towards the Alps. We did not pause. Later there would be time for sleep. Bostar, I hoped, was right. The Romans would not march at night. Each evening too, he said, they made a proper entrenched camp. That made them slow. They would not catch us. I would not fight on ground I had not chosen. I would fight Rome on Roman soil.

I was gambling. It could only be Scipio's army. What would he do when he found that I had gone? What would I have done in his stead? "Always think from two positions, Hannibal, yours and your enemy's," my father had told me long ago. Surely I would take ship back to Italy and wait on the other side of the Alps. Scipio could have no doubt now of my intentions, I thought. I was very nearly right.

Only when I was sure we were beyond pursuit, when my scouts reported nothing, day after day, did we slow. The elephants were hungry. There had been no time to collect their fodder. We were all hungry, tired and Similce's time, she said, was near. On a high plain showing when the sun shone the vast whiteness of the Alps, we made our second proper camp on that long march.

Perhaps it was seeing the Alps that demoralised the men. Perhaps I had overstretched them. Commander after commander brought me the same message of mutterings of discontent. When the Boii came, I talked to them at length in broken Latin. I saw my chance.

I ordered an assembly. I had the chieftains of the Boii stand beside me on the wagon. "Soldiers of Carthage," I began, "we stand below the Alps and many of you, I hear, are now afraid. Look at these men beside me. Speak to them yourselves. They are descendants of those Gauls who many times have crossed and re-crossed those Alps that you so fear. They will tell you, as they have me, of how two centuries ago Bellovesus led his tribe of Insubres over the Alps and founded a great city, Mediolanum, on the other side. He was followed by Elitovius who led the Cenomani over the Alps and they dwell now near Brescia and Verona. The Boii themselves, the Lingones, the Senones, all these came here from the other side. Only twenty years ago the Boians Atis and Galatas called more Gauls over the Alps. And seven years ago Concolitanus and Aneroestus led their great host, more than ours, through those mountains you so fear."

I pressed on. "Have we not always been victorious? The plunder you won in Saguntum you will know a hundred-fold when we conquer Italy. We have crossed the Ebro, the Pirineos, the Rhône. You should not be afraid." I paused. Still silence from the men. I jumped down, gently helped Similce up onto the cart where she could be seen. "And which of you is so little a man as to refuse to follow where this woman, my wife, will go?" That did it. First the ranks near me kneeled, then those behind, like stalks of barley bending in the wind. Only some pockets still stood. I would deal with them later.

Walking back to the tents, my arm around Similce, one of the Boii came up. Magalus was his name. "If your men ask me, Hannibal, I cannot lie. Yes, my people have crossed the Alps many times, but in the summer. You must wait."

I stopped. I held him with my eyes. I could trust this man. "Magalus, will you guide me?"

He did not shrink my gaze. "You are a brave man, Hannibal. I will."

149

Similce went into labour that afternoon. She would have no-one with her, not even me. "Leave me!" she panted between contractions. "Since when is Hannibal short of things to do!" but I only went outside and waited. Magalus offered to fetch a Gaulish midwife. I declined. I did not stop the many men from coming and waiting, silent with me in the rain.

Where had I heard such a cry before? At Hanno's crucifixion. Then another, then a third and I could not bear it, then suddenly there was another sound, the crying of a child and I burst in alone and then I saw them, lying on the hides and skins, my wife naked and the slithering cord still pulsing and, at her breast, my son.

She smiled weakly as I took her hand. "When my eldest sister bore her first child, she was in labour sixteen hours. But I knew you are in a hurry, Hannibal," she whispered, teasing me. She took a sip of water from the gourd I held to her lips. "What shall we call our son, Hannibal?" Still bloody, wet with afterbirth, he lay on her, sucking at her breast.

"He is half you, half me, half Spanish, half Carthaginian. What name is most favoured in your family?"

"My father's, Fuano."

"Then we shall call him – Fuabal," I said. She reached up a hand, stroked my cheek.

"Then let your army see our Fuabal, our son. Give me your knife." She cut the cord, reached for a piece of clean cotton and a skin, it was of lynx I think, wrapped Fuabal, grizzling, up. "Now let me sleep," said Similce, and she handed me our son. Then, "He's not an egg! He won't break!"

But he did cry, or howl more like, especially at the din that went up from the men when I took him outside and held him up in what was now a thin sunshine. "This is Fuabal," I shouted, "my son!" and I heard the name passed around the camp on many lips.

We broke camp only five days later. Two days after Fuabal's

birth, Similce was back on her feet and seeing once again to the sick, the wounded, carrying our son tied to her in a shawl. I saw them when I could, but I was busy. First I identified those men whose commitment I doubted, who had not kneeled, who were still grumbling. Castello and Maharbal agreed with me on who should be put in command – a Greek, Aragoras.

I sent them away, 10,000 men, to the coast with orders to send to Bomilcar for transports. With them went a sealed despatch for Bomilcar. "Where are we to go?" Aragoras asked me.

"Follow Bomilcar's orders when they come," I replied. In my despatch, I advised Bomilcar to send the force to Sicily. I did not tell Aragoras that. I trusted him, but not those he led.

That left me 58,000 infantry. Enough. I would recruit more from the Gauls, if I needed more. I spent hours and hours with Magalus and Bostar, studying and making maps and plans. We planned it all, where we would abandon the carts, the tents, anything superfluous. Fodder was the problem, for the horses and the elephants. I had cut and gathered into bundles all the greenery for miles around. The men would pull the bundles behind them on ropes through the snow. We worked out precisely how little we thought each man would have to eat to stay alive.

Led by Magalus, we began to climb along stony icy paths of scree, up and on into a narrow gorge from which cliffs rose to our right and a sheer drop fell to our left. Our line was very long. At least Similce and Fuabal are at the rear, I thought, when the rocks began to rain on our column from the crags above. The mule in front of me, two men beside it were swept away by a boulder passing in the blinking of an eye.

I ran the few steps forward up to Magalus, sheltering behind a crag. "Allobroges," he said.

"You told me they were friendly! Are they not Gauls, your kinsmen?"

"Mine, Hannibal, indeed. But not yours." Another rock crashed past us.

I passed the word. "Take shelter!" I wanted to wait like that until nightfall. Then I would find these Allobroges.

But a long column is hard to stop. Glancing down, I saw the men still marching up and bunching when they met those to whom the word had come to stop and twenty, thirty at a time the boulders caught them. I felt such rage, that I do remember. I knew that I would lose men to Roman swords or *pila*, but I had not trained these men and lived with them and loved them in my way for this.

The mules' hee-haws of alarm and fear echoed from the rocks and I saw them rear and fall, their bundles plummeting with them down below. I broke from my shelter, calling "Barca!" as I scurried up the rocks above me and came panting, the bloodlust on me, to the first group of them, eight of them, piles of boulders round them. I killed them and went after more. I saw Castello. But where is Maharbal? I was thinking. With the rearguard where I placed him, when a spear thrust missed me by a hair and I took that man through the stomach and my sword came out through his back and there were parries, cuttings, thrustings until the rocks ceased to fall.

Our way became even slower after that. I sent scouts ahead and we came on only when they said the way was safe. I had the elephants moved to the van. Magalus said they would terrify the Gauls, if there were any more. "We will soon be too high, even for them," he said. "They are not mad." We crept on. But then it began to snow, first fat slow flakes, then more, driven by a rising, whirling wind. I passed orders for all to walk, all animals to be led, and we trudged on, each step an effort of the will.

I was making my way down our long column, encouraging here, chastising there when slowly the column stopped. I ran back up, slipping on the snow, past the elephants, mammoths in the mirk. A huge rock blocked the path completely. I sent for

Magalus. "Is there a way round?" I shouted in the wind.

Snow freezing on his beard, he shook his head vigorously. "We must go back."

When a way is closed, go through and know no fear. There had to be a way.

Similce's baths. I had seen how the heated rocks split and cracked. I would heat this rock until it too cracked. But it was a weary day, passing timber up the column from the tree-line far below. All that night I had the fire fuelled and had as many as could fit there sleep within its warmth, two hours each.

I pushed the last chunk of that rock away myself, burning my hands even through the skins wrapped round them. "Three more days to the summit," Magalus said. It took us six, or was it more? Those days and nights are blurred, a black oblivion in my memory. The snow did not let up. It lay on top of the frozen snow beneath it. The foot sank through, only to slip on the layer underneath. Similce was failing, word reached me from the rear. I had her brought up to the van, and Maharbal and Castello. Bostar and his staff I had not seen for days.

Fuabal was wrapped in swaddling clothes and skins and tied around Similce, under three cloaks. I think I wondered how he could breathe. We moved him together from her front to her back and then I carried them, my wife and my son, on my back and we went on up through the cold and snow and wind.

Castello carried them too, and Maharbal. One hundred paces each, that is what we had agreed, and it was good to have to count those steps, to focus on those steps. I crossed the Alps by counting to a hundred. I heard that men were going blind from the snow. "Look only at something black or dark," Magalus said, and I trudged on looking at the black fox skin round my middle. But there was no remedy for frostbite, only death. The new boots with which many had been issued at Illerban were a catastrophe. The leather was of ox-hide newly flayed. In the cold and wet the straps contracted, freezing to the wearer's feet, cutting off the blood. Alive perhaps, these men, but unable to walk, able only to die where they sat or lay.

What could I do but go on? We slept each night where we had stopped, grouped together under cloaks for warmth, the salted fish and raisin cakes the same in mouths cracked and dry. It was hard to move in the morning, to get up from under the night's blanket of warming snow. Many did not. I lost ten of the elephants' drivers, who had slept at their beasts' sides for warmth and been crushed when they rolled. Similce always fed Fuabal in a shelter that we made from cloaks. He sucked well enough, but otherwise was still.

The cold grew unbearably intense. It shimmered around us. Each breath was such rasping pain that I remember still the fear of that which breathing in would bring, and knowing that I must. There was only, blurred but bright, the will to stay alive. The ground was leveller now, the little I could see. Magalus said that we were almost at the summit, at a plateau, from which we would then begin our descent. "Will I see Italy from there?" I asked him, speech slurred.

"Not unless this snow stops," he shouted back. We slept that night on the flat, Similce beside me, Fuabal between us, and Maharbal and Castello and two more men I had found wandering, deranged, all barely alive from that cutting wind. Soon the snow was covering us where we lay.

Something was different when I half-woke. The wind. The wind had stopped. And what was that? Light. To the east I saw a sun when I pushed up and out, leaving my sleeping wife and son. Slowly at first, stiff, then faster, frantic, I ran across that field of shining snow, falling, sinking to my waist, rising again, on to the edge. There beyond, below me, I saw Italy.

I tried to shout out, but my lips were swollen, cracked. I blundered back. Only a mound of white in the whiteness showed me where they were. "Similce, Maharbal, Castello!" I croaked, scampering towards them. "Wake up! Italy, Italy!" I clambered over their bodies, scraping off the snow. Sitting up, Similce reached out in instinct for our son, pulling back the cloaks around him. He did not stir. I have seen so often in so many dreams again those miniature teardrops, frozen, glinting in the light. I squeezed shut my eyes and I remembered his weak crying in the night. I knew that Fuabal was dead. I opened my eyes. They met Similce's. Hers were enormous, blank, black. She tried to scream, but no sound came in that crackling air.

VII

ITALY

We could not burn Fuabal in that place and so we buried him as best we could, high up there in a brilliant blinding sun, under a sky merciless and blue. Similce did not protest when I took from her the bundle that had been our son. She sat still when Maharbal and I dug, as deep as senseless hands allowed. We found some stones and covered him, surrounded as we worked by soldiers I had led there, watching silent in the snow. The bones of Fuabal must lie there still, there with soaring eagles and with death.

I thought to speak to Similce. I thought to say to her: "We will have other children," but words seemed vain. We stumbled on, away, in a bitter cold without that dulled the pain within, prayers to Melkarth and Eschmoun and Tanit-pene-Baal dying before they had even formed.

Years later, when I could not sleep because I had bad dreams, I went to Bostar in the night. "Does your past never trouble you?" I asked him.

"The wise man has no past, Hannibal, nor a future. The wise man lives only in the present."

But only the future drove me on then, there in the Alps.

Descent was worse than ascent. The snow had stopped, but now the cold was almost worse. I remember zigzagging paths on which was ice. Magalus led. He often slid down on his back, for there was no purchase for the foot. We followed. The only sounds that I remember of those days were the death screams of the many, many men and animals who fell. I forced myself back up the column, wanting to encourage those I found who had simply stopped. I meant to tell them to look down, across to the plains of Italy, its rivers glinting in the light. Instead I said to

156

them: "Stay here and you will die." Very many did just that.

We lost thirty elephants, more. They simply fell, trumpeting to death, their noise reverberating from the rocks and crags to ears immune. Amongst the horses I found Belleus, thin, panting, mangy, scared. He barely recognised me. Perhaps the sense of death was so strong on me, Fuabal's death, the death of multitudes of men. So many deaths surround me. I first saw her through those crazed descending days, strewing leaves of sure obliteration on our paths. "I am the mother of beauty. I am your mother," she called to me, shadow forming only to disappear. "From me alone shall come your dreams and your desires. And yet I make the willows shiver in the sun. Impassioned maidens wander in my train and stray among the glittering leaves. Come, Hannibal! See, I have your son." Rome, Rome, I held to Rome, I held to Similce – where is she? Up with Maharbal. He will look after her. Rome, Similce, I will not go mad and with each shambling step I banished death. That was my victory over the Alps.

First stunted and occasional, then surer, taller came the trees. There is a place that I remember where trees shelter a green valley. Through it runs a river, sparkling from the snow. There with the last strength we had we lit fires, we slept, rested. Similce said nothing, only sitting, staring far away. She refused food, even fresh goat-meat some had been fit enough to hunt and kill and cook. She drank only water that I brought her. I tried to make her talk. "Leave her, Hannibal," came the voice of Bostar, soft behind me. "Where she has gone, no-one can find her." At least Bostar was alive. "I never have enjoyed snow," was all he said.

"The maps, Bostar, the maps?" I asked.

"They, like me, are well."

"And Epicydes, Hippocrates?"

"Both have frost-bitten toes. They are saying that perhaps Sicily was not so bad after all. But they will live."

On the second day of our makeshift camp I began to take stock. I had lost much more than Fuabal in the Alps. I wrote it all down on tablets given me by Bostar. I recorded death. That was how I dealt with the death of my son, just as in action I dealt with that of my father.

So many were missing and so much. I had to restore discipline, momentum. I found Magalus. "We need a proper camp, and food and rest and clothes," I said.

"Three more days will bring us to the plain and to my people."

I passed the word. We moved on through a softening air and I remember thanking the life there was in spring, in living, growing things after so much death. I forced my mind from Fuabal. I thought of Rome.

From the Boii we had food for men and horses, mules and famished elephants. I ordered a muster. Only 20,000 infantry were left, 6,000 cavalry and 26 elephants, all exhausted, weak. The mules carrying the gold had gone, fallen or, Castello suggested, taken by deserters. Each morning found more men had left us in the night. I didn't trouble to pursue them. Similce lay still, staring into space. Rome was slipping away. I knew there were Roman garrisons to the west of us at Tortona and Stradella, at Lomello. If they learned where I was and attacked us, lame, frost-bitten, hungry and, worse still, grieving . . . Battles are lost or won mostly in the mind.

I won by will. I wanted. I believed and I renewed that belief alone. I began at the beginning. I called Castello. "Drill practice, twice a day, for all." I saw the doubt in his face. "I know the state the men are in, Castello. They can rest between their drill." He smiled. I sent Maharbal and forty of the fitter men and horses off to scout. I needed information. I needed gold, gold to hire new troops and buy more horses. Magalus told me where I could find it.

I picked the men myself. I led them myself. I had them spend our last day in camp cleaning armour, sharpening weapons, rehearsing orders. I left Castello in charge. Similce was sitting by a fire of spitting pine. I kissed her gently on the forehead. She did not respond. I turned away.

We went to Torino, chief town of the Taurinians, for generations enemies of the Boii. We simply broke down the town gate, as at Heliche, with a makeshift battering ram. They were no better before my two syntagmata, those Taurinians, than the Illergetians or the Volcae. If all the Gauls were as poor fighters as these, I remember thinking as I massacred, I would have to train hard any Gaulish recruits. With each sword-cut, each death, I thought, Fuabal. The troops followed my lead. There was no-one still alive when we left smoking Torino with our gold, no-one except the fifty prisoners, all men in their prime, that I took with me from there. For them, I had a plan.

I sent Magalus away to the west with most of the gold. He promised me his kinsmen there would again revolt, tying down the Roman garrisons. I needed that time, especially after Maharbal's report. He had done well. Scipio, he told me, had gathered in the Roman soldiers in the west and stationed them at Placentia. Bostar had the map ready.

Placentia was at the confluence of the rivers Ticinus, Trebia and Po. A good choice, I thought. A little obvious, but good. I had to cross one of the rivers. I was wondering which when Maharbal's report again held my whole attention. "The second Roman army, under Sempronius, coming from the south . . ."

"Sempronius? That is impossible!" I exclaimed. "He was sent to Sicily!"

"Was sent, Hannibal, yes, yes. But he was recalled when news of us reached Rome."

"So I am right!" I shouted. "We can draw all the Romans in, and chop off one head! Aragoras should now have reached Sicily. He will be almost unopposed! Bostar, pass this news round the men."

159

"And is Sempronius also bound for Placentia?" I asked Maharbal.

"Yes. He is. You see, we captured a Roman scout, I just outrode him . . ." and Maharbal was off, recounting his adventure, gesticulating as I thought and planned. What I had learned was good indeed.

The next morning my mind was clear. I gave my orders. The whole army, what was left of it, mustered after breakfast in a circle on the plain beyond our camp. I stood in the middle, alone. I signalled. Castello led in the Taurinian prisoners, and after them Magalus, who would translate. I spoke in simple Greek. "Taurinians, you saw what happened to Torino. This is how we deal with enemies of Carthage. And so I give you this choice: either crucifixion, or single combat with each other to the death. The victors will be given a horse, weapons, pay, freedom and a place in my army, my army which will march on Rome."

I saw Magalus hesitate in his translation. There would be cousins amongst them, brothers. They would not fight each other. He looked at me. My will has always been implacable. He finished. The Taurinians shuffled, looked about.

The first to walk over to the pile of weapons was a small and stocky man, his hair long and blond and matted. He picked up two shields and swords, walked back and gave one of each to a taller, leaner man. An interesting match, I thought, as others coupled off and I withdrew and said, "Begin."

Anyone that I trained learned that the good swordsman witholds more than he commits. Let your opponent spend his energy, expose himself. Then strike. The parry is more important than the thrust. Those Taurinians knew no such skill, but blundered at each other in brute strength, quickly spent.

Soon, as we watched, most of the Taurinians were wounded. One lost his sword and the hand that held it, but he charged his opponent and they clinched and wrestled on the ground. The stocky one, the first one to come forward, did badly at first against his opponent's greater reach. But sidestepping neatly a clumsy slash, he quickly closed and brought his own sword fatal through the other's belly.

At last twenty still stood amongst the groans and blood. "Take them away," I told Castello. "Assign each to a different *dekadarchos*." I walked again into the circle and I stood among the dead or dying Taurinians. I spoke to my army, louder now, my Greek more flowing: "Soldiers of Carthage, what you have just seen was no entertainment. It was an illustration of our position. The Taurinians fought because there was no way for them to escape but in victory or death. Our situation is identical. Which of you would go back, disgraced? Which of you would live? Our plan is working. You have already heard that the second Roman army has been withdrawn from Sicily. They must be anxious to meet us. Let us not disappoint them! Let us go forward, then, to victory and to Rome." I had a few of the *dekadarchoi* primed to cheer. I did not need them.

There was a new fervour in the drill practice that followed. But Sempronius' coming meant we would be hugely outnumbered. I needed more men. Not Gauls, I had decided. I had no time to train them — if indeed they could be trained. Ligurians and Celts, these were the soldiers I needed, traditional mercenaries of Carthage. But for them I had to go south-east. And between me and the south-east were the Romans, two or three times our number, even allowing for a legion being tied up against the Boii.

I had to win. Not a major battle, but enough. Cavalry. I could only do it with my heavy cavalry. I had 6,000 in all, but 1,200 were light Numidian. Of the rest, how many horses were fit? I went to the cavalry lines. Belleus whinnied in recognition. He was looking better already, new hair beginning to shine

161

where it was growing through the patches of mange. I was stroking him and talking to him when I felt a hand on my hip.

Similce was beside me, weak and thin and drawn. I put an arm around her, her head on my shoulder. We said nothing, sharing pain that binds. Reaching to draw her closer, my hand touched her right breast. She flinched, looked up at me with tired eyes. "It is the milk," she said, "the milk for – " "Fuabal" was just a whisper. Her eyes dropped away.

"Veg – " She cleared her throat. "Vegetables," she said softly.

"What?" I asked, unsure what I had heard. She turned her head, looked up at me again. I saw her blood-shot eyes, her wrinkles new and clear, her cracked and peeling lips.

"Vegetables. The horses too, we all need vegetables."

I smile as I remember. Piles and piles of them, radishes, celeriac, beetroot, salsify, fennel, beans, shallots, broccoli, samphire, gourds, sow-thistles, cardoon, tender shoots of ruscus, bryony white and black. From far and wide Similce had them gathered in, even the bulbs of gladiolus, asphodel, wild orchid, scilla, eastern star that she mixed into her stews. And then the herbs, the eryngium leaves, purslane, orach, amaranth, sorrel, patience dock, bugloss, heliotrope, for days she busied herself with these and made of them great vats of steaming tea which, sweetened with honey, each man was made to drink. They joked, they pretended to protest, but drank. Hannibal's army rose up from the vegetables of his wife.

Was it twelve days later, more? I knew that we were ready. These things are an instinct. We struck camp and marched a day and a half. When I ordered "Halt and camp!" a half-day's march west of Placentia, Castello rode up.

"We are well within the range of Roman scouts, Hannibal," he said, bemused.

"That, Castello, is exactly what I want. Trust me."

I trusted myself, that is more important, trusted my belief that Scipio or Sempronius or both could not resist coming out to meet me and so that night I ordered many campfires lit. I meant to save their scouts any trouble.

I wanted the Romans to cross the river, not me. They were not Volcae. That is what I forced them to do, but first I forced them to divide, by dividing my forces into three. Maharbal I sent south to the river Trebia, Castello north up the Ticinus. Both had orders to seem to be preparing to cross by felling trees, building rafts. Leaving a small force of my Hammer Guard behind at our camp with Similce and Bostar and the elephants, still unfit, I took 4,000 cavalry – two squadrons of Numidians, the rest of heavy cataphract – towards Placentia and the river Po. They were almost bound to cross there, I had thought, if only for the simple reason that at Placentia there was a bridge.

I saw the dust of the Roman column. My instinct was to charge. The ground was level, perfect. But our horses were still weak. Wait, Hannibal, wait. I ordered Δ-formation, the Numidians at the rear, and I sat at the van as Belleus trembled.

From round a low hill then I saw them coming, my first force of Romans, cavalry. I counted the standards, one for each squadron, eight, ten. So they were 3,000, fewer than us.

I saw one standard that was red and blue. It could not be. I rubbed my eyes and looked again. It was. Red and blue. I had learned from Epicydes. He was an authority on these things. They interested him. He was always trying to get me to issue colours to my different troops. It could only be, it was – the standard of a Roman consul.

I drew out my javelin, I wound the throwing thong. The Romans stopped. I heard their trumpets. They deployed into one long line, three deep. So they would try simply to envelop us. I chuckled, turned, gave my silent commands – arms outspread for the "fly", then, pointing to the Numidians, crossed forearms for the command that they should stay back. Their *hemiloxarchos*, what was his name, I should remember, leant forward along his

163

horse's neck to show he understood. We had practised so many times.

I waited, waited as the Romans cantered. Then they broke into a gallop and I closed my eyes. I thought of my father and of Fuabal. I let the fury grow. I seized it, rolled it round. We charged to meet the Romans, our formation so tight I was each horse and man among us, and they were me. Rising up on Belleus, I spread out my arms and like a bird my delta's wings unfolded to a line as long as was the Romans', now a hundred strides away. I threw my javelin, willing to it death.

It caught the horseman riding with the consul's standard, perfect, just below the throat. Belleus was bursting through the Roman line when I felt the swinging sword and twisted from it on his back and turned him, bearing round. I saw Romans dismounting, gathering round one lying wounded on the ground, their lances outwards to defend him but I was past them, wheeling, slashing, fending with my shield and we were forty, fifty knots of men and horses fighting. Now, I thought, come now.

I did not see them, but I heard them, the ululation in the throat of those Numidians, coming from the Romans' rear and then I knew that now we had them in the dust and noise.

That one group of Romans stayed unbroken. Three times I charged, three times was checked and turned away. No horse could bear down on such lances. I was off Belleus and running, screaming "Bar-ca!" as he was still turning from his pass. There were eight or ten of my men with me in the mêlée, seeking out that consul and I burst through the first rank of lances. I cannot now remember more than two of the first rank turning on me from behind and the screaming of the Spaniard there beside me, a lance through his groin, and just beyond there was the consul's standard, planted in the earth. Someone called, "Hann-i-bal! Hann-i-bal!" through the din, and I looked and saw.

Young, perhaps eighteen, slender, graceful, all that I took in at a glance of him who was now leading two maniples or more towards us. A troop under Maharbal attacked them, but they came on, shielded, straight towards us. The lancers round me called out "Scip-i-o!" and again, louder, and I knew then who was lying just beyond me on the ground. But I had to get out, to re-group. The Romans were retreating in good order, before I found Belleus again and the semblance of command.

As we stripped the Roman dead, I thought, that was a brave man. I found one of the Roman lancers alive, bleeding from the shoulder. "Who was that leading the maniples?" I asked him.

"That was Scipio," he said.

I put my dagger to his throat. "Scipio was lying here wounded. I will not ask you again. Who was that?"

"Scipio," he said again, then coughed some blood. "*Erat etiam Scipio minor, consulis filius* – that was Scipio minor, the consul's son." I cut the lancer's throat, for Fuabal.

Morale was high when we returned to camp. I let the men brag and sing. "So Romans die like any other men," I joked with them. Over 600 Roman dead, eighty prisoners and we had lost only a hundred. But I knew it was a skirmish, nothing more. I had proved the superiority of my cavalry, of our training. But we had not faced a Roman infantry attack. It was time we did – on our terms. And I had been wrong. The next time, I did not intend to fight myself. I had to plan and watch and keep control.

I was perturbed by what young Scipio had done. He had saved his father's life. Mine had lost his in saving mine. I sent for Bostar. "Who are these Scipios?" I asked him.

"Epicydes knows more," he said.

"Bring him."

He told me they were an old and noble Roman family, who had served Rome for generations. "Well, one is wounded now. Soon, perhaps, we can do the same to the son and stop the service of the Scipios to Rome."

"Perhaps. But what about the uncle? Where is he?"

"Uncle? What uncle?"

"There is another Scipio, Hannibal, Gnaeus Cornelius Scipio Calvus. He defeated the Insubrian Gauls some three years ago. Has he not been sent to Spain?"

I did not know. "Thank you, Epicydes," I said. "Soon we will stop the Scipios or any other Romans being sent at all."

Maharbal and Castello returned. The Romans had not crossed after them. "Then they are more cautious than I had hoped," I said. "Bostar, question the prisoners. I want to know what Sempronius is like. With Scipio wounded, he will have sole command. Castello, go with him. They may need some persuasion."

"Sempronius is a hothead," Bostar said when he returned. "A *cerebrosus fervidusque* in Latin. Those are the words they used. Interesting words."

"An interesting trait, Bostar," I replied.

Maharbal's scouts returned. The Romans had re-grouped at Placentia, breaking down the bridge behind them.

"At least we have no gear to hinder us," I joked with Maharbal as we rode north.

"And this smaller army is a quicker one," he replied.

I thought it would take two days to follow the Ticinus north and cross it, then another two to march east, cross the Po and come up behind Placentia. It took only three, not least because I sent Castello and 200 of the Hammer Guard ahead to forage. Castello grinning from ear to ear, they returned on the second day with grain and meat, several hundred horses and a troop of new recruits, Cenomanians dressed in skins and armed with axe and targe. They said they did not fight for pay, but against Rome. I said I shared their sentiments. "Watch them," I told Castello. But they were to prove good troops to Hannibal.

We went a day's march south of Placentia before we turned. We made a palisaded camp. Our sentries' cries were clear in the still evening air. There were perhaps 2,000 of them, Celts, deserters from Scipio's auxiliaries, and with them came ten wagons of grain and salted beef. I was delighted. Word was spreading, word that Hannibal had come to destroy Rome, that is what they told me in their curious Latin. They had found the Roman grain store at Clastidium deserted and they thought they would save me the trouble of going to collect it. All the Romans, they said, were at Placentia behind its walls. I told no-one, not Maharbal, not Similce, but I knew a huge relief. The odds were shortening.

Maharbal and I rode out alone before sunrise. I needed perfect ground and all that long day without resting, Maharbal and I were searching for the place I knew I had to find.

We were climbing up the sides of a defile. The bank was thick with wild roses and their thorns and I remember still that luscious, lingering smell. Maharbal swore when he tripped and fell into the thorns. "Let's go back, Hannibal!" he shouted. "I'm not a goat!"

"No, you're an old woman!" I shouted back. "Get a move on!" He caught up with me, scratched, sweating, panting and we stood together, both the same size and build, in the red and yellow roses of northern Italy. "You're looking at the lie of the land as if your life depended on it, Hannibal," he said.

I put my hands on his shoulders, looked at him. "It does, anda, it does."

Rising from the Apennines to the south, the river Trebia flows into the Po, a few miles to the west of Placentia. Its banks are high and covered with thick scrub. Deep gorges run down into it, watercourses for the winter floods but dry then in a summer sun. We had become adept at crossing rivers. The Trebia was cold, but neither fast nor deep. We simply waded across, Similce on my back. We made our camp beyond the high western bank. I checked each step of the ground, preparing my battle order, waiting for Maharbal to set the trap.

With 2,000 horse, he was to lure the Romans out by riding up to Placentia. Surely Sempronius could not resist. He was gone a day. I had Castello and one syntagma of heavy cavalry rest that morning and eat. By mid-afternoon I had them re-cross the river to take up their position in a deep defile that ran into the Trebia on the eastern side, north of our position. "Your breakfast will be cold, Castello, but you will feast tomorrow night," I said, and he smiled.

Maharbal was breathless and excited – he so often was – when he returned in the late afternoon. "It's working, Hannibal, it's working! The Romans are perhaps an hour behind us. I did exactly what you said: engaged their van and then withdrew, engaged and then withdrew. I lost a few of our men, but not too many."

"You have done well, *anda*," and I hugged him. "Now go and wash."

They came in the early evening to the east bank. I had half my army and the twenty-three fit elephants out of sight beyond the rise. And Castello, of course. I had been to that defile myself. The scrub was so thick, they would never find him, even if they looked. The Romans would have seen perhaps 10,000 men across the river from them, a quarter of their number for I counted up the standards of their maniples. Four legions in all. So, both the consular armies. They withdrew east to camp. Later I saw their fires, heard their trumpets sound the watches through the night.

I did not sleep. Again and again I went over my dispositions: Spanish and African infantry in the centre, heavy cavalry and elephants on each flank. I had to drive the Roman flanks in on their centre before it broke mine, as it surely would through sheer force of numbers. I walked back to our camp. Similce was cooking. More of her famous stews, and bread from Roman grain. She kissed me, I remember, quickly on the neck. "I thought I'd do that before you put your helmet on," she said. "And no, don't ask! Yes, they will be fed on time. Now go and check your sentries."

They were fed on time, all of them, beginning three hours before dawn as I had planned, the Numidians first for they would first see action, then the rest, each man a bowl of stew and bread, and then with muffled arms they moved down to position in the dark. Still in the dark the 2,000 Numidians crossed the river. I had had them rub their bodies with olive oil against the water's cold. "Remember, lots of noise. Attack their outposts. Engage and then withdraw," I told the *loxarchos* in charge. He simply nodded. Always men of few words, Numidians.

I heard the noise, the shouts, the trumpets then, in the half-light, I saw the Numidians swarming back across the Trebia and Romans hard behind as I sat on Belleus up the bank above my army, its full numbers still enough concealed, I hoped, in that poor light.

On they came, the legionaries of Rome, wading through the icy Trebia on empty stomachs, just as I had planned. I waited, waited to give the signal to my slingers on the wings, waited for the Roman maniples to form. I knew they would be beyond the slings' effective range. The hail of stones that I then unleashed did, though, what I had hoped. It made the Romans raise their shields, made more difficult their climbing up the bank.

The Romans threw no *pila* at the Trebia, up that bank. They could not, as I had anticipated. I had thought that my infantry's spears would take their toll, but they bounced harmlessly off the rows of locking shields and it was a formidable sight, the Romans moving steady up. My centre charged them on command, sweeping back the *velites*. But they could not break the Roman line. It was too deep. I signalled for the elephants' advance, the pincer movement from the wings. But perhaps the elephants were still too debilitated. They were sluggish, slow. I remember thinking that I should have had their drivers make them drunk. I saw one fall, its hamstrings cut, and then another, but at least their bodies slowed the Romans' advance and slower,

slower, they came on. "Now!" I shouted, but of course no-one could hear me and I gave the signals.

One syntagma of heavy cavalry from each of my wings came charging down the hill in perfect order, Maharbal leading on the left. We broke the Roman line and pushed them back and back onto the others climbing still the bank and "Good!" I shouted as I saw my *dekadarchoi* seek out and kill the Roman trumpeteers. The legionaries could not form a line. I saw in the now bright light a Roman on a white horse crossing the Trebia with a maniple on each side. That must be Sempronius, I was thinking, when Castello caught them from behind.

I wanted with all my being to ride down and kill. I had to stay. Command. Control. Yes, I have fought many battles, but the hardest have been with myself. I would have stayed, I am sure, had not Sempronius turned his rearing horse, moved up-river avoiding Castello and his men and, four other mounted Romans with him, fled. I had left a squadron of my Hammer Guard behind me, to guard Similce and the camp. There was no need of that now. I signalled for them, saw them start to come and then I plunged down the bank to catch Sempronius and my shout of "Bar-ca!" echoed off the further bank.

Bostar used to say that from right mind come right actions. The Romans were caught on the flanks and the rear. The battle was won. There was only slaughter left. If I could catch the consul, my victory would be crowned. Was that not right mind?

So I pursued Sempronius, I and my squadron. But all our fresh horses I had given to the cavalry on our wings. I sensed how tired Belleus was at once. Lying on his neck I whispered to him "More!" but he had no more to give and the Romans' dust grew distant as we rode. Why did I not turn back? I might have been in time. We rode on until I was alone, just Belleus unfoundered, and only then turned angry back.

It was dark when we returned. What was I expecting? My mind was far away, planning, considering. "There are no fires," that is what I noticed first. My pulse quickened. Belleus protested at the dark cold water of the Trebia. I soothed him in, across. The dead lay where they had fallen on the farther bank. Belleus stumbled on a shield, a buckler. Why had the Romans not been stripped? Maharbal knew my orders and then I saw him, alone, sitting on the ground. I slipped off Belleus. "Maharbal, what — ?"

His voice was unfamiliar, the tone of those two words: "*Anda*, come."

He took my arm. We walked up the bank, tripping, silent, faster, dread in my heart, dry mouth, and at my throat. On we walked to what had been our camp. There were three torches burning, three, planted in the ground, and now I see them, those three torches, burning in my mind.

She lay where they found her, where the Romans tied her, my naked wife spread-eagled, stripped, profaned. What I see is blood, the bright blood and the dark blood, I see as then I saw the many colours of that blood between her legs and on her curving belly that I knew more than my own. Spreading, drying still upon her breasts that I had sucked and licked and nuzzled there was a brown blood and a blood black red, that is what I saw, my wife raped, roped to stakes beside her ankles and her wrists. And to the right of her, I see them now just as too many times before, I see four taller stakes to which Bostar, Epicydes, Hippocrates and a Spaniard were tied. All around them and those torches, disappearing in the darkness and the dancing shadows, stood the victors of the Trebia who had won but who had lost some sacred, sacrificial thing. It is only once and it was then that I have known pure evil and I know the smell of it, the feel of it, the taste of it and, yes, I, Hannibal, great Hannibal, yes, I was afraid.

I could not move. I could not comprehend. The eyes see, the mind does not believe. She groaned, she lolled her head. I ran. There was a crumpled shift, her shift beside her and I covered her and I fell down to lie upon the ground, the bloody ground beside her and gently and so gently then I took her living hand. I do not know how long I lay there with the dust of Italy in my mouth. I turned my face towards the Spaniard and to Bostar and "Tell me!" I rasped. Bostar began to moan and swing his head, back and forth in madness, and he was fighting for his mind that time, that only time that Bostar failed me. "You," I whispered to the Spaniard, "you," from deep in my throat then howling "Tell me!" and he was sobbing, weeping, and then I knew him, a simple man, a cook. He raced and raged, a torrent in a mad voice. Only now, for the first time and the last, do I allow myself to remember what he said.

"We were cooking. We were cooking. She wanted a special meal. She said that we would have a victory to celebrate. I do not know where they came from, but suddenly they seized us and they held her and they stripped her and they tied her down and formed a jostling file before her, did the Romans, and she screamed and screamed and writhed and someone hit her and they stuffed a cloth into her mouth and one after another they, they – "

"Tell me!" I screamed.

His voice was quiet now. The torches spluttered in a gust of wind. "One after another then they took their turn on top of her. They entered her and moaned and groaned and pumped. If one took too long he was pulled off but they each took their turn, again, again.

"But that was not enough for them, not," he sobbed and shuddered, "e-nough, -nough for them. They had a pole with them, a painted pole." A standard. A legionary standard. There rose in me a bitter bile and that is why I said I know how evil tastes. The cook's voice was a whisper. "When they had done with her, one of them took that pole and thrust it into her, in and out of her, until his arms were red with blood. They were, they were" – and now his voice I could just barely hear – "they were still laughing when they went away."

172

She died in the night, on a bier within a makeshift tent where I had carried her, inert. I could not stop the blood. I put my head between her bleeding legs and treated with the blood to stop but it flowed on over my head and down my face, stinging my eyes. I was anointed by her blood and I taste again now, taste the taste of my tears tempering the blood of Similce my wife.

When she was dead, she simply slipped away, I lay down on top of her and ran my fingers up and down her ravaged sides, through her matted bloody hair, my face buried in her neck. I did not sleep. I also died. There are so many forms of death.

I heard from very far away, it seemed, the call of "Hannibal", insistent, soft. He did not often call me by my name. I was up and pulled him down and I was straddling him in one movement, a knee on each of his shoulders and my dagger drawn. I still believe I would have killed him, but for those eyes, those mute, those trusting eyes and then not resisting he reached his chin out to expose his throat. I looked and looked, blood booming in my ears. I dropped the dagger, started hitting, pounding at him, screaming at him, "Why, Why, Why?"

The frenzy passed. I felt inutterably weary, winnowed, worn. I sat back on his belly, closed my eyes and Maharbal began to talk, a monotone. "I saw them break away, most of one maniple. They must have been *hastati*. They were young. I saw them climb the bank but I was fighting by the river. I had been unhorsed. There were many Romans round me. And I knew that you had left a squadron of your Guard behind. I saw no danger from a hundred Romans marching to their death."

"But you must have seen me go, Maharbal, you must have seen me go, and then the Guard!" I cried out, squeezing tight my eyes, fighting with the pain.

He took the fingers of my right hand in his. Level, truthful: "No, *anda*, no. I neither saw nor heard. I saw only Romans to kill. Hannibal, I, I – "

I knew. He loved her too. He loved me. It was I. I who had killed Similce. Control, command, communicate. I had failed in these. I had failed my wife and that which now began was in atonement for that failure, for that hurt.

"Did you take any prisoners?" I whispered to Maharbal below me. You see, it was only vengeance that brought me back, that saved me.

"Yes, many. Should I – "

Unseeing, my eyes open now were staring ahead. "Go and bring them here."

There were more than 400. I ordered a hundred of our men to dig the pit. I did not stop the many more who also dug, unbidden, all that day and through the night by torches as I stood unwashed and watched. It was a deep pit and a dark one, as my mind. We castrated those Roman prisoners, four men holding, one man cutting. I did not need to give the order for them, moaning, to be thrown into the pit. I did order that each man of my army throw down on them some earth. Then above those immolated Romans quickly next we built a pyre. We left Similce burning on it and we went from that place, setting on our solitary way.

I ceased to be a man. Emptiness clutched and seized me. I ate, I drank, I slept, I pissed, I crapped, I gave commands but I felt nothing, nothing. As if from far away I can remember many things, but they do not matter. Victumulae, that matters because I am ashamed of what I did there. No, that is wrong. I am not ashamed for me. I am ashamed for man.

We needed food, recruits and gold and horses, many things. All these we got at Victumulae. But there I also fed the yaw of my revenge. I spared the Italians of that town I sacked when I was making for the Apennines, for Rome. I sent them to their homes, saying I had no quarrel with them, that I had come to liberate them and their kind from the tyranny of Rome. But there were many Romans in Victumulae, merchants, tax-collectors, clerks. I remember looking at them herded in the town's small square, remember how the hate I let it grow.

She was small. Her hair was brown, her face was oval, her shift was wool and blue. It was her belly. I saw her pregnant belly. I said to Maharbal beside me: "Find me more of them, any who are pregnant. Have all the rest impaled." For many years after Similce's death I barely spoke but to give orders. I was never disobeyed.

We were ready to leave. There were eight pregnant Roman women, each held for me by four of my Guard. Four limbs, four Similce's staked limbs. I shook the vision off. I used my dagger. In that square, surrounded by the impaled, writhing Romans I cut into those pregnant Roman women as you cut into the half of a melon, cutting out the fruit. Neat and quick I cut and I pulled out from them their foetuses, for Fuabal, for Similce, for my pain. I left them lying in the dirt, among the buzzing flies, the vultures wheeling in the sky, eight dying Roman foetuses bound to their dying mothers by their throbbing cords.

I was inviolable, invincible, immune. Man can be a god. I know, for I have been one, a god of blood and death. I was cold, efficient, clear, infectious. Even Maharbal, bubbling Maharbal changed, living in the shadow of my darkness. He scouted. He brought me reports. We marched on, south, to Rome.

The elephants were sick with fever, all but one, the giant bull we knew as Surus. We left the sick to die. Many bones mark the ways of Hannibal. When people have asked me by which route I crossed the Alps, I have always said: "Go and look. Look for the bones."

It shows me what I was then when I say that I felt nothing when Belleus also died. If life is nothing, what is death? It was his heart, Maharbal said. I knew that I had over-reached him when I pursued Sempronius. "Shall we bury Belleus?" Castello asked me. I simply stared at him until he turned away. And then I mounted Surus and rode on at the van.

I knew all about the Romans, the Romans famous for their bravery. Each day my army and my information grew, from deserters, mostly auxiliary Celts and Ligurians. The Romans were skulking, Scipio at Ariminum, Sempronius at Arretium. Both, I learned, had been given fresh legions and had recalled those of their troops that they had sent against the Boii. Under Magalus, 2,000 of the Boii joined me. "We have killed many Romans, Hannibal," Magalus boasted to me when he came.

"Not enough," I replied, and I dismissed him.

Many of our horses now were sick again with mange, showing great patches of hairless, suppurating skin. I did not care. I would have marched on, through the winter.

We had camped in and around some little village in Liguria, I cannot now recall its name. I was asleep. Castello woke me. "Hannibal, a troop of Gauls are looting, raping, drunk." For the last of these alone I crucified the thirty men. But it was the four women raped that stopped me. Even now I savour that irony. I have been as cruel as any man. I have done everything that any man could do to wound and to hurt Rome and Romans, but never, never since that thing they did to Similce did I forgive rape.

The rapes made me see I could not march on Rome with a rabble, ill-disciplined, untrained. I turned. We went to winter quarters at Bologna to the east, the capital of the Boii. We built proper barracks, exercise grounds. I trained my men without mercy. Those who were inferior, I dismissed. Tribesmen came, asking to join us. The small, the old I turned away. When we left Bologna in the spring, I had again an army, a new army of Ligurians and Celts and some Etruscans, at its core the old. This, the second army that I made, was an army of the coldness and the pitilessness of what was then my ruthless heart. Before Bologna, I would have marched on Rome alone.

I heard from my brothers. I had almost forgotten them, since the Trebia and, and what happened there. I scanned the report:

"Hearing that the Romans were planning to land a fleet at Cartakhena, we returned there . . . We left half our force under Ezena's command. He, and we, grew in confidence when you were no longer there to guide us . . ." The attempt at humour, if that is what it was, was lost on me. "Sent Ezena north of the Ebro . . . strategic reasons . . . town of Cissa his base." Cissa? Yes, inland of Emporiae. As good a place as any, I supposed. I would, I think, have chosen Emporiae myself. But I had left my brothers only the baldest instructions: hold Spain. Otherwise, I had discounted it. By the time the Romans could make any impression there, I would be at the gates of Rome.

"But, under Gnaeus Scipio, the Romans landed at Emporiae, not Cartakhena. We had been deceived . . . they marched on Cissa . . . Ezena defeated, killed . . . Spanish chieftains taken as hostages . . ." I groaned. Rome, Rome. I was still so far from Rome. I had an inspection to do. I almost read no more. But the hand changed from that I had recognised as Mago's, bookish Mago's, to one I had not seen before: Hasdrubal's.

"Thinking you would not want this slight to go unavenged, brother, and having learned from you the pleasures of winter campaigning, I marched from Cartakhena with four syntagmata. We crossed the Ebro and attacked the Romans as they were marching back to Emporiae . . . chose my ground . . . Romans routed, heavy losses . . ." Well, well! I thought. I almost chuckled, the first lightness I had felt since, since Similce – died. So the soldiering blood of the Barcas is not confined to me!

I called Castello. "The troops are wait – "

"I know. But read this." Castello frowned. "Of course." The despatch was in Punic. "Get Bostar to translate it for you. Then pass the word that even the scholar Hasdrubal has seen off Rome."

When I returned from my inspection, Maharbal was back from a reconnaissance. He was toying with a plate of stew.

Neither of us had much will for food. "They're still there, at Arriminum and Arretium."

I nodded. "Thank you." I went to my tent, shut the flap. I took out maps. Arriminum and Arretium were so obvious, guarding the routes to Rome, the first on the Adriatic, the second south of the easy central passes through the Apennines.

I called Magalus, who knew the country, and Castello and Maharbal. I pointed at a town called Pistoia, at a route between Ariminum and Arretium and down beyond the river Arno. "We will go this way. Any questions?"

"Yes, it's impossible, Hannibal!" Magalus exclaimed. "There are trackless marshes. We cannot – " My look silenced him. There was a burning madness in my eyes through all those years.

"Trackless, Magalus? We know where Rome is."

There was only one more comment, from Castello. "You cannot leave two Roman armies at your back."

"I won't leave them, Castello," I said. "I will lead them. Now, strike camp."

Magalus was almost right about the marshes. I remember well those stinking, steaming marshes and their seething flies. I did not care. My army followed, bound to my will. I did not care about the men and horses drowning in the sucking mud. I did not care about the pain as I was losing my left eye. Weeping sickness, Magalus called it, transmitted by the flies. I welcomed the pain, the throbs and pulsations of the pain. Savouring, I licked with thickened tongue the puss that went on streaming from that eye. It is as close as I have come to the enjoyment of food. "Come, come, you cannot reach me," that is what I said to pain. I wondered if it was like the pain Similce felt.

I squeezed the rotting eyeball out myself, pressing with my thumbs before the men who told me I could not go on. I stuffed the empty socket with a piece of cloth. It oozed for days, blood drying on my beard among the flies and in the sun. It bleeds less than Similce bled, I thought. I ordered it to stop. I shrugged off Bostar and his poultices. It seemed right, as it does now, that Hannibal should be denied two eyes. I have seen and known enough with one.

We captured four Roman scouts before the town called Faesulae. I made them talk myself. They told me of the new consuls for the year, Flaminius and Servilius, the former now with the army at Arretium.

"And where is Scipio, Publius Scipio?"

"He has been sent to reinforce his brother in Spain."

"*Quot milites*, how many men?"

They said they didn't know.

"*Et aliquid novi apud Siciliam*, and what is happening in Sicily?" My Latin has improved since then.

Again, they said they didn't know. I believed them. Anyway, I didn't really care.

Between Faesolae and Arretium were rich and fertile farms. I burned them all, slaughtered all the animals we could not eat or herd. It took time. I sensed Maharbal's impatience when I sent a troop of my Guard, no less, to round up some steers that had broken away. "People who are hungry cannot fight," I told Maharbal. And then I led my army right under Flaminius' nose. Of course he followed me south. They marched so slowly, Romans, with their proper camps and kitchens each night, that I had to slow our march. We passed Cortona.

I rode ahead to reconnoitre. The lake I saw was called Lake Trasimene. I left Maharbal and 4,000 infantry as rearguard to draw the Romans on. I led the rest of my army on at a proper pace. We had part of that day and a whole night to prepare.

On the north side of the lake there is a narrow valley, almost a gorge. The Romans followed Maharbal in. I have heard it said there was a deep mist that morning, that Flaminius would not have entered such a trap if he had seen it. That is a lie. The day was sparkling, clear.

I gave only two orders in that battle. The first, three flashes of the bronze mirror in my hand to each side sealed the valley, west and east: a syntagma of heavy Spanish infantry at each end, their line ten deep. Nothing could break through. The second, three more flashes a hundred heartbeats later, sent my army charging down both hillsides on the Romans, still in their column of march, below.

The Romans could not form their line. Their legionaries did not have the room. I heard the battle. Even the sound it gave was trapped. I saw it. The Cenomenians were lethal with their axes on the first rows of bunched and herded Romans, as were the screaming Celts, naked to the waist, swinging, hacking with their cutlasses. On those in the middle my slingers from both sides kept up a steady rain of murdering stones and the close-packed Romans could not even raise their shields for shelter. Thousands fell, with neither sword drawn nor *pilum* thrown.

I watched, I studied, cold, detached. If I had done that at the Trebia . . . I defied the thought to grow. As the ranks of Romans thinned, those left managed to form their maniples on the bodies of the dead. Nine of these locked shields and broke out, marching up the southern hillside of the valley. They cannot have known about the lake. I did not have to signal. Magalus took his Gauls, went after them. He simply drove them into the lake, he reported to me later, and let them drown.

We killed more than 15,000 Romans on that day. I know. We counted as we stripped them. An Insubrian Gaul – was Ducarius his name? – brought me the head of Flaminius. That is why despite my doubts I had taken on those Insubrians when they came to me before I crossed the Arno. Their lands I knew had been ravaged by Rome. I thought that they would want revenge. I know its power.

I sat that evening to eat with the head of Flaminius in front of me on the ground. As was usual, Bostar brought his plate to eat beside me. We often talked then, planned. He was walking towards me when he saw the head. He stiffened, stopped and turned away. "Bostar!" I called. "Where are you going?" Those around me fell silent.

"I prefer to eat with the living, Hannibal."

"But we have killed a consul, Bostar, a Roman consul!"

He took two steps towards me. "You have killed one. There will be many more. Now, may I go?"

I nodded. He went. Perhaps I should have reprimanded him and made him stay, but his views could not affect the men. They were exultant. I heard them talk, joke about the spoils they would take from Rome. They didn't understand Bostar. Nor, then, did I.

We took no prisoners at Lake Trasimene, not even from the *extraordinarii*, the allies. Such were my orders. But prisoners we got, unexpectedly, the next day. We were stripping the Roman dead, burying our own, though they were few. Pickets I had stationed to the north rode up, two Numidians, men and horses sweating from their ride. "A Roman column. Cavalry," one panted.

"How many?"

"Four thousand, perhaps more." It had to be the vanguard of the second consular army under Servilius. Maharbal was close to me. I was enjoying my work among the dead, the dead broad foreheads, dead brown and staring eyes of Roman dead, imagining that such as these had raped Similce. I cut the nose off the one below me. I threw it to the ravens. I wiped the blood off my dagger on my sleeve. "Go, *anda*," I said. "Take all the cavalry." There were 8,000. Most had been well trained. They had not been needed at Lake Trasimene.

He brought back 1,800 prisoners the next day, hands tied on their horses. "The horses are fresh and sound, Hannibal. That's why I – "

I cut him off. "I understand." I questioned the praetor in

command myself. His name was Caius Centenius. I had no need of torture. He was so arrogant, so confident.

"You will be crushed, Carthaginian, crushed." I let him have his say. I learned much from him, of Roman dispositions, plans, before I cut his tongue out and before I next put out his eyes. "Now, Roman," I whispered in his ear as he lay blubbering on the ground, "Now you will not be able to tell how you met Hannibal, nor see the ruins he will leave of Rome." I gestured to Maharbal. "Give him a horse and an escort. See that he gets to Rome. And Maharbal. Many of his men are *extraordinarii*, not Romans. Let them go." His jaw dropped. "We have come to set them free, Maharbal, not make prisoners of them. Tell them to go to their homes and spread the word that Hannibal is bringing to an end the tyranny of Rome."

Rome, Rome. Many have asked me why I did not march on Rome after Trasimene. I have had faults, like any man, but I have never been a fool. I knew I had to break the Roman confederacy. So far, not a single Italian town or city had declared itself for me. For allies I had only Gauls I did not trust. And my army was small, barely 40,000 men. Rome had, I knew from Centenius, ten legions already raised and armed, far more than double my number, and garrisons in many towns fortified and strong. And I had to break, I knew, the Roman mind. Trebia and Trasimene, these were nothing like enough. "Well, am I a Pyrrhus?" I had asked Bostar after Trasimene.

"You are Pyrrhus after Heraclea. May you not have an Asculum to come."

When I heard from deserters a week later of what had been announced in Rome about Lake Trasimene, I knew that I was right. The people were expecting a long speech, an explanation. "*Pugna magna victi sumus* – we have been defeated in a great battle," that is all the praetor, Marcus Pomponius, said of

Trasimene, and then he left the Rostra, that is what I heard.

Bostar simply nodded when I told him. "Yes, that is the Roman mind," he said.

"The mind that I shall break, Bostar, break."

Then there was Rome itself. I knew of its mighty walls. Yes, I could have built the seige equipment, but as Silenus had said to me many years before, only a fool learns from his own mistakes. Demetrius Poliorcetes. He it was I thought of, his mistake I learned from. A hundred years before my time he had sought to beseige Rhodes. He took with him the whole panoply of seigecraft and yet he failed, because Rhodes continued to be supplied by sea. Rome could be supplied from Ostia. I had no fleet. For this alone, for many other reasons, no, I did not march on Rome.

Is this the truth? That was the reasoning of my conscious mind. Another part of me had yet to hold the funeral it craved, the funeral of Similce. And so I gave to her the greatest funeral ever known, the funeral of Cannae. And that same reason is perhaps why I ignored the news from Carthage.

Bomilcar's messenger had taken two months to find me, even though a galley had taken him to Genua. "I went west first, Hannibal. I did not think – "

"Whatever you thought, you thought wrong. But now do your job at last. Did Rurio reach Sicily? Is it held?"

The man blushed, fidgeted with his hands.

"Speak, man!"

"Hannibal, Rurio and his men are in Carthage. Or at least – "

"In Carthage!" I exploded. "At whose command?"

"Bomilcar's, or rather the Council's. They feared an attack from Rome."

"Any attack from Rome will come through Sicily, you fool! Does Bomilcar know nothing?"

It wasn't worth the effort. I would give them Rome. In fact,

I learned, Bomilcar had sent some of my men away, but to Sardinia, insignificant Sardinia. Apparently some Sardinians had revolted against Rome and appealed to Carthage for help. "That is what we gave them," said the messenger proudly.

"How many of the Council have estates there, eh?" I gave him back. I was suddenly tired. "Go back to Carthage. Tell Bomilcar that I said Sicily is the key. No, don't bother. Tell him that of Rome's many heads, I will chop off the foremost. If he could spare me a fleet, my task would be easier."

"But, but – "

"Yes, I know." What was the point. " 'Carthage needs her fleet for trade and for her own defence.' Leave me."

I shut Carthage out of my mind. Let others record my ravaging of Umbria, then southwards the same in Apulia, Luceria, Arpi and Campania, followed by Fabius, appointed dictator by the Romans, Fabius and his four legions who would not fight. It was as well. I was brooding, healing. My dreams of Similce began to ease. I did not want to fight – yet.

Castello did. I sensed his impatience. We were riding together on our march across the Ager Falernus. Many were the farms of vines and olives we destroyed. "This is the richest land in Italy," Castello said, "and Fabius just lets it burn." I looked back, saw the dust of Fabius' army following. Castello spat. "This Fabius is a woman!"

"If he is, Castello," I said, "he is a wise one."

I knew from many sources that Fabius was winning the Romans time. They were reinforcing Rome, I heard, breaking down the bridges over the Tiber, repairing walls. They were raising new legions. By refusing battle, Fabius had not won, perhaps. But neither had he lost.

Fabius' tactics suited me well. "Do you have apples trees at your home in Spain, Castello?" I asked.

"What? Yes, but – "

"When do you eat the apples?"

184

"Why, when" – poor Castello was even more puzzled – "when they're ripe, of course."

"Exactly. Castello, we must let Rome's apple ripen before we bite."

We were not ripe either. That is why I too waited. Each day I hoped for a Roman town to open its gates to me. Epicydes had cousins in Capua. I had sent him there, with gold. His reports were hopeful, encouraging. I did not burn the lands of Capua in Campania – nor, later, the estates that belonged to Fabius.

That is because I had a plan. From scouts, deserters, spies, I knew all about Fabius' colleague and Master of Horse, Marcus Minutius Rufus. He was another hothead. When I fought, I wanted to fight someone like him, not Fabius. I hoped that Fabius would be dismissed.

So we burned. Burned, and worked. I worked hard at drilling my army as we wandered at our will. I had four syntagmata armed with the Roman arms we took at Trasimene. I trained those men and trained them until they knew those weapons as well as they knew themselves.

Maharbal did the same with the horses captured after Trasimene. They were small, but sturdy and adapted quickly to our ways. Month after month, Fabius' scouts watched us training. Ours never reported much activity in the Roman army. "Perhaps they do not need to train," said Castello.

"Perhaps," I replied. "But we do."

At Teanum Fabius at last acted. He tried to trap me. Even then I did not fight. I drove away his legion blocking the valley of my encampment not with men but with oxen, 2,000 maddened oxen, faggots tied and burning on their horns, in the middle of the night. Then we slipped away. I had the oxen rounded up later. We fed on them all through that winter as I waited, as I grew. "Remember the cow that you are eating is a cow from which the Romans ran," I used to tell the men. They were confident, relaxed, well fed and paid. There was no shortage of good things in Italy. I even agreed, eventually, to some camp-followers for the men. I left Castello to arrange it. The Balearic slingers were especially grateful, I heard.

I teased the Romans from time to time, of course, in part to keep my men sharp. Twice I used my Numidians. We would strike camp and march away, the Numidians lying concealed, having taken their positions in the night. Fabius would follow me. The Numidians, under Maharbal, would sting the Romans in the rear.

Then, I heard, Fabius had been recalled to Rome to justify his tactics, the fiasco of Teanum. Minutius was in command. I was almost ready, laying my plans with Castello and Maharbal when Minutius actually attacked one of my foraging parties.

The Romans hailed this as a great victory, it was said. They had killed thirty of my men. But Minutius was promoted to joint command with Fabius, who returned. "We have missed our chance, Hannibal," Maharbal said.

"Perhaps," I replied.

But then, we learned, Minutius and Fabius had divided their command. Two legions each. We were near the town of Larinum. Minutius and Fabius had formed two separate camps. I was still brooding, healing, dreaming of Similce, but I thought that it was time to make the Romans dance.

I reconnoitred myself, alone. In front of Minutius' camp there was a hill, around that broken ground. Perfect! I thought. I even chuckled at the prospect, the first lightness of heart that I had felt since, since – No, Hannibal, no.

That night I sent Castello and 800 infantry to the hill, Maharbal and four syntagmata to the broken ground. "Don't worry, Hannibal. They won't see us. We'll look like bushes." There was an excitement to us all.

"Don't just look like bushes, Maharbal, be them!"

In the morning early, Minutius responded to the sight and noises of Castello on the hill. At first, he was cautious, committing only few but, as he saw them die, more and more, at last a whole legion, now the second coming forward to swamp the rises of that hill.

Only then I signalled. The trap was sprung. As Maharbal engaged the surprised Romans on their flanks and from their rear, I sent two more syntagmata forward from our camp nearby. I was tempted to join them. It is as well I stayed on that high ground.

Just in time I saw them, Fabius' legions, coming from the north. We would be massively outnumbered. My best troops were now engaged. They would be taken from behind. No silent signals now. "Ride, ride!" I called to my trumpeters. "Sound the retreat!"

Fabius did not pursue us. We had lost 300 men. "Not as many as the Romans, *anda!*" Maharbal exclaimed. His high spirits were returning. I did not say so, but I knew that I was glad.

"You were right, Hannibal," is all Castello said. "The apple was a little sour."

I went to Cannae because we needed food. It was a major Roman store. We ate our fill as, my scouts reported, both consular armies were approaching under their new consuls Varro and Aemilius with instructions to engage. Dictatorship was ended. Of Fabius and Minutius, I heard no more.

I did not worry when I learned the consuls' armies had been doubled, each four legions strong. I was used to being out-numbered. I cancelled drill and musters. "Let the men relax," I ordered. I liked to walk among them, dozing in the summer sun. I knew a deadly calm. It was time. I called in all of my commanders. I explained, I set out my orders, I went through them again, again.

And not just with my commanders. As the Romans drew up on the north side of the river Aufidus, I had my plan of battle passed by each *dekadarchos* to their men. I felt their confidence, as they mine. I was standing with Castello that early evening in front of my Spanish infantry in the centre of our line, looking across the level ground to the massing Romans. The men behind me joked and gossiped, played with dice.

"They are very many, Hannibal," Castello said.

"They are, Castello, they are," I replied. My one eye passed along the Roman line. I remember wanting to itch the empty socket of the second. It still tries to follow its neighbour, even though it is not there. There came to me the first true warmth I had felt since the night Similce died. "But there is one thing you haven't thought of, Castello," I said. "In all those Romans, there is not one whose name is Castello."

He burst into laughter, slapped his knee. I heard the story passed among the men all through that night, heard the guffaws of appreciation. That was the spirit of Cannae.

The battle itself is well recorded. I believe they study it at military schools. Our line followed the river. I preferred the safety of knowing I could not be taken from the rear to the danger of being pushed into the Aufidus.

Again, I had my men fed in the small hours of the morning. I sent my Numidians across the ground between the armies at first light. As I had hoped, Varro sent his *velites* to meet them – it was his day of command – and from my right wing Maharbal, sweeping with the heavy cavalry, drove them from the field. The Roman maniples advanced.

I was at our centre, with the Spanish infantry. At Cannae I did not stay back to command. I gave the simple order. I led our centre out myself, shield-sheltered from the rain of *pila*, and the Romans met a convex, not a straight line as they knew. We gave them back the unthrown *pila* of Trasimene and many died before our two lines closed. I killed a few who broke my guard but mostly we blocked and parried as I had ordered because what we did was draw them on and just in time we drew back and I still remember now each measured, careful step to make from convex, make a concave line, sucking Romans in.

Maharbal had been waiting, to the west as I had planned. Now he closed the net, his men dismounted, armoured, killing at the Romans' rear. I threw away my shield, far into the close-packed Romans. I had my sword and dagger and I paused, called out "Sim-il-ce!" and my men took up the cry.

The Romans were encircled in the killing fields of Cannae and they died there in their thousands, under a blazing sun for hate and for revenge, for sweet, how sweet revenge.

I love the softness of the belly when my sword is in it, sharp. I love the quick cut of the dagger to the neck. I have known the poetry of death. That is what I most remember now of Cannae, that and the coursing sweat under my helmet and my armour all that long day of death. My sword broke on Roman armour. I took another, then an axe. For each Roman that I killed I thought there are now more Romans without father, husband, friend. We fought and killed for hours, for a lifetime, until there were no Romans left to die and stretching all around and far beyond me as the sun sank were the piles of Roman dead.

Italy was mine.

VIII

DELAY

Perhaps it was exhaustion. Perhaps no man should ever know such power. Perhaps it was the darkness I had lived in for so long. Perhaps it was the wounds I had not noticed as I fought.

I left my men shouting, cheering, splashing in the river to be clean. Alone I waded across the Aufidus, alone walked to our empty camp. I took off then my dented helmet, my hands caked and crusted red with Roman blood. I lay down on some hides. They were brown and mottled. For an hour, a lifetime, I dreamed and dozed.

"So, Hannibal, you have won." A voice, Bostar's soft voice, deep.

I turned my head to him. "Yes, Bostar, I have won." I sat up, stiff and sore. I noticed I was bleeding, bleeding from my belly, arms and legs. I thought of Similce's blood. Should her spirit not now be at peace? Now had she not crossed beyond Ashroket's further bank?

I heard the sounds of victory. The men were singing now, snatches of singing borne to me on the evening breeze. Victory?

My tears were sudden, silent, thick, stinging the cuts and scratches on my face. The words came wrenched from a part of me I had not known was there. My voice was level, steady. It was the only way to deal with a pain beyond what I could bear. The pain was not of the body, but the mind. "But now I see, Bostar, there is, there is – " I could not admit.

"There is?" His gentleness was ineluctable.

"There is a thing worse than a battle lost."

"Yes? And what is that, Hannibal?" He knew. He knew, he had to draw the pain. I should have burst without him.

"Worse than a battle lost, Bostar, there is a battle won."

190

Only Bostar knows how I then wept, racked, convulsed by tearing sobs. He took me in his arms. In time, I lay back, spent. He began to treat the wounds of my body. "None are deep. But these other wounds, Hannibal," I heard him say, "these I cannot heal."

I lost something at Cannae, something I did not know was mine to lose, something I have never found. I lost the capacity to change, the innocence and the humility of change.

There was a moment, though, a moment. It was dark. I heard the horse hooves drumming. "*Anda, anda!*" Maharbal calling, calling me back to the world.

"What world?" Hannibal asked himself.

"The world," answered another Hannibal, "the world that you have made."

"But I did not know what I was making!"

"What you now have learned, you have now learned."

Maharbal was breathless, urgent, now dismounted. "The Roman camp, Hannibal! The men are looting the Roman camp! They have wine and women. You must come!"

I could not let Maharbal see me weak. That is why I went. I came back from a different and I fear a better place and to the Roman camp I went. Thirty-five years have followed in their bloodshed and their hate because I, Hannibal, great Hannibal, because I could not be just a man.

Seeing me, the men gave off their looting. They surrounded me, jostling, cheering, until they heard the menace in my voice. "Who is responsible?" I asked in Punic, then louder again in Iberian, then Greek. My head was pounding, my wounds were sore. A *loxarchos* I recognised stepped forward.

"Hannibal, it started with my men. I thought – "

"I don't care what you thought!" I snapped. "You deal with them. Then I will deal with you. You know what is ordained. Maharbal, burn this place."

"But Hannibal, those wagons, those oxen!"

"Burn it, Maharbal. Burn it all."

The habit and demands of command took over, and masked my empty heart. Was I not born to this? We were four days counting, stripping first the thousands of the allies then seven times 7,000 Roman dead. Seven for my marriage. Seven for my marriage's revenge. Revenge was sweet. Revenge was bitter. I heard the cheers, the laughter when a dead senator, a praetor, even one of the consuls' cadavers was found. "Where were his wounds?" I asked Castello when he came to tell me.

"Why, there were many: in the chest and neck and arms."

"None on his back?"

"No, none."

"Then he died an honourable death, fighting for his country."

Castello spat. "Pah! He was a Roman." Castello was taller than me. I had to reach to grab the tunic at his neck and pull his face to mine and say so soft to him, "Castello, he was a man."

It was in such a mood that I rode out alone. For hours I rode through country deserted, away from Cannae and its blood. I heard the sound of laughter and of shrieking. I dismounted, followed the noise up a wooded rise.

Below me was a gentle river. Shielded by the trees, I saw them playing in the water, a young Italian peasant and a girl, both perhaps sixteen. The girl ran out from the water, naked, sparkling in the sun. I saw her nubile breasts, firm belly. I felt the promise and the power and the pathos of the young. The boy chased her. They ran down the bank, beyond where I could see them, but their laughter lingered long.

That is why I did what I then did. It was to flame again my will, to stamp out the pity in me, pity not for Romans but for man. It was to resume the old, rather than face the terrors of the new. I was afraid to leave the Hannibal that had been for a Hannibal who might not be.

I knew the trees which, cut, would serve as chopping

boards. I knew the axes of the Gauls and Cenomenians were perfect for the job. Still we were a long time, chopping off the hands of 20,000 of the Roman dead. "How many prisoners do we have, Maharbal?" I asked when it was done.

"At least 6,000, perhaps more."

"Bring a thousand here. Add their hands to those." I gestured to the wagons loaded with the hands of dead men, blood running through the wagons' boards and down their wheels. Similce's blood was much more red. "Then bind their stumps. Send them with the wagons to Rome. Tell them to give this message: 'Hannibal the Carthaginian returns to Rome two of her eight legions that he has destroyed.'"

Was this the action of a madman? Was this the fruit of hate? It is so hard to know. My mind was cracked and slipping and, save Bostar, there was none to know. What could I say to Maharbal, to Castello, to so many men? That because I had won a great battle, I could not go on?

It was in my loneliness after Cannae that I turned to my home. Was it my home? I did not, do not know. I had none other than that city shown to a boy by his father long before. "Never, Hannibal, never ignore her when she calls." I thought that she was calling me. I called to her with rings, four bushels of gold Roman rings that I ordered gathered from dead hands of Roman knights alone at Cannae. I sent those rings to Carthage by a ship that we had captured in the small port of Salapia, near to Cannae. I sent a Ligurian with those rings and with my message. Fierelus was his name. I had to send my message by his mouth, this I remember, because my hands were stiff and swollen from the grip of Cannae's many weapons, many dead. I could not hold a stylus.

"Tell Carthage that I greet her," I told Fierelus. "Tell the Elders of everything that we have done. Say that I need money and need men. But most of all, tell them, I need ships. If they give me ships, be sure you tell them, I will give them Rome."

He turned to go. "And Fierelus," I called him back. "Bring news to me of Silenus." He looked puzzled. Of course, how could he know Silenus. He had only joined me after the Trebia. "Silenus of Caleacte. He was my tutor. Ask for him," I said. "There will be many who will know."

I was seeing to the stacking of the Roman weapons that had come to us from Cannae. The messenger of the northern Boii was a savage. I remember how he scratched and stank. "Two legions, near Modena, dead." His rank and toothless grin. "We caught them in the forests. We all drank from the victory cup, made from the praetor's skull."

Another, smaller Cannae. Surely Rome must yield. I sent to her a hundred Roman prisoners as message. The ransom I asked for the rest of them, 5,000, was a token, nothing more. Why, was I to beg?

The whole century returned in three days. Rome cannot have listened to them long. The Senate had replied, they said, that Rome had no need of such poor soldiers as Hannibal now held. I repeated that message to myself: Rome had no need of such poor soldiers as Hannibal now held.

"Why have you returned," quiet I asked them at last, "with a reply such as this! Do you not fear death?"

Their centurion met mine with an honest, simple gaze. "*Civis Romanus sum* – I am a citizen of Rome," is all he said. Before Cannae, I would have killed him. Now, I set him free.

I should not have held a council after these things, in that still shifting mind. But the aftermath of Cannae was over, our dead burnt or buried, our wounded treated, our order restored. I knew the troops were getting restive. I heard the talk of "Rome, now Rome!"

Maharbal began the talking. "In five days, Hannibal," he said, "you will be sitting in the Capitol of Rome." His face was flushed and proud before me, among Castello and the *loxarchoi*.

The awning under which we sat was flapping in the wind. Even now I hear it, flapping, flapping, flapping in the tunnels of my mind.

I should have explained; our lack of ships, of seigecraft. I should have said that 40,000 men could not begin to invest Rome. Not even Alexander, that is what I should have said, not even golden Alexander would have tried. But was I now not greater then Alexander?

Or should I just have told them that I did not have the will, that I had found the pith of my revenge?

I stood there before them, these men that I had brought across the Alps to destroy Rome. I said softly "No," that one word "No."

Maharbal was on his feet. His voice was loud and angry. Never before, never had he challenged me. "I see the gods do not give to one man all the gifts they have, Hannibal. You know how to win a victory. But you do not know, Hannibal, how to use it." He turned, and stormed away.

Castello and the others sat, bewildered. "I, I am — " What was I going to say? That I was sorry? "Castello, full drill for all the men. Issue as many as you can with Roman arms. We will speak again. Now go."

I went to find Maharbal. I wanted to explain, to share. I wanted, I needed his help. I found him in the horse lines, lying drinking, drunk. He wanted to forget, he said, forget. I understand that now. I did not then.

"Forget, Maharbal, forget? The weak forget. The strong remember."

"Then go, strong Hannibal," my *anda* slurred, "go and be strong. Remember for us both."

I found Bostar in his tent. He was working on a map. I sat down beside him. "Do you remember, Bostar, how I asked you for a map of the Roman mind? Now I need one of my own."

"What is in your mind, Hannibal?" I looked up, away. I felt, I –

"Nothing, everything, I, I don't know, Bostar. I don't know what to do. For the first time in my life, I don't know what to do."

Bostar rolled up his map. He turned to me. "Don't know what to do, Hannibal? Or is it that you don't know why to do it?"

"I know neither. I have done what I was born to do. Now, I think I could destroy Rome. The seige would be long, but there are other ways. And Carthage, surely now Carthage will help."

"Do not look to Carthage, Hannibal. Look into yourself. What do you see there?"

Even the question was strange to me. I thought of the story that Honesty has her dwelling in a high place, above rocks difficult to climb, and she is not to be looked on by every mortal, but only by he who, with clenched concentration and sweat, climbs to the peak. "I see fear, Bostar," I said at last.

"Of what?"

"Fear of things I don't understand, things I haven't even considered."

"Such as?"

"Assume we do march now on Rome. Yes, she still has six legions in Italy. I could deal with them, and then Rome would yield, yes?"

"Perhaps, Hannibal, perhaps. Go on."

"But what then? That is what I fear. I fear my own ignorance. I fear myself for never thinking about these things. I have been a soldier, that is all. What would I do with a world without Rome? How would it be governed, and by whom? It is the enormity of what is now before me, Bostar, that is what I fear."

We talked on, late into the night. Owls hooted, flying

downwards in the dark. "Do you know the Greek word *hamartia*, Hannibal, and what it means?"

"Yes," I answered, puzzled. "Error, fault. Silenus told me it implied innocence. Is it not often applied to Oedipus in the Greek tragedies, Oedipus who in all innocence killed his father and married his mother?"

"You were well taught. But not just Oedipus suffered from *hamartia*, from tragic error. Ajax, Orestes, many more did what they did unknowing of the consequences it would bring. You were born to do what you have now done. Yet perhaps now you have a chance to change." I was so weary, so confused. *Hamartia*? "Hannibal, you must sleep now."

"Yes, I must. But what do I do?"

"Wait. It is all you can do. Do not seek the answer. When the answer is ready, it will come to you."

So I waited. I marched my army unopposed through Samnium and on into Campania. Towns and cities opened to me their gates. The men ceased to talk so much of Rome. Maharbal and Castello barely spoke to me at all. I did not mind. They carried out my orders. I started to have seige equipment built, to bolster a belief I was not sure I had. At least each month, I wrote to Carthage. I heard nothing back.

I ceased to be a soldier. What did I become? I would like to think that I became a statesman, an administrator. But that is not true. I became no more than a pedlar, a market hawker. The truth is that I wandered as I waited, like Odysseus, to reach my home.

My hair turned grey after Cannae. The weeks and months slipped by. Some things I remember clearly. A port. I needed to have a port. I tried Puteoli. I remember how they stood and, silent, watched me from their walls. I sent an emissary in, an Etruscan. "Tell them I have come to liberate them from Rome," I told him. Their reply was simple. It was, the man said, a Roman proverb. "*Non generant aquilae columbas* – eagles do not beget doves."

I marched on along the coast to Neapolis. They met me with a hail of arrows. I rounded up the peasants from the neighbouring farms. I had them disembowelled in the stream that ran into the city, under its walls. I waited for three days. They sent a message. "The citizens of Neapolis thank Hannibal the Carthaginian for polluting their water. They have turned to their springs and cisterns sooner than they had thought. The water is sweet and cool."

I burned everything. Every hovel, every stubble field, every olive tree and vine. My men were sullen, restive, hungry. So was I. Can you imagine how it was, to have been conqueror of Cannae and find that you had conquered nothing at all? I knew where the Romans were, waiting, watching, silent. I was a Pyrrhus, a Pyrrhus who had won a battle but was losing a war, a war of the mind.

Maharbal was hardly ever off a horse, not since that night after the council when I would not march on Rome. He grew gaunt and haunted, thin. Each report he brought was an accusation. I knew he knew: I still had no answer.

Still I did not hear from Carthage. The winter rains began, the winds. Epicydes came. Whether through gold or conviction, I did not care, but Capua offered herself to Hannibal. Capua at least turned her back on Rome. That cheered the men. That bought me time.

I disliked Capua from the first moment that I saw its marble glisten in a weakening, fitful sun. Their Elders oozed and fawned upon me when I walked through their gates. They gave a banquet in my honour. Had I been in Capua a day, a week, a month? The courses were interminable. I ate little, but I could not stop my hosts' exulting explanations. Sea-hedgehogs, oysters and asparagus, sea-nettles, beccaficoes, chines of roebuck and wild boar, fowls covered with a perfumed paste, potted river fish, leverets, roast fowl, a dish of pike livers, pheasant brains, flamingo-tongues and lamprey-milt, then cakes from, they proudly said, the marshes of Ancona. "They do not even eat like this in Rome," the paunchy, sweating Capuan beside me leered. "Nor do they have the likes of this to please the liberator of Italy."

I remember now his jowls, his hanging fleshy jowls. It was the girl, the dancing girl that followed. I saw only from another banquet long ago another girl, another dance. This was not Similce. This was a harlot, like her city, swinging her sweating, swaying breasts, her heaving hips before me as she danced. It was repulsive to me. And as I saw Castello lick his lips I thought, how many men have known her, nibbled those nipples, shoved their penises inside that pouting mouth? I know, I know the things men do. I have lived more than fifty years with soldiers. I can still remember now those lines of Anakreon that I remembered then, those lines Silenus had taught me and, do you see, I, Hannibal in Capua, I, Hannibal felt suddenly alone and so afraid?

ἀγανῶς οἷά τε νεβρὸν νεοθηλέα
γαλαθηνὸν ὅς τ' ἐν ὕληι κεροέσσης
ἀπολειφθεὶς ἀπὸ μητρὸς ἐπτοήθη.

Gently, like a new-born fawn, dropped but lately, still a nurseling, that is separated from its horned mother in a wood and trembles, terror-struck and dumb.

That is what was in me then. That is everything the dancing girl and Capua was not.

I left that night. I left my army to its wenching and its drinking. Yes, I was allowing even those. How else could I keep my army happy so far from their many homes? "No rape" was my only order. I went to Mount Tifata alone.

I had chosen Tifata for my base before we entered Capua. Its high and grassy plateau sat above the plains, the passes that I had to control. I had my Guard there, watching the Romans watching me. They had another hill-top camp across the valley. I meant to destroy it. When?

The Roman will was waxing as mine waned. I felt its shadow. Did they never even think to yield? Many were the stories brought to me. After Cannae, the Senate issued a prohibition on weeping and wailing. Widows of Cannae were forbidden to mourn. The Romans consulted their gods, their sacred books. They carried out a sacrifice, a human sacrifice. "And they call us barbarians!" I stormed when I heard. Two men, two women were entombed alive on the Capitol of Rome, two Greeks and two Gauls. "What am I fighting?" I demanded of Bostar. "Magic or men?"

"Neither. You know, Hannibal. The Roman mind, the Roman mind."

It was the next morning at Tifata. Maharbal brought them to me, four Romans he had captured on a raid. He was doing that more and more, without even asking. He and some hundred of his beloved Numidians would ride off to scout, to harry and to kill.

These Roman soldiers were different. Their armour was poor, none of the four's the same. "*Estisne milites?*" I asked them, puzzled, "*Are you soldiers?*" They nodded, afraid. "*Auxilarii?*" They had to be.

"*Nullo modo,*" one replied, "Not at all. *Novae legionis servilis sumus*, we are from the new legion of slaves."

"Can this be true?" I asked no-one in particular, "that Rome is raising legions from her slaves?"

One of Maharbal's Numidians spoke out. "So I found out, Hannibal, from a centurion that we – that we did not bring back. The Romans have bought 8,000 healthy slaves from their owners, at public expense. They have released criminals and debtors from prison, and pressed them into service making arms. They – "

I held up a hand to silence him. "Tell me no more. Maharbal, let them go."

"But they are Romans, Hannibal!"

"Romans they may be, Maharbal, but I will not wage war on slaves." A part of me was still trying, I think, to change.

I heard at last from Carthage. Fierelus returned. He bore a long scroll, written again in old proto-Punic. That angered me. Did they not know that each day I heard and spoke Iberian, Numidian, Latin, Greek, Ligurian, Gaulish, even the babble of the Celts? To whom was I to speak the Punic of my boyhood, let alone their Punic of the past? They did not know what Hannibal had become. Is that why I was so angry, or is it that nor did he?

Bostar translated for me. "We have the rings of Cannae lying on the Senate floor, a sign you say of a great victory. And yet you ask for reinforcements, gold and ships. What then would you have asked for having lost, not won? You name the cities in alliance with you, Trebula and Saticula, Telesia, Compsa, Melae, Fulfulae, Orbitanum, Blanda and Aecae. We do not see the name of any Roman no, nor even any Latin towns among them. Our orders were that you should return to Carthage. Instead, you sacked Saguntum and brought on us this war. This Council is divided, but narrowly believes that you must finish what you have begun. We have no ships to send you. We need them for our trade. Take them from the Romans, if your position is so strong. As for men, we are sending 20,000 infantry but not to you, to Spain. That is where the mines and interests of Carthage lie and, we learn, because of you the Romans plan to invade it. For you we can spare 4,000 Numidians and forty elephants. Inform us when you have a port to which these may be sent."

Fierelus had sat throughout Bostar's translation. "What of Silenus?" that is all I asked him more.

"Silenus, Hannibal, is dead."

"I see." I replied to that so calmly. "Where is his grave?"

"None knew of that, Hannibal. Most turned away when I even asked for him. They seemed afraid."

I nodded, dismissed him with my hand. I got up, burned the Elders' scroll, and I was glad to see the ashes grey.

There were silent Roman armies all around me. And yet I won my port. No, I did not. I sent Castello down to Bruttium in the south with half my army. There were no Roman soldiers there. He captured Petelia and sacked it, then Cosentia and Crotona and Locri. There we had our port to which in time there came the help of Carthage, if help is what it was. The elephants were untrained, the Numidians were raw levies. I sighed. How many armies did I have to train? Castello sent a message that at Locri he had captured four Roman galleys. Did I want them sent to blockade Ostia?

Sooner no ships than four, I thought. To blockade Ostia I would need a hundred ships, not four. I told Castello to beach them, leave them guarded, garrison the towns, return to me. By the great and giant elm tree on Ashroket's bank there is a spring, its waters running from the lake of Memory. There are those who stand guard before that spring. Those who wish to cross the river must say to the guards: 'I am a child of the earth and of the starry heavens, but my generation, it is of the sky. You yourselves know this. Now I am dry with thirst and I am dying. Give to me then quickly the water running cold from the lake of Memory.' And they will give you to drink from the sacred water, and you will cross in peace.

Yet the water of my memory of those years after Cannae is not cold and clear but warm and dark. Each day brought more and petty questions. I remember the many deputations, like that of the Atellians. The town of Atella had joined with Capua in welcoming me. They came to see me at Tifata. They wanted to talk to me about coins.

"Coins?" I asked. "You want to talk to me about coins?"

"Yes," their leader said. "We are minting new gold and silver coins, commemorating our alliance with you. We thought to put the face of Hannibal on these coins."

He was so unctuous. I was so weary. He would not meet my eye. I know how people see my sightless eye and look away. So many Roman legions in the field, and they talked of minting coins. "Put whatever you want on your coins," I said. "Now go."

I once saw some of these coins. On one side was the Atellian god Sol, and on the other an elephant. An elephant. All my old elephants were dead. My new were untrained. Carthage had not thought to send me any drivers.

I began to hear regularly from Carthage. Nothing of what they said brought me any cheer. I had kept pressing them — why? from habit? — for men and ships and gold. Bomilcar still held the upper hand. "Your father's war in Spain was self-sustaining. Why is yours not the same?"

"This is not *my* war," I replied. "It is *ours*. To kill a snake, you must cut off its head." But even as I wrote, I felt confusion. I believed what I wrote, but was it true? Whose war was this? It could not be, must not be only mine.

It could have become Philip's war as well. For a week after the ambassadors of Philip, King of Macedon, had left me, I felt elated, strong. Philip had heard of Cannae, said his envoys who came. He too hated Rome. Understandably, I thought. For some time had Rome been sniffing Greece, as dog a heating bitch, expelling Demetrius of Pharos, tinkering in Epirus and Dalmatia. It could not be long before she turned to Macedon and its passes to the north and to the east. Even now, I thought, the Romans would be knocking at Philip's door were I not preoccupying them.

Philip wanted a treaty with me. Was this the answer? A confederacy of those who opposed Rome? There were other kingdoms to the east. I could ignore Carthage!

"Tell Philip that I greet him and I thank him. Tell Philip to come." We discussed the terms of our treaty. I liked those Macedonians. They were blunt, direct. I took a new interest in my army, in their training. I passed the word the Macedonians would come.

The ambassadors' ship was captured by the Romans at sea. They were tortured and they talked. The Romans sent a fleet to patrol the Adriatic coast, denying Philip a landing. The Romans did not wait for him. They sent an army over to Apollonia and burned the Macedonian fleet. Hannibal remained alone.

The desertions hurt me more. Castello brought the news. "Twelve hundred, Hannibal, Gauls. And horses."

"When?"

"Last night."

"But the sentries?"

"They cut their throats."

"I see."

I wanted to ask why. But I knew. In the shipyard at Gadez I had once seen an old trading galley of Hasdrubal's beached. Her caulking was gone, her mast had slipped. She was to be stripped, and what was sound, salvaged. Somehow, her rats knew. Even before she was being pulled to the shore, I saw them jumping off her and swimming away.

My question to Castello was more particular, then. "Is there any special reason, Castello?"

"Well, it can't have helped." He shifted, uneasy. He spat out the word. "Pay."

"Pay? What about it?"

"They hadn't been paid. And you've forbidden looting."

I sighed. "Tell me." I had no idea. Pay was in arrears for a full third of my army. "Castello, we have three captured galleys at Salapia. Take them, with as many men as you think you'll need. Be quick. Go to Fuano. Bring back gold."

He nodded, left.

I was more bemused with myself than angry. There had been so much on my mind. The two new Roman legions in Sicily, for example. I heard that Carthage had sent 25,000 men and 3,000 cavalry. Part of me was raging that Carthage had not sent them to me. Part of me did not care.

It was the first part that drove me to action. It was time I stung the Romans once again. Maharbal was surprised and delighted. We took only 500 Numidians with us from Tifata. I wanted only to scout and think and see. We left in the darkness of the very early morning, to be past the watching Romans before light.

We were tired. Many of us were dozing as we rode. They came on us without warning, very many, riding hard. I saw him, my friend Maharbal, surrounded, slashing, blocking, but I was fighting too. We all dressed the same, as simple soldiers. So we had done for many years. But Maharbal had always worn a florid Boeotian helmet. Perhaps because of that they thought that I was he and there were hundreds round him, his troop fallen, Romans mounted and dismounted, swelling round him. There was nothing I could do. I broke off, led my men with me and we charged them and we charged them and they broke. I found him, blood streaming from the side of his buckler. Its straps, I saw, had not been tied. He smiled at me, my *anda*, my friend Maharbal.

"We have not talked, Hannibal," he croaked. "I suppose that I am getting slow. There should have been many more Romans lying here with me." He coughed. The light caught the little foaming bubbles of blood on his lips. "But Hannibal," a whisper now, "can you really have forgotten Rome? Will you – " His eyes wandered, circled, closed.

I had ridden two-up only once before, with my father dead. I rode back to Tifata with Maharbal dying. It is remarkable he lived so long. I have told of that. I have not said of the blackness that came.

205

For many days and nights I lay in my tent at Mount Tifata. "I am not to be disturbed, at all," I told the guard. My body was weak when I got up at last. My mind was clear. I opened the flap. The guard was startled. "Get me Bostar." The man stared at me, uncomprehending. I cleared my throat. "Get me Bostar, do you hear!"

I was lying down when Bostar came. It was night. I sat up when he entered, I gestured to him to sit down. "Bostar, I have the answer. In the morning, you will ride for me to Rome. On behalf of Hannibal the Carthaginian, you will offer peace to Rome."

He said nothing. The lamp-light flickered in the dark. I lay back.

"On what terms, Hannibal?"

I did not look up. "On any terms you choose, Bostar, on any terms you choose."

He always moved so softly, Bostar. I hardly heard him leave. A cook brought me soup, and bread. I thanked him. I ate.

I must have slept. I half-heard the trumpets of alarm. I was fully awake when I heard the shouting. "Hannibal, Hannibal!" Castello's voice. He had made good time. He burst in. "Hannibal – " He looked exhausted. He was filthy, limping.

"Castello, sit down. Have you brought the gold, Castello?"

He stared at me. "Hannibal, you look so thin, so gaunt. Are you ill?"

I waved a hand at him in annoyance. "Have you brought the gold? They must be paid before, before . . ." My voice trailed away.

Castello rested his head in his hands. He did not look at me. "No, Hannibal, I have not."

"What!"

"Hannibal," his voice was stronger, insistent, "Fuano is dead, or rather killed. And there is worse. The brothers Scipio have defeated yours in a great battle. We lost many men. The Romans then attacked the loyal tribes . . ."

When he was done, we sat in silence. At last I said, "Then it is as well."

"What is 'well', Hannibal! We are losing Spain! You talk of 'well'! Have I served you for this!"

I got up, walked over to him. I squatted down in front of Castello and fixed him with my eyes. "Castello, tomorrow Bostar rides to offer peace to Rome."

Castello shrank. He crumpled. First his face, then all his limbs relaxed. He shut his eyes. And Castello, the veteran Castello, began to cry. I moved from squatting to sitting on the ground before him. Time passed as I let him cry. I felt nothing but a still and distant peace. Maharbal's peace, for I too had died.

Slowly, Castello stopped. Even the well of sorrow has an end. His eyes red, his body trembling, Castello reached out his and held my right arm, just above the wrist. "Hannibal, I have one more thing to tell you."

"Yes, Castello?" I was so calm. "What is that?"

His eyes broke off. He let go of my arm – we have never touched before, I thought, I and this man I hardly know – got up, walked to the far side of the tent. His back to me, straining to keep a level voice, he began.

"The Romans could not capture Cartakhena, Hannibal. Your brothers saw to that. But they were camped outside it. They found" – his voice almost died – "they found your father's grave. They, they, they – "

"Go on, Castello."

"They took his bones from the urn and threw them into the sea. Then one by one" – now Castello blurted – "one by one the centurions pissed into that empty urn. Then they levelled the grave-mound of Hamilcar, with oxen and a plough, and they sprinkled salt all over it and their priests came and cursed that place, it and the Barca name."

It began in my toes. I drew the anger right up from the earth, along my legs, up. It tingled first, then coursed, raced, raged through me, bursting in my brain and in all of my body, all around me. I began to shake, to sway. The moan began in my stomach, swelling, growing. It exploded in a wailing cry that billowed round the camp.

For a long time I fought the anger, to contain it, hold. Slowly I pulled it, slowly back as I had counted each step up and through and down from the frozen Alps, until I made it yield.

I was looking down on myself from a great height. I heard my voice. "Thank you, Castello. You must eat and sleep now. Go first to Bostar. Tell him his orders are cancelled. Is that clear, cancelled? At first light, I want all the *loxarchoi* here. All of them. I shall inspect the whole army at noon. Now go."

The true answer had come. Let others think of empire, of government, of trade and statecraft. I was a soldier. I was Hamilcar's son. I would be what I was. I would confound *hamartia*, philosophy. I would destroy Rome.

IX

DEFEAT

I spoke to the *loxarchoi*, then the whole army. I told them what the Romans had done. "I have come back to you," I told them. "Remember with me how we won at the Trebia, at Trasimene, at Cannae. Now we will complete that which we have begun.

"As for pay, I know that many of you are owed. I will pay you, many times over. I will pay you from the treasuries of Rome. If any doubt that, let them take their gear and go."

There were mutterings, glances. I do not know who began to cheer. It started at the back, and was taken up by my whole army, cheering as one.

"We will fight like that," I told them, when the noise had died down, "as you have cheered – and as we fought at Cannae."

For four days I did nothing but digest information and plan as, under Castello, the whole army drilled below Mount Tifata. Bostar, Epicydes and Hippocrates knew much. I rebuked Bostar for not telling me earlier. "You cannot tell people things, Hannibal, they do not want to know."

The Romans now had twenty whole legions under arms. I wrote it all down, so as to be clear. Had I not learned the usefulness of lists from my father, whose desecration I would now avenge? There were two legions in Sicily, two in Sardinia, two in Spain, one at Brundisium on the south-east Italian coast and two in Gaul. I understood the legion at Brundisium. I still hoped that Philip would come. The Romans expected him, evidently. "He is said to be building a new fleet," said Bostar.

"But two in Gaul?" I asked. "Why?"

"To prevent reinforcements reaching you from Spain,"

Epicydes said. There were two legions in Rome itself, and nine more scattered all over Italy.

"They have me, they think, at bay. Why don't they attack?" I asked Bostar.

"It is the Roman mind, Hannibal. You thought you won at Cannae. You hurt the Romans, yes, as they have never been hurt before. But you drove them in on themselves. Now they will seek only to contain you as they block or destroy any hope of help."

"Will they attack Carthage itself?"

"Yes, I think they will – once they have control of Sicily."

"There is little I can do there," I said.

"There might be more than you think, Hannibal," Epicydes replied. "Send me there, with Hippocrates."

King Hiero had died, his place being taken by his young grandson, Hieronymus, who, safe in Syracuse, was continuing to support Rome. "But without Hieronymus, matters would be very different, Hannibal. Carthage has many friends in Syracuse."

"Without Hieronymus, Epicydes?" I asked, blankly.

"These things can be – arranged."

I understood. "Then go," is all I said.

I felt strong and clear when I led my army from Mount Tifata. I had been eating everything placed before me. I thought of Similce's stews. I smiled. Castello was riding beside me. "Rome, Hannibal?"

"Soon, Castello, soon." The knife was sharp. I wanted to hone it before Rome.

We marched towards Venusia. Why Venusia, a town of no consequence or gold? Because it was a Latin town. I had waited long enough for the Latins to abandon Rome. I meant to destroy Venusia and show the Latins the price of peace with Rome. Between us and Venusia were the armies of both consuls, with two more legions at Tarentum on my right.

One of those was tracking me. It was the old Fabian game.

I was scouting on my own, very early in the morning. Near the village of Petelia I found the Roman camp. I saw the valley near it through which I meant to slip that night. I was walking through a vinefield. The morning was cloudy. A flash of sun shone on the vines and in that light I saw the grapes before me. They were blue.

The battle of Petelia, then, was not, as I have heard, a brilliant, careful, measured plan. I fought because the grapes were blue. Since then have I always looked at grapes with care. I have seen them black and beryl, perse and purple. But never since Petelia have I seen them blue.

We caught the legion in the valley. It was the only way. I sent a syntagma quiet behind the Romans, another up the valley's sides. I waited and I dallied, practising at drill. You could not rush the Romans now, as I had at the Trebia. I led the charge myself against them as they were forming up at last to march and the sky had cleared above me and the sky was blue.

They followed when I broke off and turned away, followed up the valley, Trasimene again. But this valley was broader and the Romans formed and held their battle line even against my slingers and my soldiers charging down the valley's sides. We broke the line of *hastati* but then the *principes* held. I was cutting, swinging, killing. Hannibal had become a better killer than he was when he had two eyes. I did not need to see. I sensed more than I saw. I favoured now the axe in left hand, flailing, knocking down and then the right-hand sword thrust, quick in to the throat or groin. I knew we could not win as we had at Cannae but still I knew the grapes that I had seen were blue. Then I saw him, the Roman consul, behind the *triarii*, his legates and his trumpeters about him and, to my right, I saw among the press of fighting soldiers a riderless and rearing horse.

I used my shield, a ram to break through the fighting. In one bound I was on that horse that knew at once that I was not then

211

an ordinary man. We galloped, weaved between the maniples. I felt invisible, majestic, as a man should who is his father's revenge, and with my axe I caught the consul's charger square between its eyes. Its brains splattered my face, its blood my buckler. The consul was down and I was on him, my right foot on him, calling "Bar-ca!" as my bloody axe swept down, cutting off that consul's head.

They broke at that, the Romans, but they could not run. I did no more fighting, but they died as long as there was sun. I remember sitting on a sorrel horse, holding by the hair the head of a Roman consul. I knew that it was but one head of a Hydra. But I might be Herakles to win. I dropped the consul's head and rode away.

My dry spring was filling. I beat the Romans again on the plain at Asculum, in my way. There were three legions there. I held my main force back. I could not afford again the losses of Petelia. So I rode out with my Guard and one syntagma of cataphract cavalry, one, just one against three legions. We were riding poor and ill-trained horses, but from the shelter of our hillside we rode out into the light. Four times we broke the line of the Romans, smashing, bursting through, killing as we charged and wheeled. We fired the Roman camp and rode away.

My brothers' messenger found us moving towards Capua. I had heard that the Romans were going to beseige it. I meant to drive them off. "A great victory, Hannibal!" The man was some relation of Similce's.

"I am sorry, sorry about Fuano," I said.

"They have paid the price," he carried on. "We beat one Roman army on the river Baetis, and a second at Ilorci. And there, Hannibal, there Scipio was killed!" "Scipio? Which one?"

"Gnaeus, Gnaeus Scipio."

I did not know that I could feel such pleasure still at death.

"This is news indeed! What's your name?"

"Salio, Hannibal."

"Salio, you have done well. Ride with me, and tell me of my brothers. Castello, pass this news to all the men." He turned his horse. I called him back. "And Castello. Tell them that we are marching now – on Rome."

He shrieked, and galloped away. I was unable to speak to Salio for some time, so loud was the chant of "Rome, Rome, Rome!"

We could all hear the calls within the walls of *"Hannibalis ad portas! Hannibalis ad portas!* – Hannibal is at the gates!" the orders, the alarm. I had the rivers fouled. I found and blocked the two tunnelled aqueducts of Rome. I had the country looted, stripped and burned. The walls of Rome were silent as we worked at repairing a bridge over the Tiber; yes, I meant to go in by the door, and the walls stayed silent until the fourth day.

I saw myself the people thronging on the battlements above the Collina Gate. I saw no soldiers there. It seemed something formal, planned. I heard snatches of the talking that the breeze brought me. There was a *loxarchos*, what was his name, beside me, an Etruscan and brave. "Do you speak Latin?" I asked him in Greek.

He spat. "All Etruscans were forced to speak only Latin, until you came."

"Choose your men, twenty, and long shields. No weapons. *Synapismos*, crouching. Go as close as you have to to hear." I turned, to assign slingers their position, just in case this was a ruse.

Nothing was hurled at my men from the battlements. No one took any notice. The Romans started to disperse. Whatever they had been doing was at an end. The *loxarchos* looked puzzled on his return. "Well?" I asked.

"Hannibal, they were, they were holding – " He shook his head.

"Get on with it!"

"They were holding an *auction*." He pronounced the Greek word *apokeruximon* as if it were the name of some strange Celtic god or river-sprite.

"An auction?" I asked. "What were they auctioning?"

"They were auctioning this ground on which we are camped."

"And did they find a buyer?"

"They did. Hannibal, they were saying the ground fetched its normal price."

I ran alone towards the gate, throwing the javelin in my hand as I had never thrown before. Its iron burst the sheeted bronze and struck the splintering wood. The shaft quivered, quivered, snapped.

The scouts were frightened, their horses foundered. "Hannibal! Three armies! A day's march away!" I could not fight, so massively outnumbered, on the open plains of Rome. I called for Salio. "Go back to my brothers. Tell them they must come."

The men were disheartened, sullen as we struck north, then east. My mood was black, our stomachs empty. Everywhere we went, it was the same: the Romans had ordered all grain to be held in walled towns or burned. We had to scavenge, digging like miners for buried grain pits. The Roman legions shadowed us. Castello asked me what we were going to do. "We cannot fight so many, Castello. And they will not fight. We must wait for help from Spain."

Yet so often still I won. Take Tarentum, when Hannibal showed that he still merited the Romans' fear. I captured Tarentum by a stratagem of which I am still proud. The Romans held it garrisoned. It was a Greek city, and an old trading friend of Carthage. I learned of the Roman cruelties there as I spent that winter nearby at Metapontum. Anyone whose loyalty was suspected was executed, their homes and goods forfeit, their women given to the legionaries' brothel.

The Romans did let out to hunt for boar and deer those Greeks they thought were loyal. My pickets captured some of these and brought them to me. Philomenus is the one that I remember. He was amazed by my Greek. I told him of Silenus. Philomenus was a good and cultured man. "The Romans, Hannibal, they are barbarians. They have no literature, no art, no science, no architecture, no philosophy. Anything they think, if they think at all, they take from we Greeks."

As he was talking, there came to me a plan.

We arranged that Philomenus and his friends would seek permission to leave Tarentum hunting every five days. "Be sure to give the garrison commander, the *legatus*, the best cuts." It pleased me to think the Roman would be well fed when I killed him.

For two months Philomenus went hunting, hunting to my camp. I always had the meat ready for him, freshly killed. "They open the gates now for us at our whistle when we return at dusk," he said. I almost laughed.

There were only fifty with me, our faces black with soot, our arms wrapped in cloths, as we crept up in the half-light to Tarentum's northern gate and hid under its walls. Philomenus gave his usual whistle. I heard the sentries laugh and joke, the bars being drawn back and my heart was pounding but my mind was clearest blue. "Come and help us!" I heard Philomenus shout to the sentries. "We have three boars. They are too heavy for us to manage." "Bloody Greek nancy boys, bloody – " He said no more, that sentry walking out, because I caught him from behind and slit his throat, as my men did the throats of the other three.

Now I whistled, and my syntagma came, all men that I had picked myself, silent, running in the dark and that is how I captured Tarentum and killed its Roman garrison, each and every one, and cheered my men and on the strength of it wrote again to Carthage – I had written so many times before – for help to destroy Rome.

I could not hold Tarentum, of course. I knew that even before I took it. It fell in time to Rome again and all her siegecraft and her legions, as did Capua. But I still hoped. I heard from Epicydes. Hieronymus had been murdered – he did not say by whom – and the Syracusans had revolted, killing the Roman garrison. Good, I thought. That will draw more Roman legions from Italy.

I was in Bruttium, in what they call the toe of Italy, when I had more news from Sicily. The Romans had besieged Syracuse. Under one Himilco, Carthage had sent more troops. They captured Agrigentum from the Romans, but failed to relieve the siege. Instead, they were themselves besieged in Agrigentum. Another force was ambushed by the consul Marcellus near Panormus. The Romans had done to Himilco what I did to them at Trasimene. So, they are learning, I thought. Finally, incredibly, Syracuse itself had fallen, despite the ingenious defences of Archimedes. The Romans had killed him in the sack.

"Now, brothers, you must come now!" It was the summer. I had heard nothing. Had they crossed the Alps in the spring? I moved north again, back to Tifata. There had been more desertions. I had Castello pass the word that my brothers were coming. Together, we would march again on Rome.

I heard the calls of alarm in the night, that night at Tifata. Our outposts had been disturbed. Castello in person brought the reason. He put it gently on the ground beside me, in the flickering lamp-light of the night. It was the head of Hasdrubal my brother, the face contorted still in terror, bruised and bloody, purple, blue, the sticking spine where they had cut him making his head tilt and roll. I stood, I stood, I looked but I felt nothing. "They rode up to the stockade, threw it over, and were gone," Castello said. I simply nodded, and he went away.

Was it macabre to keep that head beside me? I hoped, I think, that it would make me feel, that it would make me kill or live again or die, I do not know. I saw in my brother's head the fate of Carthage. I needed to watch it rot, decay. Each morning when I woke, I saw it. "Feel, Hannibal, feel!" I said. But I did not and the skin of my brother's head turned from red to brown to grey.

We moved south. I was not even wearing armour when, that day at our camp near Locri, I saw five Roman maniples marching to our palisade. Out, it was so usual, was so normal, marched the columns of our men. The Roman probe, and then withdraw. Red, everything before me was red: red in all its colours, lurid, shrieking, garish, tender, creamy, crimson, ruby, dingy, orange, patinated, deathly, many-hued and deadly red.

I seized a sword and ran after our soldiers, on beyond them, running on. I shouted, "I am Hannibal, *Aegherghi*, Romans, come to me and share my red!" and I ran then at those maniples, neophyte of death and red.

Warm, I remember was the *pilum*, greeting me is what I thought. There was no pain that I remember, only warmth and it was red. A sea, a mother's womb, an artery, a world of blood, of my heart pumping blackness that was red.

The part of me still living was very far away. I used I think to hear a man's voice, was it Bostar's, calling from the wakened space below. Free as water, pure as fire, effortless as air I travelled, searching, seeking in a singing silence and I found there was no end beyond the stars. Then I heard a voice there, the voice not of any man, and the voice was soft and strong and urgent, calling in that ethereal and incandescent air. And I knew then that the voice was my voice, the voice of my life leaving, far away and far. It did not entreat me but it asked me, asked me was I sure.

I had a choice, the voice was telling, the choice of peace so much of me was craving but it was a choice that knew that I had failed. The other was to return to my body, far below. And I put on my father, Similce, Maharbal, my brother, that which their absence taught me and I was ashamed and I was curious and I chose the struggle that is man, that lay below.

Many weeks I lay there in that hut at our camp at Crotona, weeks of fever, vision, healing, tended by Bostar. I see the scar now as I write this, on my stomach, purple, knotted, yellow, lurid, speckled white and ochre even so long after, reaching far.

The messengers came often. Now Carthage was concerned. Suddenly she had the ships to cross the sea with messages for Hannibal. I heard that Scipio, young Scipio, had invaded Africa. Still I would not go. Yes, I was held there in the toe of Italy, Italy where I had spent so long, but even with twelve legions round me, still the Romans did not dare.

In despatches now in simple Punic, the Council told me how they fared. At the battle of the Great Plains, Scipio had destroyed their vaunted army, the army that they never sent to me. I was interested in how Scipio had won. I asked. They sent me a full report. I saw what Scipio had done, what Scipio had learned – from me.

It was simple, brilliant, brave. This was the man that I had seen at the Ticinus. I knew our fates were joined. He had learned from me, but also from himself. At the Great Plains he had rejected centuries of Roman tactics. The armies had engaged. As Scipio's *hastati* held the line, he did a thing unheard of, a thing I would be proud to have done. Instead of leaving the *principes* and *triarii* to stand in case the first line failed, he sent them wheeling round the flanks. Our army was enveloped, slaughtered to a man.

Carthage was now beseiged. Only I could save her, said the despatches. They reminded me of how my father did the same against the mercenaries, came when Carthage called. Fulsome sycophants, I thought. I replied suggesting they make their own peace with Rome, that they ignore me in that, as they always had.

I was not surprised to learn that they had tried. Neither was I surprised by the Roman Senate's answer, that they would not consider peace while Hannibal remained on Roman soil. The Elders' order came to me to come.

I was still undecided. Each day I walked, inspected my men. Did they have the will? No, not for Africa, but to break out, northwards. A new Carthage in the north perhaps, in Spain, where Hannibal would rule and be a man?

Our camp had acquired its followers. That was only natural. I execrated prostitutes and brothels. I had executed those of my men who raped. But there were many women living in those last years with my men, if not as man and wife, then as much the same, Greeks and Illyrians, Corcyrans, Locrians, Syrians, Italians. I saw no harm in that. I liked, as I was healing at Crotona, to walk among them, see them living, men and women, washing clothes, laughing, talking in the sun.

Tychaeus was the soldier's name, a Numidian, a good horseman, one of very few now who had been with me all the time. He was known as *oikaner* in the coarse Greek of my army, *househusband* that means, because he had taken up with an Italian girl, Flavia. They had a tiny hut they shared together, just beyond the horse-lines, and Tychaeus was famed for going there when off-duty, leaving his fellows to their dice and brawls and games. I went there once and saw that he had made a table for their hut from planks of rough-cut brushwood, and chairs and other niceties of home. The Celts and the Gauls did not like this. They hated Italians and Romans. To Tychaeus as to his people, mercenaries for generations, Hannibal's was just another war.

I had heard of the child born to Tychaeus and to Flavia. Accompanied by his friends, Tychaeus brought what they had left of her to me.

She had been still a baby, that much I could see. Tychaeus

219

brought a tiny naked torso, nothing more. And then he unwrapped a cloth before me and I saw two arms, two legs. "*Dikasterion*," he said. It was the formula in my army for demanding justice when a wrong had been done.

I set up an inquiry. I presided myself. I had been absent with death for so long it was time my army saw me theirs again and there was not a man among them to whom this tortured baby was not great right or wrong. Amulgo was the Gaul, a *loxarchos* no less, who admitted to being ringleader. "I am not ashamed," he said. "I am proud!" and all the Gauls cheered, noisily confirming their approval, their support. This had become an issue of more than a dead baby. You cannot keep idle still 30,000 men and not expect their rivalries, their jealousies to burn. It was hard enough when marching, campaigning. For fifteen years I had kept an army of as many nations and yet seen no trouble such as this before.

"Let this teach those black-skins that Italians are filth. Are there not enough of them before us, all around us, that we should breed even more? Anyway, I thought the darkies liked their women the other way round!"

"Women?" came a Celtic voice. "I thought they liked doing it with dogs!"

So it went on. I let them have their say. I called Tychaeus to speak.

He explained that he had been on patrol. His woman had left the baby to fetch water. He pointed to his daughter on the ground. "We are all of us children of the one father. Her mother is Italian but a woman, and she was the daughter of a man." He threw down his sword before me. "I ask, Hannibal, for *aextheran*." *Aextheran*, in Punic, was an ancient custom of justice in our army: ritual single combat, to the death, and with that came the ending of the wrong.

"Do you accept, Amulgo?" I asked him. He guffawed, huge and yellow-bearded, still young and strong. Tychaeus was typical of his people, slight and light and wiry, older, a completely different man. For the time it takes to groom a sweated horse they fought, the time it takes to mend a buckled shield. Amulgo spent his strength on nothing, for each time he swept or stabbed Tychaeus was not there. He caught him, though, and Tychaeus' blood was flowing from the sword cut and the axe head by the time he killed Amulgo, lying panting on the bloody ground. In one hand only the sword went up. He called to the dark gods of the desert that he had not seen for so long and down into the throat of Amulgo, unguarded, plunged the sword of his revenge.

I stood there in the sun, when it was over, looking at the limbless baby lying in its shroud of flies as Tychaeus' friends tended him and helped him away. I dug the baby's grave myself. I have seen so many wrongs and lives begun and ended. I knew that I must start again.

When the Elders sent their further messenger, I told him: "Tell the Elders, Hannibal will come. Tell them I am coming for a limbless baby. You will see her grave beside you when you leave the camp."

We built the ships we needed, very quickly. Why had I not done that before, that is what I used to think as I was watching, in the forests of the Sila, trees being felled and timbers split. I thought, how strange it is that my war has been fought on land but lost at sea, where it was never fought.

Then, in a temple on that cliff-side above the sea that was not room enough for the power I was born to, Carthage, and the power, Rome, that had come to be, there I set down what I had done in Italy so that men might always see. In Punic and in Greek, I had written on bronze sheets the numbers of my men and, beside those, the numbers of the multitudes of Rome.

My last action in Italy was to set many of my soldiers free. They were Gauls and Celts for the most part, enemies of Rome. I knew that they would mutiny in Africa. Without me, they

221

would have been crucified by the Romans. So I had them killed there, more than 4,000, by the shore.

We set sail at last in the early evening. Our sails were a motley of canvas, cotton, hide and leather, anything that we could find. I had lost so much in Italy. Perhaps, I thought, perhaps I have found more. The helmsman set his course. We caught the evening breeze. I looked about me, at the fleet of ships, the men, the horses. "Where is Bostar?" I asked the men beside me. No-one knew.

I turned and with my one eye then I saw him, standing alone on receding shore. He raised his right hand up, palm towards me, higher, nearer in the dusk. An elegy, a eulogy, a blessing. I understood. I walked back to the stern of my transport, through the supping soldiers. I stood and watched him, Bostar standing, until I could see no more.

I slept under Bostar's will that night, slept as I had not slept for years until the helmsman came to wake me. "There is Carthage, Hannibal, there!" What was it to him, a Syrian? Just another port? What was it to me?

My plan had been to try to sail straight into the harbour. It was morning, very early. I thought the Roman fleet would be beached, and not at sea. But I needed to find Africa again. I needed Hadrumetum to find that which I had been, to think and to prepare.

It was as I had known it in my childhood, a long and sandy beach of turtles, palm trees, caves. The memory was more tender for its distance. We drew up our ships and I was first to set my feet again on Carthaginian soil. We made our camp inland. There was a place of shelving plateaus, from which we could see all round. And there was a spring. The men ate fish, fresh-caught, in plenty, dates. It was a good place, where we camped.

I sent ten men to Carthage at once, Numidians who knew the trackless ways. Tychaeus was one. I asked for men and arms, provisionings. Scipio had three legions, that I knew. I had three syntagmata and 800 horse. I trained them and I trained them as we waited. We had come lax from Bruttium. Libyans and Moors came to join me, broken men welcomed by neither Carthage nor Rome. I sighed, accepted.

"Can we train them, Castello?" I asked him. "We can try," is all he said. He was now an adept of making soldiers was Castello, though by now an old and wizened man.

Carthage sent me two syntagmata of Celtiberians, newly hired from the west of Spain that Rome had yet to conquer. So Carthage had ships for these, I thought. There would be time enough for such thoughts, with the battle won. They were good soldiers, ordered, practised, fit. With them came eighty elephants and drivers from the walls of Carthage, richly equipped. I thought less of the billowing caparisons. These I had removed. I wanted my army, when it marched, monochrome. The colour that I wanted was black. All arms, all armour I had daubed with ash mixed with the ink of squid and octopus.

The Elders sent me gold. My troops were paid. Each day there came another message: when will you come? and I replied each time: Hannibal will come when he is ready.

This was to be a different warfare, open on the plains. I trained my troops to make them mobile, wheeling, flying as a bird. My only hope lay in my elephants, to counter lack of men. To them I looked to break the *hastati* of Scipio. I wondered, would they do.

Another thing delayed me. I never told of it, nor let it be known, but each step I took was an agony, each breath a rasping pain. I had never cared as I moved among my men, washing, swimming, bathing, working almost naked in the sun. Now I ensured that none should ever see what lay under the tunic that I wore.

Where the Roman *pilum* caught me, where the scar pulsated, shone, there was the pain. My stomach had healed, yes, but somehow it was stuck to my ribs. It all lay tight upon me as a drum-skin. Only lying did I not feel the pain. And I was so often dizzy-headed, for I could not hold down food. Secretly by night I made and drank the brews as Bostar taught me, of ground weasel bones and marjoram and thyme. If I ate anything solid, my sticking stomach threw it up again. I still did not feel ready when Scipio came to me. My scouts reported his army moving towards a town south-east of Carthage, a town called Zama, famous for its olives and its wine. I marched to meet him, anxious if I could to choose my fateful ground.

I learned that Scipio's *extraordinarii* were Numidians from the far west, under their king Masinissa. I had to know Scipio's dispositions, plans. I called Tychaeus, told him to mingle if he could with the Numidians and get into Scipio's camp. He laughed, that I remember, a rare thing in his kind. "So I am to be a spy now, Hannibal! I will do what I can."

He came back four days later, cheerful, at ease, calm. "What have you learned?" I asked him.

"What have I not?" He gave me long and precise details of Scipio's arms and men and plans. He had no fewer than 12,000 cavalry. "So many?" and immediately I began to plan. "This is remarkable, Tychaeus. How did you learn so much?"

"Oh, I had a guide, the best that I could find."

"And who was that?"

"My guide was Scipio, the Roman who commands."

Tychaeus had been detected and brought to Scipio for sentence. Tychaeus told him of my orders. Scipio said: "Release him. Now come, Numidian, come!" and had showed him round the camp. "Tell your master," Scipio had said before he sent Tychaeus back, "tell your master I am looking forward to our battle. Tell him that I feel our fates are joined."

"What was he like, this Scipio?" I asked Tychaeus. They often have a wise way with them, Numidians, as sparing, distant as their sandy lands.

"Scipio?" Tychaeus answered, and I remember now the words of Greek he gave. *Ti de tis; ti de oo tis.* What is he, what is he not; Scipio, he is a man."

I was still surprised then when he asked to see me, asked the day before the battle joined. He had beaten me to a strong position on the hill of Khoudiat Bexthene: well, no better, but he had water there. A plain lay between our armies, and I camped opposite, on the hill called Khat Bourene. I think I was surprised that I agreed to go.

I walked out alone to meet him, alone as he had come to me. I wore armour, blackened. He wore white, his toga bordered with the purple of his rank. His skin was fair by Roman standards, his hair curling, his eyes blue. He was slight and lightly walked towards me. What did I look like, stocky, smaller, hoping I was not limping as my stomach tore me as I moved? I was, I guessed, ten years his senior.

We talked in Latin. His was polished, careful. Mine was rough, direct as I was used. It was the only time that I talked with a Roman as my equal. I am glad it was the last. Where has the hate gone, that is what I asked myself. I said to Scipio, "I will kill you if I can."

"I saw you fighting at Ticinus," he replied. "I am glad we meet again. I have been your pupil, Hannibal. It is from you that I have learned."

His hands were long and tapered, that I noticed. He brushed a fly from his face. "Must we fight at all, Hannibal?" he asked. "Can you not offer Rome a peace?"

"That is not mine, nor in my nature to offer. You have already Spain and Sicily, Scipio. I cannot rest while Rome still stands."

"Why, Hannibal?"

I looked beyond him, saw his legates and his praetors standing, sitting on their horses, fretting in the sun. I almost said, "Because of what you did to Similce, to my father's grave.

Because – " The truth is, I did not know why. "Because, Scipio, I know nothing else."

"So," he said, "the pupil and the master. Do you know Plato's *Symposium*?" I did, thanks to Silenus. So Scipio and Hannibal discussed Plato before Zama. "Plato's is a better world than this, do you not think, Hannibal?"

"I do, Scipio," I said. I saw he was a man as I am. It was fate and it was circumstance that made us fight, the destinies of birth. That, and nothing more.

We joined battle the next morning. I had planned an early feint. But as I was having my light cavalry fed in the darkness, my scouts reported Scipio was doing the same. So, move and counter-move. I smiled, cancelling that order. We all lay down to sleep until the dawn. I should not have eaten soup. My stomach gurgled, frothed and swelled and ran.

Still my dispositions were as I had planned them, as the two armies moved down to the plain. Four lines I formed, expecting the Romans' three. The fourth and last was half of my Italian veterans, 200 strides behind the rest in case Scipio should release his *principes* and *triarii*, as he had done at the battle of the Great Plains.

But so my front rank, half of the Celtiberians and the Moors, the Libyans who had joined me, was greatly outnumbered, only two deep. The Roman front line, I saw as they grew closer, was five. Castello led our line. He flashed to me on his bronze mirror, five times. I acknowledged. I had already seen.

I saw the Roman cavalry, very many, waiting on their wings. I sent mine, many fewer, to charge them, perhaps too soon. Perhaps. What is perhaps? Any battle turns upon the slightest thing. I saw them break off and the Romans follow westwards. The odds are shortening, Scipio! I thought. Now let's see what you can do!

When the two lines were still too far apart for sling or *pilum* throw, then I ordered and it happened, just as exact as I had planned. My first line flew, but inwards on my warhorn's blaring order. From one line, the Romans now faced ten marching columns. Between each of these, the goaded, maddened, charging elephants came, their drivers' orders clear and cogent, my only hope against so many men. "Break the first line of *hastati*, smash them, trample. If you reach the second, do the same."

The speed, the ease of Scipio's reaction is the finest thing that I have seen in fifty years of war. It was done, it seemed, before the Roman trumpets' sounding ended. From chequerboard, Scipio's maniples were forming their straight line just as my elephants charged. In the time it takes to run that distance, in that time the Romans changed their forming and my elephants met only bristling columns, with wide avenues between. When I saw the great beasts passing almost harmless down them, I knew that I was fighting a general who had learned from me. A cramp seized my stomach. I winced and looked away. When I looked again, the gap was closing, front lines running. The sounding and the clashing of their meeting was familiar, pungent, as the sour-sweet of my sweat. Stomach aching, I put on my helmet. I felt my old friends, sword and shield and dagger, axe and javelin. I greeted them. I felt their comfort. I prepared to join the fray.

Such were the new tactics of the battle of Zama, tactics that the world had never seen before. Yet the battle after Scipio's manoeuvre was just the same as many battles fought before our time; just, no doubt, the same as many yet to come. It was bitter, hand–to–hand. There were no flourishes, no fancies. The first lines killed each other. The second lines fought on the corpses of the first. My third line foundered on the planted *pila* of the *triarii*, but I broke that with my hardened fourth. I might have done it, myself fighting, though I was tiring, stomach aching, spinning head, as I stabbed and parried in the gore. Along the line beside me we were winning, killing, pushing back. Swing and block and step and swing and block and step, back went the thinning Roman line.

I caught glimpses of Scipio, beyond me, sitting on his charger up the hill. Did he wonder as he watched us, wonder if he might beat me still?

Or did he know about the cavalry? He cannot have known. Perhaps he just believed. Anyway, they came, the Roman cavalry and when I heard them, felt them, saw them at our rear, I knew. I gave the orders, shouted. Enough heard me, understood. In good order, more than two syntagmata, first we fought and then we marched back to Khat Bourene, up into the rocks where Roman horses could not follow.

It was night when we reached Carthage. I left her as the son of Hamilcar, young, plenipotent. I returned defeated, tired, old. I told the guards to find my men good billets, to send the Elders to me. I went to Megara alone.

It is the flapping shutters I remember, the weeds and the decay. In the starlight of the darkness I saw the great gong in the courtyard of the Barcas hanging loose upon its frame. I found the hammer, swung and swung it until the sound it filled my brain. I lay down beside that gong still humming, I lay there exhausted, I lay there alone, thinking of the battle, of Scipio, of my childhood, of my father, of Similce, of Rome.

I did not know the men who came. What was I to them but a name. They accused me, said I had failed Carthage, given her to Rome. I was Odysseus amongst the suitors. "I would have won if you had – " It was pointless. "We will make peace," I said, "with Rome."

Two days I stayed, or was it more, sleeping, hiding in what had been my home. I heard them come and heard them call me. I wanted just to be alone, walking in the midnight halls and darkening corridors, rooms of rot and silent groans.

I found the secret doorway from the garden, pushing through the blocked and bursting paths. I could not hear the gravel crunch before me that I hoped for. The ways were weedy and forlorn. The door opened. Up I climbed, again I saw her, wakening in the rising sun. Greater than me, far greater, I had to serve her while I breathed.

The children ran from me, the adults stared when they saw me, walking through the streets of morning, mourning for a battle that they thought I might have won. Mine were other battles, other places. All that in me was silent, dumb. I found my men and gave my orders, walked on to the public square, past the place of Hanno's crucifixion, past the place where that was done.

"Where is Astegal?" I asked the robed attendant by the Council's doors.

"Astegal is dead. I am High Steward to the Council now."

"And where is Bomilcar, the Sufet?"

"He too is dead."

"That is a pity. I would have liked to meet him. But, High Steward, call the Council. Tell them Hannibal has come."

"But it is early, they will be – "

"Do it man, before I cut out your tongue."

I was sitting in the great chair when they came in, sleepy, angry, in ones and threes. I remember their cacophony of voices, telling me what was, what was not to be done. I let them speak and shout and clamour. I have heard much of the babellings of men.

They were ashamed at last and silent. One spoke out, clear. "I am Salicar, High Sufet. I say let us hold a proper Council and decide what is to be done." He walked towards me, across the hall and up the sacred steps of gold and ivory, up towards me, sitting in the chair. They say now that I seized the chair of Carthage. I did not. I simply refused to let it go. "You will give way to me, the Sufet!" Salicar intoned.

"That I will not," and I shouted out my order, "*Bainomen!*" in Greek, "*Advance!*" as I had so many, so very many times before. Still in their blackened armour, my men came through the silver door.

"This is outrage, madness, sinful," cried the Elders. I told them to go home.

I tried so hard in the two years that followed, tried to be a man of peace and not of war. First we made our terms with the envoys of Scipio. His terms were generous. Carthage was to remain independent. It was not to build a fleet of more than ten warships. It was forbidden to wage war on any people outside Africa, or on any within Africa without Rome's consent. They say Scipio wanted done, wanted home to have his triumph. I say I do not think that true of him. Even the indemnity he asked for was not crippling, 10,000 talents over fifty years. I had walked round all of Carthage, seen the wealth of many men. Were they to give, there would be ample for a new fleet and an army. With both only would I try again. I knew well and I remembered the vow that I had made of enmity to Rome. I swore the vow would not die when there was life in me. But it must have its season and its proper time.

So it was not me who then attacked the Roman envoys, sailing to Rome to have their Senate ratify the peace that should have come between Carthage and Rome. Their names were Fabius, Baebius and Sergius. I sent the only three triremes we had, I thought, as escort with them. The Romans say I killed these envoys, the Carthaginians that I lost three ships. Only twelve of the sailors on them returned to Carthage to say what had been done.

As they came from the river Bagradas, hoisting sail to course the sea, three quinqueremes from somewhere rammed them, then discharged their slaughtering marines.

I had done much in Carthage, restoring order, hope, supplies. I had the outer harbour re-dredged. I had begun the re-planting of the farms fired by Scipio. I had done many things. These counted for nothing, when news of the envoys' killing came. I was a stranger in Carthage. To all my questions on the killings, I met sullen silence or blame.

Salicar was at least honestly dishonest. "You did this, Hannibal, we know," he said in Council.

"Truly you are Bomilcar's son," I said softly to him.

"How dare you name his name!" he shouted, "You who have done so much harm. Why, you never even knew him!"

"I know that someone had Hasdrubal killed, long ago in Cartakhena. The killing of the envoys, that is something much the same." We have a Punic saying that I gave them, of the dogs that eat not flesh. "Which of you," I asked them, "is in league with which of Rome?"

Of course they did not answer. I was so tired. I was born to this but could not understand it. I was part of it, but separate. I was master, but a servant. Which hurt more, my stomach, heart or brain?

I would have stayed, still, until they killed me, by a steady poison or a knife thrust in the night. I would have stayed until the task was done, until Carthage knew a peace of honour and could grow and build again and heal.

These were the dreams of a man, not of the boy who marched on Rome. Rome had to be exhausted as was Carthage. I, of all men, ought to know. And she was fighting still the Boii, stretching more her hold on Spain. Antiochus, the King of Syria, was conspiring against Rome. There would be war. Meanwhile, she had defeated Philip at the great battle of Cynoscephalae. Now she had Macedon to rule. Rome could have no will for Africa, if Africa left her alone. All this and more we heard from the trading ships that had begun to come again, as swallows in the spring.

But then the Romans sent for me in Carthage. The Senate had said the peace could only be established when I was held captive in Rome. They would not speak of peace until the man who killed their envoys of peace was theirs, "*perdomitus in vinculis,* abject and in chains". Had this been arranged in Carthage, in a council in a hall-room, by some fat and reeking man?

Castello had died at Zama, and Hamilax long before. For my men I had no fear. Carthage always kept and paid her soldiers. They would respect and pay mine, were I away. There was nothing else for me. My father's house in Megara, ruined, empty, with only memories of a childhood love for Carthage, perished, empty, gone.

They had not found my father's secret treasury, deep below the slabs of porphyry, underneath the echoing hall. I prepared to take from it as much as I could carry. There was one more thing I had to do. I had learned of Silenus' time in Carthage. He had been despised and shunned because of me. They would not keep him, so he trimmed his sails, as Greeks have always known.

He had found work of sorts and lodgings in a dank and squalid corner of the dyers' quarter, Malqua, where he kept accounts for pimps of catamites and whores. I found his room there in the dark hours, waking up the crone who stank and swore. I made her bring me tallow, candle. "Where are his things?" I asked her.

"What do you think! I sold them. He was a Greek, old and stooped and wrinkled. Here he had neither friends nor kin."

"If you speak like that of him, you slut, I'll kill you. I'll send your shade to wait on him." That silenced her, though I meant it. "Now, again, where are his things?"

"I told you, I sold them. There are only some old parchments left, for which no-one was prepared to pay. Why, I even offered them to Axhnego, the Syrian who sells tablets and papyrus, for one copper xthet, but he laughed and turned away."

I asked her where she kept them and she showed me. In the sputtering light I saw what she had held. One cracked, dried scroll of Plato's *Theaetetus.* "I never understood that, Silenus," I

232

said. "I am here now, in your honour. Can you hear me, far away?" Sophocles, Euripides, no Aeschylus surprised me, but then I found it, that which I expected, what was in my mind. The *Iliad* of Homer, in a sheath of calfskin, the scrolls loved and worn. One unrolled almost of its own will before me, and I read in that hovel for Silenus, for my father, for Similce, for Carthage, for my soul. Hector is explaining to his wife Andromache why he must go out and fight, though he knows that he will die:

ἔσσεται ἦμαρ ὅτ' ἄν ποτ' ὀλώλῃ Ἴλιος ἱρὴ
καὶ Πρίαμος καὶ λαὸς ἐϋμμελίω Πριάμοιο.

The day shall come when sacred Troy shall perish, and Priam and the people of Priam of the ashen spear.

Such was my valediction. The old had ended. Something new, it had begun.

X

DEATH

The world was all before me, myself my only guide. My boat was ready. So I had arranged, a fishing yawl, well decked and timbered, strong. Worked by three men, she could be sailed, they said, by one. The last of the Barcas had yet some friends among the fishermen of Carthage.

I sailed that night only as far as Cercina, the island, off the coast of Carthage. They would not think to look for me so near. Also I needed time to rehearse the rudiments of sea-craft. Hannibal the soldier became a sailor in the night, I thought wryly, as I worked the sheets and sail. But in the morning the sailors of a trading ship surprised me. They would be sure to tell.

I asked them to share my breakfast, dates and olives, dried fish, bread. They joked at the porridge I made of mine with water and a pestle. I did not tell them of my stomach. I said without thinking that I had rotting gums. And gums are what we talked of for a long time, sailors' gums. They often swell and blister on a long voyage, that is what they told me, without lemon juice or limes.

They wanted peace, they said, to trade. I felt strange and humbled. Had I brought war to people who would only trade? That was the way of those I thought of as my people. Rome would let them trade. They did not care if they were truly free. That I would not exchange my lot for such servitude, was that not a way of living just for me?

"The sun is growing hot," I said to them. "Let us sit and talk, but we need an awning for shade. My sail is too small for all of us. Bring yours." It suited them to stay. Fair winds had brought them swiftly there from Tyre. They and their cargo of cinnabar and silphium, green porphyry and dates were not due in

Carthage for another day. They were a long time bringing in their sail. As long to rig her again, I thought. I left Cercina early the next morning, sure that by the time they had rigged their sail and told of me in Carthage I would be far enough away.

I went to Crete. It was an easy sail of nine or ten days, sleeping having lashed the tiller forwards to the masthead. To good purpose had I questioned passing sailors when I knew I would be leaving, learned of winds and currents, ways.

Knossos was a large and bustling harbour, heart of Crete. My boat was only one of very many and in the town, its streets or markets, in the simple lodgings where I stayed, Hannibal was but one man of many. Never before had I been no-one. Those were settled, human days of thoughtlessness and waiting, living as a desert spring. You must let it slowly fill again its basin, when man or beast has drunk of it too deep.

I liked to walk the streets of Knossos, to see and feel and touch its crumbling mighty walls. This had been the centre of a rich and spreading empire, the Minoans, which had perished. Like men, leaves in the forest, peoples wither, pass away. The day would come when Rome too would be a memory, for all its waxing power.

There were so many in Knossos, refugees from Rome. There was one inn where they liked to gather, drink the Cretan wine and talk. I used to go there to eat, for the food was plain and wholesome, and to listen. Three men in particular I came to know by name from listening to their conversations as I sat alone.

Hamiscora was a Sardinian, Malalas an Illyrian. Abgar was from Macedon. All three talked in Greek of how they had been driven from their native towns and cities by Rome. They became maudlin sometimes as they drank. "I have lost everything, everything!" Hamiscora complained. "And Rome is invincible."

"Yes, I learned that at the battle of Cynoscephalae," Abgar said. "The cursed Romans defeated even our great Macedonian phalanxes."

"But only by applying what they had learned," said Malalas.

"Learned?" asked Abgar. "Learned from whom?"

"Why, from Hannibal, you fool," Abgar replied. "They would never have won at Cynoscephalae if they hadn't learned from him, especially that general Scipio. And Hannibal showed they aren't invincible, Hamiscora. I met a fellow Illyrian who was with the Roman *extraordinarii* at Cannae. What Hannibal did at Cannae was incredible – "

"Pah!" Hamiscora broke in. "But where did it get him in the end? They say he ran away from Carthage. I heard he'd been captured, skulking somewhere in Numidia." I almost laughed aloud.

Hamiscora went on. "Nothing, I tell you, can stop Rome now . . ."

It was good to be unrecognised, to see if the Hannibal I heard talked of was the same one that I knew. I was buying figs and halva in the market, I remember, when one man did recognise me and call out my name. A big and swarthy bow-legged sailor, a shipowner, I thought, a memory from Carthage. "Hannibal, I know you! There is a bounty on your head." By this time he was close beside me. Behind him were his men.

"And how much is the bounty for Hannibal?" I asked him.

"Two thousand gold xthets for your body, five for you alive in chains."

He had a squint, that I remember. His face was pock-marked and his lines were many, leathered by the salt and sun. I did not want to kill him. I wanted to ask him why he would trade me as a bale of cotton: the money, yes, but why he wanted Hannibal, a fellow Carthaginian, dead. Perhaps my war had spoiled his trade. I had wanted to give Carthage freedom from Rome's shadow. Perhaps most people prefer shadow, Rome's or any other shadow, and the comfort of their daily bread.

His men were all around me now. "Will you come or must I take you?"

I did not trouble to reply. The market was emptying, traders quickly shutting up their stalls. He nodded. I sensed two of them, reaching out behind me. I rolled and twisted, an old trick, though my stomach tore. I drew my sword and, rising, stuck him, then a second and the others ran. Now Hannibal has killed a Carthaginian, I thought. I sheathed my sword unwiped. My wanderings began.

For many years I wandered. Very many are the places, peoples I have known. I liked those where they did not know me, first those islands where I spent a week, the passing of a moon, a season; to Kasos, Karpathos and Saria I wandered, Kalimnos and Levitha and Kos. Only once was I ill-used by people, on the island of Sifnos, in the winter, in the rain.

They were surly people, in-bred, poor. Their diet was as bitter as their land. My gold and jewels from Carthage were with me. I was uneasy for them, saw the many glancings, heard the whisperings about the treasure of the man with one eye and no name.

Even the meanest Greek island has its temple, some of wattle, some of stone. They believe, the Greeks, that their gods walk among them. They see their gods as men. That has always drawn me. You see how they behave in Homer, how they fight and cheat and lie as mortal men. And I liked that, through those years of wandering. My gods were still the gods of Carthage, but I saw that they were gods of pitiless abstraction, like their city, pure idea.

The temple of Sifnos was to Artemis the hunter. I bought two amphorae and placed them there. "There are in these things of great value," I told the priestess as I sealed the jars with wax before her, the jars containing sand and shells. My three bags of gold and precious stones I had elsewhere. I heard the noises, saw the torches as the Sifnians went to take that which they thought my treasure. My boat was ready. In a swelling sea and in the darkness I sailed to another island. Like my heart, from then I kept my treasure hidden. Now what is left of it lies here on the floor beside me open. Let Prusias have it, let the Romans, as a dog a bone.

Slowly as I journeyed on I felt again the purpose rising, as the sap, as desert after rain. The roots of Rome ran deep in me. What rose in me, purer, calmer was again my hate for Rome. Where was I? I cannot remember, but in the morning before windbreath I was walking on some shore. In the sea a single dolphin broke the surface, shining, gleaming, free. There is no more than that to tell. Why did I sell myself as a mercenary thereafter, fighting against Rome? Because I had put on again my nature, as a dolphin in the sea.

Everywhere that I had been there was talk of Antiochus, King of Syria, builder of an empire, they were saying, that would engulf even Rome. I took a ship to Antioch. I sold my faithful yawl.

Antiochus was said to boast of finding Antioch of brick and leaving it of marble. It was astonishing, I admit. But I have never cared for buildings. These, it seemed to me, were made for show. So was their builder, the king.

I got past the first doorkeepers simply by staring when they questioned me and walking by. I knew my former power. Only the guards at the doors of the very palace stopped me. My cloak was dirty, and my *chiton*, my sandals old and worn, the heavy bags I carried weathered, cracking. "You!" they laughed. "You want to see Antiochus the king!"

"Tell him," I told their officer, "tell him a man has come to see him, and Hannibal is his name."

"You, you are – " Few could look at my one eye for long. He went away. Soon I was shown in.

Yes, I thought, yes, I have become a name.

On and on we walked, I remember, to the throne room of the king. Without number were the courtiers and concubines simpering and whispering in vaulting halls and rooms. He rose to greet me, a great honour, I was told. He was tall and handsome but he knew it and he even wore a crown. "So you are Hannibal, the Carthaginian," he said in mannered Greek. His voice was high and strained.

"Yes, Antiochus, that is who I am. I have come to fight with you against Rome."

"So simple?"

"Yes, so simple."

I have never been a man of conversations. The one that followed was the longest I have known. It concerned mostly Antiochus' ambitions. We went to his map room with his generals, talked of –

The chamberlain of Prusias has just come to tell me. Prusias himself is too ashamed. He has not been to see me now for many weeks. The Romans have come. They have docked ten triremes in the harbour. They have thought it necessary to bring a whole cohort to arrest me, this Hannibal, this old and tired man. I know how long they will be marching from the harbour. I can finish, and be done.

Antiochus made me an admiral, not a general. He was that sort of man. I had said my war with Rome was lost where it was never fought, at sea. He gave me a fleet. He was to command on land, I at sea. His fleet was at Tyre. I sailed there to bring it to Ephesus. The Romans knew. The fleet of Rhodes, allies of Rome, attacked us unsuspecting. The Rhodian ships all had the Roman *corvus*, a hinged gangplank, and with these they grappled us and then their soldiers boarded. The Roman method now was to fight as if on land at sea. On both now they learned, they innovated.

Mine was a fleet of sailors, not of soldiers. I shook my head and sailed away, leaving forty galleys to the Rhodians. I explained all this to Antiochus, said we had to train our fleet to fight that way. He agreed. He always had some other project. He left me making soldiers out of sailors in Ephesus. He marched away the many pennants of his gilded, strutting army. His favoured troops wore armour of alligator skin. I told him I thought they would find bronze a better foil to Roman *pila*. "The sight of so much bronze fatigues me, Hannibal," he said. "The skin of alligators is a finer thing."

The Romans beat him at Thermopylae in Greece and then Magnesia near Smyrna. He tried to use his gilded war-chariots in the hills. He sued for peace. He did not have to tell me one of the many terms. "Hannibal the Carthaginian must be delivered up to Rome." Antiochus at least did not prevent me. I left as I had come, although my cloak and *chiton*, they were new and clean.

I travelled by camel through Aremenia. King Artaxias was a kinsman of Antiochus. I built a city for him, Artaxiata, though I did not choose the name. From there I came to where I now am, to Bithynia where Prusias is king. He was not at war with Rome. But at least, I thought, he is fighting Eumenes of Pergamum, allies of Rome.

I won my last battle for Prusias, if battle is what it can be called. He had a fleet of fine ships but no soldiers. I found him some. I found him many snakes, vipers, adders, jade and emerald and hissing and I had them put in earthen jars and we sailed against Eumenes with no soldiers, just with oarsmen who were slaves and jars of snakes. When the ships joined then we threw them onto the decks of Eumenes' galleys and it was with snakes we won the day.

Rome's power now was strong and growing. Still I meant to try. I liked the hillmen of Bithynia. I could have made of them an army, still surprised the Romans when they came. But they heard of me in my training, learned of me from Pergamum. "I know, Prusias," I said when he came to tell me, now not quite a month ago. "They have demanded Hannibal in chains." I did not and I do not blame him. "Do not be afraid, Prusias," I told him. "I am a bird grown now too old to fly."

Rome is waxing. Those who fear or hate her can stand only in her shade. She will reach her zenith. Even the sun of Rome, in time, must cross the sky and die.

I must hurry. Let the Romans have me. I thank the light and love that I have known. I am sitting steady in this chair. My legs are spread. My back is straight. My feet are firm upon the ground. The dagger here that I shall draw across my throat is sharp and ready. I am not afraid to die. I must only move these many tablets on which I have written what I here have told you, where they may not be spoiled by my blood.

May the shades of all the many dead forgive me. May I see again Similce on the other side. The river. What is beyond?

Life is boundless and measureless, a river whose water no vessel can hold. I dreamt of Rome's destruction. It is not a thing of shame that I have failed. Let men think of me, remember. Has my failure been the result of *hamartia*? If so, what has mine been? I do not know. Hannibal has been as man, a shadow of a dream.

EPILOGUE

Quintus Furius Bibaculus, Coss., Pr., Aed., Tr., Pl., Senatui Populoque Romano. Si valetis, bene est. Ego exercitusque valemus. In Bithyniam itinere feliciter confecto, Hannibalem Carthaginiensem reperimus emortuum . . .

Quintus Furius Bibaculus, to . . . the Senate and People of Rome. We reached Bithynia without incident. We found Hannibal the Carthaginian, but he was dead. He had cut his throat. He was naked and alone. There is no evidence that Prusias or any other was involved.

On the table where he lay we found many tablets lying in the pool of his own blood. Written in Greek, they seem to form an account of some kind. There were a few clothes in the room, the dagger of his suicide, and a sword. And there were gold bars, marked with a scorpion, and jewels and precious stones, lying uncovered on the floor.

I had not thought to find so old a man, so ugly. Can this have been the enemy of Rome? The heat is very great here. The corpse will quickly rot. Knowing that you would not accord to Hannibal the Carthaginian the rites of burial, I will have his body thrown into the city's cesspit. We shall then take some hostages as punishment for sheltering this Hannibal, as ordered, and then we shall return to Rome.

APOLOGIA

I have drawn in writing this novel on such classical sources for the life and times of Hannibal as survive. Polybius, Livy and Appian are principal. Plutarch's *Lives* of Fabius Maximus and Claudius Marcellus are useful, as is Cornelius Nepos' *Hamilcar* and Diodorus Siculus. Silius Italicus' epic poem *Punica* is splendid stuff, even if one sympathises with Pliny's judgement – *maiore cura quam ingenio*, more distinguished for its sweat than for its genius. Plautus' *Poenulus* is revealing. All, however, are Romanophile. Hannibal can hardly have been that. Of the culture that begat him we know little, notwithstanding such works as B.H. Warmington's or Serge Lancel's *Carthage* or Gavin de Beer's *Hannibal*. The Romans were a thorough lot, and Carthage is a memory.

Professor Michael Whitby saved me from several errors. If, despite his advice, I have courted controversy by making Hannibal a familiar of Alexander's *Ephemerides*, I am delighted. If scholars protest at my suppositions regarding cartography, I refer them *inter alia* to Aristophanes' *Nub.*, 200 ff. If they find improbable the indiscipline apparent in the rape of Similce, I refer them to the mutinies that Scipio faced in Spain, or the conduct of Pleminius at Locri. The army of the early Roman republic is not, I believe, the army after Marius.

I have taken other liberties with history, as novelists are generally allowed. If I have helped to understand Hannibal, *satis superque* – it is enough, and more than enough.

I am very grateful to the Scottish Arts Council, whose bursary enabled me to complete this book, to the many friends who have encouraged me, to my mother and my father for their unflinching support, and to Canongate, for their diligence and care.

Ross Leckie, Edinburgh
July 1995

245